SUMMONING

SUNY Series in Modern Jewish Literature and Culture
Sarah Blacher Cohen, Editor

SUMMONING

Ideas of the Covenant and Interpretive Theory

edited by

ELLEN SPOLSKY

State University
of New York
Press

Grateful acknowledgment is made to the following for permission to reprint essays that have appeared elsewhere:

Paul Contino, Editor of *Religion and Literature,* for Susan Handelman's essay, "Facing the Other: Levinas, Perelman, and Rosenzweig," *Religion and Literature* 22, 2–3 (Summer–Autumn 1990)

Daniel Walden, Editor of *Studies in American Jewish Literature* for Sharon Deykin Baris' essay "Intertextuality and Reader Responsibility: Living On in Malamud's *The Mourners,*" which appeared in Vol. 2, 1 (1992) of that journal

H. M. Daleski, Editor of *Hebrew University Studies in Literature and the Arts,* for Elizabeth Freund's essay "Binding and Unbinding: The Summons to Interpretation in *The Merchant of Venice,*" which appeared in *HSLA* 19 (1991)

Published by
State University of New York Press, Albany

Production by Susan Geraghty
Marketing by Bernadette La Manna

Printed in the United States of America

For information, address State University of New York Press, State University Plaza, Albany, N.Y., 12246

Library of Congress Cataloging-in-Publication Data

Summoning : ideas of the covenant and interpretive theory / edited by Ellen Spolsky.
p. cm. — (SUNY series in modern Jewish literature and culture)
Includes index.
ISBN 0-7914-1525-2. — ISBN 0-7914-1526-0 (pbk.)
1. Religion and literature. 2. Literature—History and criticism—Theory, etc. 3. Covenant theology in literature. 4. Covenants—Religious aspects—Judaism. 5. Judaism—Essence, genius, nature. I. Spolsky, Ellen, 1943– . II. Series.
PN49.S84 1993
809′.93382—dc20 92-23258
CIP

10 9 8 7 6 5 4 3 2 1

In the fall of 1989, honoring a debt to the seminal scholarship of Professor Harold Fisch on the description of Covenantal Hermeneutics, the Lechter Institute for Literary Research in cooperation with the Kaplan Fund for American Literature, held a conference at Bar-Ilan University, Israel, for the purpose of exploring the implications of that work for current interpretive theory. Since its founding in 1981 the Lechter Institute has held several conferences on aspects of the relationship between contemporary literary study and scholarship in Jewish Studies. Two collections of essays have been published: David H. Hirsch and Nehama Aschkenasy edited Biblical Patterns in Modern Literature, *Brown Judaic Studies 77, 1984, which gathers the essays from a 1982 conference.* The Uses of Adversity: Failure and Accommodation in Reader Response, *edited by Ellen Spolsky, Bucknell UP: 1991, collected the papers from a 1985 conference. This conference focused on the similarities and differences between the notion of a contract or a shared grammar, the prototypical example of which is human language, and the clearly related though distinguishably different concept of the covenant, the prototype of which is the covenant made between God and the Israelites at Mount Sinai. This volume is dedicated, with appreciation and love, to Harold Fisch.*

CONTENTS

INTRODUCTION

Ellen Spolsky

Recent discussion of traditional Jewish forms of text interpretation has emphasized the parallels between valued forms of open-ended literary interpretation and Midrash Aggadah as exemplified in the Talmud. It is worthwhile, in this context, to insist again on the distinction between principled resistance to closure and covenantal hermeneutics. The attempt to describe this difference has been central to the work of Harold Fisch. The openness of interpretation discovered by various post-new critical structuralisms rests on the model of the grammatical contract, and derives from features of natural language grammars which are not necessarily features of the covenant that Fisch understands to govern biblical interpretation. Crucially, while aspects of the grammar of natural languages are innate and universal, a literary hermenuetic is more like a grammar of fashion or of telephone etiquette. Although it is largely tacit and is internalized by all members of a culture, it is neither innate nor universal. Furthermore, because the grammar of a language is detachable from the function or the intentionality of any speaker of the language, there is an infinity of possible recombinations among the subsystems of the language grammar and between the language and its changing functions. Any citation can always be reinscribed with a new meaning in a new context.

The covenant which installed the Jewish tradition of Talmud Torah (the learning of the law by interpretation), is considered to have been revealed at a specific and never to be repeated time in history. That revelation, accompanied by blasts of thunder and lightening and the blast of the shofar, was just about as far from tacit as could be. The text of Exodus records that the covenant was explicitly and intentionally accepted by a specific population. Furthermore, its acceptance entailed the permanent and unnatural sign of its acceptance—the circumcision of all male children. The crucial difference between a contract that is a grammar and the contract that is the covenant becomes clear as the two are differently understood in relation to the texts to which they give meaning.

Meaning in a literary contract may derive from (be satisfied by) narrative closure, often in the form of genre conventions. The beginning predicts the end, as Frank Kermode described it in *The Sense of an Ending*. In this understanding, of course, the reader finds closure in the identification of authorial intention and authority. When that authority has been deconstructed, then openness is a result of the detachability of speech act from intention. The covenantal contract, however, is satisfied by an openness which does not deny the authority of the founding intentionality of the text; in fact, it acts within an ongoing responsibility toward it. Closure is neither implied nor enforced by the authority of the code itself nor by the intentionality of the text. That intentionality, in fact, insists on the open-endedness of the interpretive activity, and doesn't promise satisfaction.

Harold Fisch, in the opening paper in this volume, aims to enrich his description of the particular interpretive engagement he calls covenantal hermeneutics and to distinguish it from other kinds of open interpretation. He constructs the boundaries of post-rabbinic midrash as a genre of interpretive activity on a subtle distinction between two poems by John Milton. As the poet of *Paradise Lost,* Milton qualifies as a covenantal poet; his *Samson Agonistes,* however, fails as midrash. The project of describing Jewish interpretive forms is far enough advanced, not only in Fisch's own considerable scholarship on the subject, but also in the work of Boyarin (1990), Bruns (1987), Handelman (1982), Hartman and Budick (1986), Kugel (1981), Rojtman (1986), Stern (1986), and Sternberg (1985), so as to make two of its conditions uncontroversial. First, although the original covenantal hermeneuticists were rabbis, both Renaissance poets and twentieth-century readers may qualify as midrashists as well. The midrashist—and this is the second necessary condition—displays a talent and a taste for interpretation that is sufficiently open to allow not only multiple, but even contradictory interpretations to stand together as equally valid.

Fisch claims further (and here is the source of his insistence on the adjective "covenantal" as a descriptor of the midrashist), that an appreciation of openness and multiplicity does not entail the rejection of the authority of the prior text. On the contrary, covenantal hermeneutics is not inconsistent with, but rather requires, the greatest respect for the authority of the text under interpretation: this is the primary condition distinguishing it from other kinds of open-ended reading. With this authority, the respondent makes a covenant; toward this authority the reader undertakes a moral responsibility. Following from this undertaking, that is, because the authority of the author is recognized, covenantal openness exposes the reader to great risks. One can make a wrong choice, even a fatally wrong choice. It is the riskiness of covenantal hermeneutics, Fisch suggests, that separates it from the kind of historicizing rereading that Bruns (1987) calls "midrash" and that Bloomfield (1972) had called allegory. If one misreads Biblical texts, chooses wrong, the result is specified as nothing less than the fate of the soul.

What Milton shares with the Rabbis, thus, is a commitment to what they all acknowledge as a moral responsibility to divine law. The interpretation of the biblical text is bound (covenanted) to respect the "authorial intention" of the law. What the author intends, however, is not a single meaning, but a commitment to interpretation. For Fisch, the question of moral authority does not arise in connection with the interpretation of a non-biblical source text. Openness, there, as it were, is what the Renaissance called wit, and it is risk free.

Fisch goes on to suggest that the double requirement of covenantal hermeneutics—the simultaneous necessity for openness and respect for an earlier text's authority—puts serious strains on the genre aspirations of the later poet/reader, and complicates the judgments about genre that an experienced reader and would-be midrashist depends on. Genre is a master, or at least a master code, and the God of the covenant is a jealous God. An interpreter (e.g., the author of *Samson Agonistes*), might be seduced into producing an interpretation which, by its own generic closure denies the continuing openness of the prior text.

Issues of genre, then, are crucially involved in covenanted interpretation. Thus, Fisch claims that although the theological exploration of *Samson Agonistes* appears similar to that in *Paradise Lost,* especially when one looks at single lines or incidents, *Samson Agonistes* is finally disqualified as midrash by its global aspiration to the closure of tragedy and its flirtation with the beauty of pastoral. Successful midrash cannot ultimately allow itself to serve the generic archetypes of western culture.

In his earlier study of *Hamlet* (1971), Fisch discussed and exemplified another aspect of covenantal interpretation. There, Fisch identified the struggle for a moral reading—both Shakespeare's struggle and his own, as a struggle against the power of the genres inherited from Greek and Roman literature. In *Hamlet,* of course, the issue is the revenge motif, which has seemed to so many critics either pagan or, worse—"Old Testament" or "Mosaic." Suggesting that "the Hebraic component of [Shakespeare's] work . . . may be as important as the Senecan-Stoic or medieval-Christian components," (p. 10) Fisch himself was the covenantal hermeneuticist there, rereading the revenge demanded by the ghost as informed not by a primitive Greek natural law "visiting punishment on those who have offended the gods," but rather as a "Biblical sense of a law justifiable to man, accessible to his reason and his sense of right and wrong" (p. 6). This "Biblical" law is "patently less abstract and otherworldly" than the Christianity of some of its critics (p. 2).

The larger issue here, following directly from the this-worldliness of the Hebraic concerns, is one of the mutuality of responsibilities between God and the humans He created. Fisch declares the moral substance of Shakespeare's drama to be asking these questions:

> How is human destiny viewed? to what sort of task is Man summoned? and in what form is that summons issued? In the experience of Biblical man the key to these matters lies in the covenant, a transforming encounter between man and God, from which many mutual obligations flow, but also trials, disaster, and salvation as well. . . . The covenant involves a choice of paths. To choose aright is a matter of immense responsibility, the sort of responsibility from which a hero such as Orestes or Oedipus is exempt, since in their case the path is . . . determined before they are born. In the covenant type of choice there is, as we have said,

> human freedom, but there is also a sense of a commanding voice. Once that voice is heard, its commandments live all alone within the book and volume of our brain. (1971:9)

In *A Remembered Future: A Study in Literary Mythology* (1984) Fisch argues that historical archetypes (as opposed to the mythical ones described by Northrop Frye) carry within them the potential for change, indeed demand it. "Biblical history is covenant history," he writes. "This is a dynamic, not a static form, not a pattern given but a pattern unfolded through trial and error. The essence of the covenant is dramatic, the memory of an encounter in which responsibilities are undertaken and promises exchanged by both parties." (p. 11) More recently, in *Poetry with a Purpose: Biblical Poetics and Interpretation* (1988), Fisch argues again that biblical poetry is materially and functionally different from other poetry in that it assumes responsibility for the future. The texts from the past are witnesses for the present. "They do not simply echo, they invade us, they demand attention. Moreover, they point outwards beyond themselves; they remind us of duties, perils, that, likewise, invade the poem. Words and world bear witness to each other" (p. 67). For Fisch, the difficulties and risks of interpretation can never sanction the evasion of responsibility for acting in the world.

Part 1 of this collection brings together the theoretical essays on the subject of covenant. Elata-Alster and Salmon begin by sorting out the ways in which the covenant is and isn't a speech act like others, thereby opening the discussion of what consequences derive from the unnaturalness, as it were, of the covenant. Handelman sees the covenant as requiring an ethical relation between people, learning from the philosophy of Franz Rosenzweig and Emmanuel Levinas, and from the rhetorical theory of Chaim Perelman, the priority and thus the responsibility of recognizing the autonomy of the other partner to the dialogue. In this connection, Statman asks whether it is possible to make an argument that people have a moral duty to maintain the covenant, and concludes that there is not. From a religiously orthodox position, both a yes and a no to this question can be justified, but arguing as he does within the traditional of metaphysics which Levinas explicitly rejected, it is not surprising that Statman arrives at the point Levinas would have predicted—with no moral basis for following the covenant.

Menachem Fisch's essay argues that what he calls the covenant of learning in the Talmud, unlikely as it may at first seem, turns out to be cognitively parallel to the way the contemporary historian of science, Karl Popper, understands scientific learning to proceed. Learning in the Talmud and learning in science are parallel, then, because there really is only one way people learn, although the laminates of cultural variation may obscure these universals. The covenant of learning, according to Menachem Fisch, is not only natural, it's all there is.

Betty Rojtman's paper begins with the acknowledgement of asymmetry. There can be no question of mutuality, here, as there is in other contractual relationships. Because God's grace in offering the covenant is so much larger than anything humans can offer or respond with, because of what Rojtman calls the gratuitousness of the covenantal promises, God is asked (by Noah, first) to give a sign to guarantee what He has offered. God obliges Noah but then God requires answering signs, and the exchange of signs, both overt and hidden, is thus instituted as the essence of the covenantal relationship.

The essays in part 2 display some of the possibilities of a practice of reading which is at once bound and open. This set of explorations of non-biblical texts, when taken together, test the boundaries of hermeneutic or midrashic interpretation. Betsy Halpern-Amaru's essay brings to our attention the pseudepigraphic text, *The Testament of Moses,* in which the author attempts to renegotiate the interpretation of covenantal responsibility by rewriting the biblical text itself. Although the rewrite could be called midrashic for its interpretive swerve, it is, according to Halpern-Amaru's reading, an attempt to close or even compel a particular understanding of a difficult historical situation.

Elizabeth Freund reads the Shakespearean scenes of interpretation in *The Merchant of Venice* as analogical extensions of the play's thematization of bonds. She discusses Shakespeare's use of citation within the play as a way of both responding to authority and of questioning that authority by relocating the language in a new context. Citation or tradition, that is, that which is passed on, though it is authoritative, must also be renegotiated in its new location, as, according to Fisch, the covenant must be.

The significance of Boyarin's essay to the discussion here lies in its recognition that the covenanted status of the texts (including, of course, the traditional interpretations surrounding them) require a revised and historically appropriate understanding of the genre categories of those texts. Citing the inadequacy of the modern distinction between history and fiction to describe biblical texts, Boyarin begins the project of understanding the functional genres of these texts by describing the concept of "reading" in ancient Israel.

Three of the essays here expand the discussion of covenanted interpretation to texts in American literature which are double bound, as it they show, by both God's covenant and America's. Budick illustrates, in the texts of Nathaniel Hawthorne and Stanley Cavell, the American incarnations of the insistence on "uncompromised autonomy" of reader and text within the covenantal bonds which Fisch and Handelman have also argued to be crucial to Jewish hermenuetics. Girgus also finds that Jewish-American writers' sense of covenanted responsibility has roots in both the biblical and the American traditions. Baris's study of a troubling short story by Bernard Malamud, asks whether even so powerful a tradition as the American covenantal heritage can offer the possibility of a national "social security" in the shadow of the holocaust. How can one respond, or be responsible to another?

Together, these essays, by raising the issue of the relationship between grammars, literary and legal codes, and divine covenants, raise the ante of literary discussion by their insistence on the unnatural and the non-reciprocal aspects of covenant. Their importance lies not so much in their illustrating, once again, the naiveté of the structuralist understanding of codes, as in their challenge to the poststructuralist, even where the latter acknowledge the inevitable swerve of ideology and power. Covenantal hermeneutics challenges us to admit that if holding an ideology is to mean anything more that the happenstance of having been born into one cultural milieu rather than another, it means having to make choices, and having to own up to them. Poststructuralists may find this position uncomfortable, but we already inhabit it as soon as we claim that social change is desirable and that criticism should work toward it.

Fisch describes this aspect of covenant precisely as a historical process: "The covenant is a condition of our existence in time, rather than an end foreseen. We cooperate with its purposes never quite knowing where it will take us, for "the readiness is all" (1984:11).

REFERENCES

Bloomfield, Morton. "Allegory as Interpretation," *NLH* 3 (1972):301–17.

Boyarin, Daniel. *Intertextuality and the Reading of Midrash*. Bloomington, Ind.: Indiana University Press, 1990.

Bruns, Gerald L. "Midrash and Allegory." In *The Literary Guide to the Bible,* Eds. Robert Alter and Frank Kermode, 625–46. Cambridge, Mass.: Harvard University Press, 1987.

Fisch, Harold. *Hamlet and the Word: The Covenant Pattern in Shakespeare*. New York: Frederick Ungar, 1971.

______. *A Remembered Future: A Study in Literary Mythology.* Bloomington, Indiana: Indiana University Press, 1984.

______. *Poetry with a Purpose: Biblical Poetics and Interpretation.* Bloomington, Indiana: Indiana University Press, 1988.

Handelman, Susan A. *The Slayers of Moses: The Emergence of Rabbinic Interpretation in Modern Literary Theory.* Albany: State University of New York Press, 1982.

Kermode, Frank. *The Sense of an Ending: Studies in the Theory of Fiction*. London: Oxford University Press, 1966.

Kugel, James. *The Idea of Biblical Poetry.* New Haven: Yale University Press, 1981.

Rojtman, Betty. "Sacred Language and Open Text." In *Midrash and Literature,* Eds. Geoffrey Hartman and Sanford Budick. New Haven: Yale University Press, 1986.

Stern, David. "Midrash and the Language of Exegesis." In *Midrash and Literature,* Eds. Geoffrey Hartman and Sanford Budick. New Haven: Yale University Press, 1986.

Sternberg, Meir. *The Poetics of Biblical Narrative: Ideological Literature and the Drama of Reading*. Bloomington, Ind.: Indiana University Press, 1985.

CHAPTER 1

Power and Constraint: Covenantal Hermeneutics in Milton

Harold Fisch

Shakespeare owed as much to earlier writers as any author can decently permit himself to owe, but he recognized no obligation. He showed no anxiety about their prior claims or about his belatedness; he simply raided the larder whenever he felt there was something there that he could use. He exercised total freedom. To Plutarch he owed the incidents, the characters, and much of the imagery and language of *Antony and Cleopatra,* but he did not set himself up as his pupil or interpreter. To the contrary, he also turned Plutarch upside down, investing Cleopatra with a power and inwardness which threaten those very "Roman" values which Plutarch so admired. Likewise in *Julius Caesar* there is scarcely a detail or episode which cannot be traced back to Plutarch's *Lives.* Nevertheless, the general thrust of the presentation is often very non-Plutarchian.[1]

Shakespeare, we may say, availed himself of that prior text completely, feeding his imagination with its images of power and valor; he also deconstructed it. The Roman virtues as set out by Plutarch are celebrated and they are at the same time exploded. This source, a fundamental shaping force for Shakespeare's imagination, is there to be utilized in the dramatic agon, to be set free in a field of force. What interested Shakespeare was the field of force;

The writing of this essay was facilitated by the welcome appointment to a fellowship at the Institute of Advanced Studies in the Humanities of Edinburgh University from January to July, 1989.

not the exposition of Plutarch's text, but the dramatic possibilities that it could yield. He might have said that a source is but a cheveril glove to a good wit; how quickly the wrong side may be turned outward.

The inclusive Elizabethan term for such a free use of sources is "wit." Wit is the quality whereby different sources are nimbly combined with, and set off against one another (e.g., *The Chronicle History* and the episode of the Paphlagonian king from Sidney's *Arcadia* in *King Lear*) and it is also the quality which determines the total freedom of action which the author implicitly claims with regard to these sources. A synonym for wit in this connection could be irresponsibility. Shakespeare is not answerable to his source, it is not set over and against him as an authority. He is always in that sense free; he ranges freely within the zodiac of his own wit. It is a mark of his greatness.

Here precisely is a fundamental point of difference between Shakespeare and Milton. Milton too owes as much as any poet decently can owe to his sources. There is scarcely an image or idea or episode in *Paradise Lost* which has not been traced to one or more forerunner texts. The industry of scholars has, as in the case of Shakespeare, enabled us to see Milton in his workshop. We have been made aware of his mastery of the poetic resources of Shakespeare, Spenser, the Italian poets, of Ovid, Homer, and Vergil, and of his own English and European contemporaries. Above all, we are aware of what he owed to his prime text, the books of the Bible together with much of the literature of commentary and paraphrase in Hebrew, Aramaic, Latin, and Greek which had accumulated around that text over the centuries. And we are aware too of the amazing virtuosity with which, like Shakespeare, he wove all this together into the tapestry of his poems. But if he owed so much to his "sources" he also acknowledged an obligation. He does not range only within the zodiac of his own wit but stands before his forerunner in a posture of grave attentiveness.[2] He strictly meditates his muse. There is freedom to be sure; Milton like Shakespeare reveals his greatness in the originality of his selection, in the daring of his invention. His song pursues things *unattempted yet* in prose or rhyme. And yet the text before him commands, it retains its authority. It is there not simply to be utilized but to be echoed and above all, to be interpreted.

Part of the pleasure that Milton implicitly promises his reader is "the joy of recognition"—the recognition of the familiar stories of Genesis and Judges, the familiar invocations from Virgil's epic, the familiar topos of the descent of Hermes as in Homer, but newly and marvellously applied to the visit of Raphael to Adam in Book V of *Paradise Lost.* And this in turn marvellously reminds the reader (and is supposed to remind him) of the visit of the angels to Abraham in Genesis 18. To the joy of such recognitions is added the pleasure of novelty. If we respond to an anterior voice still audible in the text we respond also to the new voice which both echoes and answers it. The intensest pleasure comes from the mingling of those voices. In Shakespeare's case our attention is not thus directed. Other joys are promised us, but the recognition of the source and the acknowledgment of its power are not usually among those joys.

We have now seemingly reversed Coleridge's position on what he terms Milton's egotism. He maintains that

> in the Paradise Lost—indeed in every one of his poems—it is Milton himself whom you see; his Satan, his Adam, his Raphael, almost his Eve—are all John Milton; and it is a sense of this intense egotism that gives me the greatest pleasure in reading Milton's works. The egotism of such a man is a revelation of spirit.[3]

Shakespeare he declares is absent from his poetry; he is "the Spinozistic deity,"[4] whereas Milton constitutes both the center and the circumference of his writing. His is the sole voice that we hear. He has evidently become for Coleridge, in this respect, the true prototype of all Romantic poets. That is why "the egotism of such a man" as he terms it gave him such intense pleasure. Like Wordsworth's solitary reaper—"breaking the silence of the seas / Among the farthest Hebrides"—or like Shelley's skylark, Milton sings by himself and the whole universe is filled with the ecstasy of his single song.

Now if what I have claimed is true, there is here a fundamental romantic misreading of Milton. Milton, we could say, is least alone when he is alone. His is not the monologue of the poet who utters his word in a universe evacuated of other presences—one might much rather speak of Shakespeare's relation to his sources in those terms. Milton is to the contrary always and intensely dialogic. We have to do with his Satan, his Eve, his Adam to be sure, but they are there to be related to the Satan, the Eve, and the Adam whom we have already known; they speak to us from within Milton's text and also from beyond it. They are not "single in the field," nor does the poet in presenting them to us pour out his profuse strains of unpremeditated art. They are both meditated and unpremeditated, newly invented and also echoed from the past. The excitement of Milton's poetry is bound up with the mutual tensions, the dialogic encounter, we may say, between these two modes.[5]

"Unpremeditated" is in fact the term that Milton uses about his verse in his proem to Book 9 of *Paradise Lost*. Urania, he says,

> dictates to me slumb'ring, or inspires
> Easy my unpremeditated verse.

The line may have been in Shelley's mind when he wrote about the skylark's "unpremeditated art." The term "easy" in this context carries great force. As adverb, it suggests the essentially relaxed mode of guidance practised by his muse; as adjective it points to the unconstrained, spontaneous nature of the verse itself. The use of this term "easy" suggests that Urania's part is to release his poetic gift; far from imposing herself upon him, she enables him to discover his own individual voice. And yet she is also said in this selfsame sentence to *dictate* to him—she "dictates to me slumb'ring." Elsewhere he speaks of submitting to her governance: "still govern thou my Song," he declares (7:30). If she grants him his freedom, she also governs him.

To understand this paradox we must understand the dual role of Urania. She is the Muse of Divine Poetry, that is, of poetry inspired by the Bible, and that is because she herself is no other than the Spirit of biblical prophecy. It is she, he tells us, who inspired

> That Shepherd, who first taught the chosen Seed,
> In the Beginning how the Heav'ns and Earth
> Rose out of *Chaos*. (*Paradise Lost* 1, 8–10)

She is thus the authority behind the text that he is expounding and to that authority he submits. But a little further down in the same passage (ibid., 17–20), Urania seems to slip into another role, that of the agent of world-creation. She is there all but identified with the Spirit which in Genesis 1:2 brooded on the vast abyss and made it pregnant. She is therefore not only the author of the text that Milton is interpreting, she is also the author of the poet and thus the source of the power and freedom which the poet finds in himself. That is her gift.

From this point of view, the several invocations to Urania are no mere epic formality; they are the very dramatic ground of the poem which may be read under the sign of an unremitting dialogue between the "ephebe" to use Bloom's term and the greatest precursor poet of all, namely, the voice which addresses him from the biblical text and is, in turn, addressed by him in the poem. Both sides to this dialogue retain their independence. Urania is the sign of a power supremely independent of the poet, one he tells us who converses with eternal Wisdom in the presence of the Almighty—and is thus independent in a sense even of those august partners. Yet her name is also one of the titles of Aphrodite and she thus stands for pure invention and impulse, for a spontaneous generation of poetic images.

Urania is thus more than a muse in the traditional sense. She is the key to Milton's inventive procedure, personifying the link between the two parties to the dialogue: the voice of the anterior text and that of the new poet who addresses it and is addressed by it. She signifies the hermeneutic encounter between them. Now if text and reader can come together in this encounter, it is because there is a prior bond between the two. There is a power in the text corresponding to a power within himself. It is not just a matter of a book which happened to come Milton's way in the library. There is for Milton a prestabilized relationship, a bond between them predating his own existence. And again Urania bears witness to that bond. That is one of her functions:

> Thou from the first
> Wast present, and with mighty wings outspread
> Dove-like satst brooding on the vast Abyss
> And mad'st it pregnant: what in me is dark
> Illumine. . .

The "heavenly muse" who first inspired "that shepherd," that is to say Moses, to write a scripture relating the beginning of things, will now guide the poet's pen in his poetic interpretation of that same scripture:

> what in me is dark
> Illumine, what is low raise and support,
> That to the highth of this great Argument

I may assert eternal Providence,
And justifie the wayes of God to men.

In pondering the nature of interpretation carried out under such conditions of prior relationality, we are naturally reminded of the category of midrash. Gerald Bruns in a recent essay has spoken of midrash as "a dialogue between text and history." And he adds,

> The task of midrash is to keep open the mutual belonging of the text and those who hear it. There is a common accord between ourselves and what is written, and the task of midrash (indeed the task of any biblical interpretation that is hermeneutically informed) is to bring this accord into the open.[6]

The phrase "mutual belonging" catches the sense of an unwilled relationship, one which is almost a condition of our existence; but "common accord," the second phrase Bruns uses to define this relationship, suggests a voluntary turning towards the text, an agreement freely undertaken. We might more properly call such a belonging and accord and the readings to which they give rise "covenantal hermeneutics." From the point of view of the Rabbis, indeed, the possibility of midrash is grounded in covenant.[7] While the Written Law was public, the ongoing interpretive dialogue with the Torah, the so-called Oral Law, was the task of a covenant community, bound to one another and to the text they had received by bonds originating at Sinai, that is, going back to the same event from which the written text itself arose.

Milton conceives himself as having precisely this same covenantal relationship to the text that he was interpreting. And Urania is the person or the agency who comes to express this mutual accord. She stands for an authority to which the poet has already voluntarily submitted. It is thus accepted rather than imposed. On the other side, his imaginative freedom, that spontaneity which will find its expression for a later age in images of romantic flight and romantic individualism, is not, for Milton, a matter of simple autonomy. He is not self-created or self-inspired; his freedom also is granted within the framework of a covenantal transaction. There is a kind of exchange of pledges. If his part is to submit to the authority of his divine source, then the muse of divine poetry for her part will inspire and raise him to ever greater heights; she is called upon to guarantee his freedom:

> whose Voice divine
> Following, above the *Olympian* Hill I soar,
> Above the flight of *Pegasean* wing.
>
> (Paradise Lost, 7, 2–4)

The élan and vertiginous wonder of this flight will communicate themselves later to Coleridge, Shelley, and Byron, sometimes in the form of fantasies of space-travel, but the covenantal ground of such imaginings, the dramatic exchange of vows, the "reciprocity" will be lost sight of. Dialogue will give way to monologue.

The special relationship of which we speak also involves enormous risks. It is after all not a mechanism but a freely undertaken partnership. As such, it can be forfeited by betrayal. What is said of Adam applies to the poetic vocation as well as to the moral life:

> I made him just and right,
> Sufficient to have stood, though free to fall.
>
> (ibid., 3, 98–99)

The poet is also "free to fall." If he is lifted up "above the flight of Pegasean wing," he can also be "carried away," tempted to a wanton exercise of his spontaneity. That is a danger which Milton vividly represents for his reader in the proem to Book 7 and from which he begs to be protected:

> Lest from this flying steed unrein'd (as once
> *Bellerophon,* though from a lower Clime)
> Dismounted on th'*Aleian* Field I fall
> Erroneous there to wander and forlorn.
>
> (ibid. VII, 17–20)

These passages are from *Paradise Lost* where Urania, as I have suggested, is the agent of covenantal hermeneutics. But what I wish to argue is that *Samson Agonistes* provides us with an even better model of covenantal discourse or "midrash." There is first the sustained dialogue with his source. The original account of Samson's life and death in the book of Judges is given even more exclusive attention than that given to the Creation-story (Genesis 1–3) in *Paradise Lost;* the text of Judges 13–16 remains an active point of reference throughout the poem, its authority unsubverted, its voice never silenced. Joseph Wittreich is surely correct in insisting that Milton in this dramatic poem is everywhere guided by the biblical framework. The additions and changes that he introduces, the interviews, for instance, with Manoa, Dalila, and Harapha, are designed "not to obscure but to reveal the implications of Milton's original"—the original being the story of Samson's life and death as set out in Judges 13–16.[8] To this text he is in voluntary bondage. He could leave it behind and do his own thing—but he chooses not to do so. "His objective" says Wittreich, "is to wring from scriptural history its highest truths."[9] If the poem is an aesthetic exercise, it is no less—and perhaps more—an exegetical exercise.

The phrase that Wittreich uses to define this mode is "interpretive fiction."[10] He borrows it from Frank Kermode's *The Genesis of Secrecy* which is mainly concerned with the authors of the gospels and the way they refashion and reinvent their stories and parables, each one making his own changes and additions. But as Kermode shows, this mode of invention or reinvention goes back to the Rabbis in their interpretive homilies on the Hebrew scriptures.[11] This says Kermode was the method of midrash. So that what Wittreich is really saying, though he does not use the term, is that *Samson Agonistes* is a kind of midrash on the Samson story in Judges.

Milton of course was familiar with traditional midrash and employed many actual rabbinical glosses in *Paradise Lost*.[12] *Samson Agonistes* contains fewer direct borrowings from the Rabbis[13] but Milton's essential procedure may without distortion be termed "midrashic." The added material, such as Samson's bitter meditations on his blindness, his reflections on the justice or injustice of God's dealings with him (with frequent echoing of Job), Dalila's renewed attempt to attract him back to her and his new-found capacity to resist her allurement, the introduction by association of Harapha, a giant mentioned in 2 Samuel 21:22 as belonging to Gat—all these are metonymic extensions of the biblical story itself as Milton found it in the Hebrew Scriptures. And the same applies to the evocation of other Old Testament episodes and texts such as the story of Elijah on Mount Carmel (1 Kings 18) evoked in the confrontation with Harapha (11, 1145–55). These serve to enrich and fill out the story of Samson as set forth in Judges by associating it with other places of Scripture. From this point of view the drama he develops is continuous with the biblical narrative as he understood it in its Old Testament context. It has not been radically removed from that context.

But it seems to me that *Samson Agonistes* is not so much an example of midrashic discourse as it is a reflection on the nature of such discourse. One would almost want to say that such discourse is the subject of the poem. If Urania in *Paradise Lost* is the agent of covenantal hermeneutics then I will suggest that *Samson Agonistes* provides us with an even better model in Samson himself as a reflexive image of the poet who is both bound and free, liberated, and at the same time controlled by the terms of his contract.

Samson is of course held to his vocation by his Nazirite vow or pledge—this is the central theme of his meditations and debates, and as such the very hinge on which the drama turns. This vow, binding a particular individual to God by a special relationship, may also stand as a microcosm of the covenant structure in general as it might apply to larger groups and societies.[14] It was of particular service because it caught, as perhaps no other image might, the antinomy of constraint and power which Milton was seeking to define. He was reaching towards this in the figure and function of Urania; in Samson it is even more cogently articulated:

> I was his nurseling once and choice delight,
> His destin'd from the womb,
> Promis'd by Heavenly message twice descending.
> Under his special eye
> Abstemious I grew up and thriv'd amain;
> He led me on to mightiest deeds
> Above the nerve of mortal arm . . .
>
> (633–39)

The first line, "I was his nurseling once and choice delight" of course echoes what is said of Wisdom in Proverbs 8:30–31: "Then I was by him as a nurseling, and I was daily his delight, playing always before him; playing with the universe, his earth; and my delights were with the sons of men." But that is not all. The careful reader will recall a parallel echo of the same verse in Milton's invocation to Urania in *Paradise Lost,* Book 7:

> Before the Hills appear'd, or Fountain flow'd
> Thou with Eternal Wisdom didst converse,
> Wisdom thy Sister, and with her didst play
> In presence of th'Almighty Father, pleas'd
> With thy Celestial Song.
>
> (7:8–12)

The parallel between Samson and Urania in the echoing of this same verse from Proverbs underlines the metapoetic function of the Samson paradigm. Urania, before the hills appeared, played in the presence of the Almighty Father because she was the muse of sacred poetry ("pleas'd with thy Celestial song"). Indeed, this verse from Proverbs has been understood from antiquity as having reference to the sacred writings and their inspired exegesis, Wisdom being a synonym for Torah, for textuality.[15] Seen in this context, Samson's election, his "special calling" ("I was his destin'd from the womb") suggests not merely his Nazirite vocation, announced before his birth by a heavenly messenger, but suggests through that image the vocation of the sacred poet devoted from birth, indeed before birth, to his visionary task. Samson's high destiny conveyed in the lines, "I was his nurseling once and choice delight, / His destin'd from the womb" has thus the same primordial, covenantal associations that we noted in regard to the figure and function of Urania. Ultimately, the issue is not only the justification of the ways of God to Samson but the ways of God to the poet, to man in general, and to the world.

The continuation of the passage: "Abstemious I grew up and thriv'd amain; / He led me on to mightiest deed / Above the nerve of mortal arm"—exhibits the essential paradox with which I am here concerned, now more clearly formulated than ever before. Samson is controlled, bound by his vow, or by the vows taken on his behalf; he is limited, constrained, "abstemious", subject to an authority imposed upon him in the past. At the same time, that very vow releases in him extraordinary power, a generative force which makes him capable of "mightiest deeds / Above the nerve of mortal arm." We catch the same fundamental rhythm in the opening of Book 7 of *Paradise Lost:*

whose Voice divine
Following, above th'*Olympian* Hill I soar,
Above the flight of *Pegasean* wing.

If Urania imposes on the poet the constraining authority of a prior text, she also releases in him an unanticipated surge of power. In the figure of Samson Milton has found the precise paradigm for this phenomenon. And unlike the figure of Urania, whose Pagan name he hesitates to call ("the meaning, not the Name I call"), this paradigm is itself authorized by the Scriptures themselves. Moreover, the Samson-model works so extraordinarily well because limitation and release, constraint and unconstraint are joined together by the same covenantal transaction, namely, the Nazirite vow. If he will limit himself in the ways required by his vow, then he will have power without limit! Abstention and what I have termed "the surge of power" go together; nor is it just a case of the one being a reward for the other; Samson's vocation joins the two modes of existence in an inseparable zeugma: "Abstemious I grew up and thriv'd amain." The grant of the free exercise of power—"above the nerve of mortal arm" and his subjection to the overmastering authority of a particular divine command issue from the same moment of dedication, the same covenantal event. The one is a function of the other.

The Hebrew term *nazir* verbally embodies this potent ambiguity and perhaps Milton's knowledge of biblical Hebrew enabled him to sense this. One semantic track joins the stem *nzr* to the cognate *ndr,* (thus *lindor neder nazir*) meaning to separate or withdraw oneself by a vow. This is particularly so in the hiphal and niphal usage: *hazzir* and *hinnazer,* which clearly carry the notion of restriction or self-limitation. Thus: "He shall abstain from wine and strong drink" (*miyyayin wešekar yazzir*) (Numbers 6:3). Another track points in the direction of *nezer* which has the fundamental meaning of crown or diadem but comes to signify the actual unshorn head of the Nazirite who has consecrated himself by means of the nazirite vow. It is this "head of hair" (*roš nizro*) which would be shaved off and burnt on the altar at the end of the normal term of consecration (Numbers 6:18). Elsewhere, perhaps by association with the hair of the Nazirite, the wild growth of the unpruned vine left abandoned in the field on the sabbatical year, is called *'innebe nezireka,* that is, your "nazirite" grapes or, as Koehler and Baumgarten render the phrase: Your grapes "left to unfettered growth." The stem *nzr* thus signifies control and restriction, but also wild growth. The Hebrew language is rich in such semiotic puzzles: *hata't* means both sin and purification, *barek* means to bless; it can also to mean to curse, and so forth. But what I think interested Milton was the mystery at the heart of the Nazirite phenomenon intimated by this verbal duality. Here is the very node, the nuclear core we may say, of the covenant as doctrine and life and, we may add that here too, especially in the symbolism of the unshorn hair of the Nazirite is the ultimate key, for Milton, of his own vocation as a consecrated poet.

Milton returns in his writings repeatedly to the motif of Samson's hair—"my precious fleece" as it is called elsewhere in *Samson Agonistes*. It had a special fascination for him. In a famous passage of *Areopagitica*, he has a visionary sight of England as a messiah-nation achieving the full promise of her religious and political destiny:

> Methinks I see in my mind a noble and puissant Nation rousing herself like a strong man after sleep, and shaking her invincible locks: Methinks I see her as an Eagle muing her mighty youth, and kindling her undazl'd eyes at the full midday beam; purging and unscaling her long abused sight at the fountain itself of heav'nly radiance . . .[16]

The image is that of Samson rising in the morning with his full strength still preserved in his unshorn locks after one of Dalila's unsuccessful attempts to learn his secret. The extraordinary vigor of this "puissant nation" is here seen as seated in its "invincible locks." We note how this image gives way to that of height and aspiration. Preserved by "these locks unshorn, / The pledge of my unviolated vow" as he was later to term them (*Samson Agonistes*, 1143–44), the puissant nation of England can now rise to the height of the eagle's nest and gaze without fear at the sun, the fountain of heavenly radiance. It would seem that with the security afforded by the nazirite model (as distinct from the Urania model) there is less danger of flying too near the sun and falling like Bellerophon crazed and blind on the Aleian field. It comes as no surprise to learn that the national renewal and strength spoken of in this passage and indeed throughout *Areopagitica* are chiefly a matter of literary creativity. The evidence of newfound power and freedom is he says "this flowery crop of knowledge and new light" with which the inspired writers, and principally one feels Milton himself, greet the dawn of a new age. The sign of the unshorn hair here then seems to guarantee boundless creativity and aspiration.

Some three years earlier in the concluding chapter of *The Reason of Church Government*, a sustained oration on the theme of law and discipline, he conjured up a vision of Samson with his unshorn locks in which the other semantic option is stressed, that is, the *nezer nazir* as signifying law and control rather than boundless creativity. The passage is an extended allegory in which the "person of the king" is Samson, "his illustrious and sunny locks, the laws, waving and curling about his god like shoulders." The bishops who seek to seduce him from the true religion are compared to Dalila. As long as he guards his hair unshorn he is secure,

> But laying down his head among the strumpet flatteries of Prelats, while he sleeps and thinks no harme, they, wickedly shave off all those bright and waighty tresses of his laws, and just prerogatives, which were his ornament and strength. . . . Till he, knowing his prelatical rasor to have bereft him of his wonted might, nourish again his puissant hair.[17]

We note again the "puissant hair" but the hair of the Nazirite in this passage explicitly stands for laws—"his sunny locks, the laws." These laws the king was to guard but like Samson he surrenders them to flatterers and seducers and as a result he is betrayed and is bereaved of his strength.

But in the passage quoted the locks of hair also suggest another category, which has no basis in the biblical account of Samson's life or in the law of the Nazirite, namely *beauty.* The sunny locks are seen "waving and curling about his godlike shoulders." Perhaps in this rather surprising tribute to Charles I, he is thinking of Absalom rather than the Nazirite Samson—and Absalom we remember was betrayed, rather than protected, by his beautiful locks of hair! This stress on beauty would seem therefore to contradict the Samson paradigm. R. Simeon the Just relates the story of a shepherd-boy of great beauty whose hair hung from his head in curly locks. Finding himself falling in love with his own image which Narcissus-like he had gazed at in the well, he undertook the Nazirite-vow which would require him at the end of a set period to cut off his hair and burn it on the altar. Beauty is involved in this model but the Nazirite vow serves as a guard against the temptations to which beauty gives rise.[18]

We may note the strongly sexual character of the scene of Samson's betrayal. He is said to lay down his head among strumpet flatteries of Prelates, and whilst his head is lying among them, they cut off his tresses. This scene recurs with some frequency in Milton's writings. In *Samson Agonistes* the sexual aspect is even more explicit:

At length to lay my head and hallowed pledge
Of all my strength in the lascivious lap
Of a deceitful concubine who shore me
Like a tame wether, all my precious fleece.

(535–38)

The same scene is evoked in *Paradise Lost,* Book 9, where the shame associated with the Fall of Adam and Eve is gathered up under the image of Samson and Dalila:

So rose the *Danite* strong
Herculean Samson from the Harlot-lap
Of *Philistean Dalilah,* and wak'd
Shorn of his strength.

(9:1059–62)

The Danite Samson, his bright tresses adorning the lap of a harlot, has here become the archetypal sign of post-lapsarian sexuality. The scene gives us beauty fatally flawed through betrayal.

If we seek the equivalent moment in the Urania paradigm we shall find it I think, once again, in the proem to Book 7. After the account of the fatal flight of Bellerophon, the poet begs Urania to preserve him from the opposite danger, that which we may term "downward transcendence."[19] It is symbolized by the fate of Orpheus, "the Thracian bard." Orpheus of course stands for the enchantments of poetry but he seeks his inspiration in the nether regions—we might want to say, in the depths of the *id*—and his destiny is to be torn to pieces by the maenads.

But drive farr off the barbarous dissonance
Of *Bacchus* and his Revellers, the Race
Of that wilde Rout that tore the *Thracian* Bard
In *Rhodope,* where Woods and Rocks had Eares
To rapture, till the savage clamor dround
Both Harp and Voice; nor could the Muse defend
Her Son. So fail not thou, who thee implores:
For thou art Heav'nlie, shee an empty dreame.

(7:32–39)

If Bellerophon represents the Apollonian excess—exemplified in the "upward fall" of Shelley, as Harold Bloom has termed it, then Orpheus here represents the Dionysiac excess of the poetic vocation. The anxiety expressed in these lines addressed to Urania ("so fail not thou, who thee implores") shows how real is the menace and also the fascination of this "Orphic quest," this descent into the region of the id.

The downward transcendence or Orphic descent of which we speak finds its most accurate symbolization in the lines quoted above from *Samson Agonistes* where the image of Samson laying down his unshorn locks in the harlot-lap of Dalila marks the nadir of his moral history. Here is the ultimate desertion—Samson laying down the hair of his consecrated head not on the altar of his God but at the very entrance to the abode of instinct and sexuality, the zone which King Lear had so graphically described in his madness:

> to the girdle do the gods inherit,
> Beneath is all the fiend's:
> There's hell, there's darkness, there is the sulphurous pit,
> Burning, scalding, stench, consumption.
>
> (*King Lear* 4.6.129–31)

Here are the nether regions, the Underworld of Orpheus. That way madness lies—that is why the maenads tear Orpheus to pieces. But Samson's "descent" into the lap of Dalila implies something more than uncontrolled subjection to the id; it is the ultimate scene of betrayal, the violation of his covenant-vows. And such violation goes beyond Samson's Nazirite vocation and extends to the vocation of the consecrated poet himself, the covenant which binds him to his source and at the same time authorizes his power and freedom. To surrender to the witchery of Dalila is to forfeit that consecration and that power.

What then is this witchery of Dalila which so appallingly and so disastrously threatens the very foundations of sacred song, so that the scene of Samson's fall links itself to the scene of Adam's fall and involves no less than the ruin of a world? And in what sense does this episode also intimate the betrayal by Milton of his poetic vocation? We trivialize the pathos of Milton's vision of ultimate loss if we suppose that the issue is sexual vulnerability and temptation as such. Reversing the normal Freudian mode of argumentation, I would wish to argue that the sexual imagery of this scene is merely the index to a profounder problem and a profounder temptation. Samson's sunny locks waving and curling about his godlike shoulders brought together in this scene with the potent charm of Dalila, indeed, the very physical center of that charm, speak to us of the fiercer temptation of beauty itself, the last infirmity we may say of poetic minds—at all events an infirmity when poetic minds are dedicated to the interpretation of the Hebrew oracles. For in the end those oracles do not authorize the surrender to the beautiful, even to the beauty of their own language. They bid us beware of treating the prophecies as a performance and they seem to warn us against seeing beauty as an absolute value.[20] From this point of view Dalila not only seduces Samson, she seduces Milton as well, disabling him for the task he had set himself. Hers is a potent beauty. As the Chorus says, "Yet beauty, though injurious, hath strange power" (1003). She is not merely beautiful, she is something like the principle of beauty itself:

> Like a stately ship
> Of Tarsus, bound for the isles
> Of Javan or Gadire,
> With all her bravery on, and tackle trim,
> Sails filled, and streamers waving,
> Courted by all the winds that hold them play.

This description of Dalila's first entry on the stage recalls the first appearance of Cleopatra to Antony on the river Cydnus in Shakespeare's play[21]—a scene which Shakespeare, following Plutarch, seems to associate with the archetypal image of Aphrodite riding on a scallop-shell after her birth from the foam of the sea.[22] Samson may reject her ("Out, out, hyaena") and the poet may seek to do the same. But there is too much involved for the poet wholly to preserve his vow unviolated. There are archetypal forces at work which threaten the hard-won balance of freedom and authority, of constraint and unconstraint which makes a covenantal hermeneutic possible. Beauty will threaten all constraints and will impose its own imperious authority. In this context the flower imagery is significant. Thus the Chorus:

> but now, with head declined,
> Like a fair flower surcharged with dew, she weeps.
> And words addressed seem into tears dissolved,
> Wetting the borders of her silken veil.
>
> (727–30)

Dalila becomes for the moment the heroine of a pastoral idyll in this reminding us of Eve, likened to Persephone in Book 4 of *Paradise Lost:*

Not that fair field
Of *Enna,* where *Prosperpin* gath'ring flow'rs
Herself a fairer Flow'r by gloomy *Dis*
Was gather'd, which cost *Ceres* all that pain
To seek her through the world. . .

(4:268–72)

It is not merely the beauty of Eve which had here threatened the accord between the poet and the biblical source: it is the haunting beauty of the verses themselves celebrating their own perfection. And if we think that in "the fair field of *Enna*" passage with "*Proserpin* gath'ring flowers" we have reached the ultimate celebration of the beautiful, we have still to see Eve as Satan sees her in Book 9 of *Paradise Lost.*

Herself, though fairest unsupported Flow'r,
From her best prop so far, and storm so nigh.

(9:424–33)

It is no wonder that the prophets set their face against the pastoral with its sweetness and nostalgia.[23] There is no resisting such beauty. Not only will a Samson or an Adam lay down his consecrated head in the "harlot-lap" of such an Eve. So will the poet and his reader.

The term "harlot" need not mislead us. Elsewhere it explicitly refers to the fierce temptations of an unhallowed literary culture where beauty, in particular poetic beauty, is the problem rather than sex. In Book 4 of *Paradise Regained,* the hero's final temptation involves the aesthetic attractions of Greek art and literature. These he rejects as so much "varnish on a Harlot's cheek" (*Paradise Regained* 4:344)—a problematical rejection indeed when we consider that this very poem owes much of its eloquence to the very tradition which is here rejected. The temptation offered by Dalila and the hero's rejection of that temptation have a similar function in *Samson Agonistes* and imply similar tensions at the heart of that poem.

One temptation then is the pastoral. The flowers of the pastoral and the pastoral tone borrowed from Dalila will at the close extend to Samson himself, as in Manoa's lines of farewell:

The virgins also shall, on feastful days,
Visit his tomb with flowers, only bewailing

> His lot unfortunate in nuptial choice,
> From whence captivity and loss of eyes.

We are reminded of *Lycidas,* a pastoral elegy likewise much concerned with hair—a symbol there of beauty but also of death. We remember "the tangles of Neaera's hair" and we remember Edward King, sunk to his grave beneath the wat'ry floor:

> With nectar pure his oozy Locks he laves,
> And hears the unexpressive nuptial Song,
> In the blest Kingdoms meek of joy and love.

This puts the hair-motif in a perspective very different from that of the Book of Judges, for *Lycidas* gives us not the strenuous task of a biblical hero but the sad languors of a Thyrsis in his lament for Daphnis. But there is just enough of this in *Samson Agonistes* to make the Nazirite begin to look from time to time like the hero of a pastoral romance. In such instances, Milton's solemn commitment to the muse of divine poetry—his own particular "nazirite vow"—is being threatened by the irresistible beauty of the pastoral.

But of course the issue in *Samson Agonistes* is not so much the seduction of pastoral. It is the even more potent seduction of tragedy. At the risk of stating the obvious, let me say that as well as writing a kind of midrash on four chapters of Judges, Milton is also—as he proclaims in his Preface—trying his hand at "that sort of dramatic poem which is call'd Tragedy." This makes it a midrash and not a midrash. The question is: can the genre of tragedy be adapted, in the end, to the kind of discourse to which the term covenantal hermeneutics may be applied? Midrash is open-ended, inconclusive; it is an ongoing dialogue between reader and text. Tragedy by contrast is marked by closure, by roundedness, as in the elegiac lines of Manoa or the summarizing words of the Chorus that follow. But the problem is not so much formal as phenomenological. The allure of tragedy, like that of the pastoral, has much to do at the deeper levels of our being with the allure of death and dying. This is not a matter of Hebraism versus Hellenism but much more a matter of the aesthetic of death versus the harsher aesthetic of living, with its untied ends, its trials, and errors.

It may be asked: if midrash is truly dialogic and truly hermeneutic why should it not be possible to read the biblical text as tragedy? The interpreter brings his personal context, cultural, historical, and social, to bear on the text to be interpreted. That text retains its authority; the reader or poet—in this case, Milton—as we have said retains his freedom. If this is so, why exclude tragedy? Is there in fact a principle of exclusion, or is not everyone authorized to make his own midrash in the light of his own history, his own situation, unloading into it his own cultural baggage, whatever it may be? This would include the religious baggage of the Christian reader who would wish to read *Samson Agonistes* typologically as an allegory of Christian sainthood, and who would wish to persuade us that Milton so read those chapters of Judges. Milton could not have been so unchristian as to want Samson to kill his enemies, so if he does so, it must be implicitly condemned in the poem itself,[24] or else the killing must mean something else, something more in line with Christian teaching.[25] The typological readings of *Samson Agonistes* have been much discussed and I will not go over this ground again except to say that Milton's religion as we know it had plenty of room for the expression of human aggressions—it was a matter of what Ezra Pound somewhere sweetly called "Milton's beastly Hebraism." When he wanted to operate with typology as in *Paradise Lost,* Book 12, he tells us that this is what he was doing. In *Samson Agonistes* he is it seems to me not doing this and the drama he develops is continuous with the biblical narrative as he understood it in its Old Testament context. It is not metaphor, or figura, but as we now like to say—metonymy.[26] But the question before us is not whether *Samson* is typological, but whether, if it were, the category of midrash could be stretched to include this kind of reading. Why not Christian typology if that is part of the writer's world of experience and why not an interpretive reading of Samson's life and death as tragedy or pastoral or the story of Adam and Eve in the Garden as epic if that is the way the interpreter's mind is conditioned by his particular cultural situation? And if not, what is the principle of exclusion?

The question arises in relation to texts of all kinds, not only the Bible. Specifically, it arises as a practical issue in the case of legal texts which are constantly reinterpreted in the light of changing circumstances. In that case we generally have established institutions, accepted as privileged sources of interpretation and as guarantors of continuity. The world of poetry and criticism notably lacks such formal institutions. Many might want to conclude from this that every combination of text and personal context has a prima facie validity and that there are no criteria of value and significance to distinguish one reading as more valid or less valid than another. But if that were so, we would have to include under the category of legitimate hermeneutics the reading of the twenty-third psalm once current among the Tlingit Indians of Alaska: "The Lord is my goathunter; I don't want him. He knocks me down on the mountain: He drags me down to the beach."[27] The point is that in the cultural context of this community there are no sheep that go out to pasture; indeed there are no green pastures; there are mountain goats that are hunted. The only way you can make them lie down is by knocking them over the head. And the only "still waters" within the experience of these people are those sometimes encountered on the seashore. Here then are two contexts in dialogue with one another. This you may say is an absurd example. The Christian interpretation of Samson which would translate him into an emblem of Christian sainthood is less absurd, but some of us might wish to ask the same question of that kind of interpretation even though it comes naturally to many good scholars and writers, namely: Are all examples of dialogue between text and history of equal value and legitimacy?

Bruns gives the basis for an answer in the passage I referred to earlier, where he speaks of midrash as characterized by a "mutual belonging of the text and those who hear it" and of "a common accord between ourselves and what is written." We might disagree about the conditions for such "mutual belonging" and "common accord" and the specific examples they would yield[28] but the principle of mutual belonging is one that we should welcome. It suggests a preexisting relation between text and context. From this principle it would follow that not all encounters between the two are what Bruns elsewhere terms "modes of participation in the dialogue with Torah."[29] Where common accord is lacking, the dialogue is presumably no true dialogue and where there is no mutual belonging we are no longer speaking of meaningful interpretive discourse for which the term midrash might be appropriate.

Midrash, grounded as it is in what I have termed covenantal hermeneutics, is thus open, but it is not that open. There is an *engagement,* a prior belonging which as the Rabbis saw, took the form of belonging to the covenantal community.[30] Milton clearly felt himself to belong to such a community. He had a strong sense not only of his own prophetic vocation but of that of the nation for whom he wrote—"why else was this Nation chos'n before any others that out of her *as out of Sion* should be proclam'd and sounded forth the first tidings and trumpet of Reformation to all Europ."[31] And this as I have argued lies behind the special intimacy he enjoys with Urania and the special affinity he finds with the Nazirite Samson. He too is chosen as is the nation whose herald he is. He has prior bonds with the text he is interpreting which go back to the first revealing of that text to "the chosen seed."

But there are evidently for Milton other bonds with other texts and other traditions; there are other cultural systems to which he seems sometimes to be no less engaged. It sometimes seems as though before the hills appeared the nurseling Milton was playing in the presence of a different deity or maybe with the tangles of Neaera's hair! All the better you may say for the poetry. The resulting achievement is more beautiful than any midrash. And perhaps it is, for it is questionable whether midrash aims at or achieves the category of beauty. The truth is probably that, while the Torah bids us choose life, death is more beautiful.

In the end Milton did not succeed in writing a midrash, but he did not succeed in writing a tragedy either. Samson's death lacks the note of defiant self-assertion of the true tragic hero. It is not the lonely descent into Avernus which Tragedy requires; in fact it is not lonely at all, for we are told that the end came "with God not parted from him, as was feared" nor is it really a descent, but rather an upward curve as befits the history of salvation. Manoa says truly, "Nothing is here for tears, nothing to wail." If we ask why in this case Milton felt it necessary to turn the narrative of Samson's career from the book of Judges into a tragedy, we would have to say again that it was because such an ambition was integral to his own context, his own world, his own inherited literary culture. It is that context which he brings to bear on the biblical text and between which and the biblical text he seeks an accord. Midrash depends on such accord, such mutual belonging. It is defeated in Milton's case because, in spite of his profound understanding of the text he was interpreting, ultimately there can be no accord between the closures of myth and romance and tragedy and the openness of biblical narrative and of biblical history.

In the end we have a case of "radical translation," of a brave attempt, to "resituate the text within an alien conceptual framework."[32] At that point we reach the limits of midrash. Milton's exegetical effort, an effort which often seems to be synonymous with his poetic enterprise as a whole, is therefore doomed, if not to failure, then to something like the partial success which attended the efforts of the Tlingit Indians to translate the twenty-third Psalm into their own cultural context, namely: "The Lord is my goat-hunter, I don't want him."

NOTES

1. This includes the pervasive imagery of stone statues whereby the martial valor and stoic virtues of the Roman leaders are so often commemorated. There is frequent mention of such statues in Plutarch. But in Shakespeare's hands this imagery becomes the focus of the play's profoundest ironies. Caesar is never less like a Colossus than when Cassius so defines him in Act 1. And see further, H. Fisch, *Hamlet and the Word: The Covenant Pattern in Shakespeare* (New York: Ungar, 1971), Appendix, "*Julius Caesar* and the Bleeding Statue," pp. 224–30.

2. I would want to argue that such a posture hardly fits Harold Bloom's notion of an oedipal struggle between Milton and his precursors. See *The Anxiety of Influence* (New York: Oxford University Press, 1973), pp. 22, 32–34, and idem, *A Map of Misreading* (New York: Oxford University Press, 1975), pp. 125–43. Bloom recognizes the importance of the dense echoing of precursor-poets in Milton but treats this as a "transumptive strategy" aimed at affirming his own priority.

3. *Specimens of the Table Talk of S. T. Coleridge* (London: John Murray, 1851), pp. 278–79 (entry for April 18, 1833).

4. Ibid., p. 71 (entry for May 12, 1830).

5. I am using the term dialogic here in the sense it has for M. M. Bakhtin. Cf. *The Dialogic Imagination,* ed. Michael Holquist (Austin: University of Texas Press, 1981), pp. 69, 280.

6. Gerald L. Bruns, "Midrash and Allegory" in *The Literary Guide to the Bible,* ed. Robert Alter and Frank Kermode (Cambridge, MA: Harvard University Press, 1987), pp. 633–634.

7. Cf. R. Yohanan's statement that God's covenant with Israel is solely on account of the "Oral Law" (B. T. *Gittin,* 60b and parallels).

8. J. A. Wittreich, *Interpreting Samson Agonistes* (Princeton University Press, 1986), p. 60.

9. Ibid.

10. Ibid., p. 61.

11. F. Kermode, *The Genesis of Secrecy: On the Interpretation of Narrative* (Cambridge, MA: Harvard University Press, 1979), pp. 81f.

12. Discussed by several scholars; most recently, Golda S. Werman has illustrated the considerable use Milton made of an eighth-century midrash, *Pirke D'Rabbi Eliezer,* which had been translated into Latin by Vorstius. See "Midrash in *Paradise Lost: Capitula Rabbi Elieser,*" *Milton Studies,* 18 (1983), 145–71.

13. An exception to this is the notion, nowhere mentioned in the text of Judges, that Samson was married to Dalila. Cf. S. S. Stollman, "Milton's Samson and the Jewish Tradition," *Milton Studies* 3 (1971), 189.

14. Milton's thinking on society, politics, and religion is, like that of his Puritan contemporaries, saturated in covenant terminology. Relations between subject, parliament, and king are ordered by covenant; marriage is a covenant. Above all, the inner life of the individual (typically that of the poet) is the locus of a covenant drama. For further discussion, see H. Fisch, *Jerusalem and Albion* (London: Routledge and Kegan Paul, 1964), pp. 113, 120–25.

15. Cf. the famous midrashic comment on the first verse of the Bible: "R. Oshaya commenced: 'Then I was by Him, as a nursling; and I was daily all delight' . . . God consulted the Torah and created the world." (*Midrash Rabbah,* edited by H. Freedman and Maurice Simon, Genesis 1:1, translated by H. Freedman [London: Soncino, 1939], vol. 1, p. 1).

16. *The Works of John Milton* (New York: Columbia University Press, 1931), 4:344.

17. Ibid., 3:277.

18. Cf. *Midrash Rabbah,* ed. H. Freedman and M. Simon, *Numbers* 10:7, trans. J. Slotki (London: Soncino, 1939), vol 1, pp. 371–72.

19. For this term see Gwendolyn Bays, *The Orphic Vision: Seer Poets from Novalis to Rimbaud* (Lincoln: University of Nebraska Press, 1964), pp. 4–14; for the trend see also Mario Praz, *The Romantic Agony,* trans. Angus Davidson (London: Oxford University Press, 1988), pp. 15–25.

20. Cf. H. Fisch, *Poetry With a Purpose: Biblical Poetics and Interpretation* (Bloomington: Indiana University Press, 1988), pp. 15–25.

21. An echo not always noticed by critics and editors, but see, M. Roston, "Milton's Herculean Samson," *Milton Quarterly,* (1983), 91; J. Guillory, "Dalila's House" in *Rewriting the Renaissance,* ed. Margaret W. Ferguson, Maureen Quilligan, and Nancy J. Vickers (Chicago University Press, 1986), pp. 113–15.

22. Cf. *Shakespeare's Plutarch,* ed. T. J. B. Spencer (Harmondsworth: Penguin Books, 1968), pp. 201–02. This may help to explain the imagery of ships and tempests noted by Barbara K. Lewalski as pervasive in *Samson Agonistes* (*Notes and Queries,* 6 [1959], 372–73).

23. Cf. *Poetry With a Purpose,* p. 60.

24. Cf. Irene Samuel, "*Samson Agonistes* as Tragedy" in *Calm of Mind,* pp. 235–51.

25. Representative studies of this kind are F. M. Krouse, *Milton's Samson and the Christian Tradition* (Princeton, NJ: Princeton University Press, 1949) and T. S. K. Scott-Craig, "Concerning Milton's *Samson,*" *Renaissance News* 5 (1952), 43–53. Important reservations about the typological understanding of biblical and renaissance texts have been voiced in recent years, notably by Kenneth Gross (*Spenserian Poetics: Idolatry, Iconoclasm, and Magic* [Ithaca: Cornell University Press, 1985]); Herbert Marks, "Pauline Typology and Revisionary Criticism" in *Journal of the American Academy of Religion,* 52 (1984), 71–92; J. A. Wittreich, *Interpreting Samson Agonistes,* pp. 57, 244; and Mary Ann Radzinowicz, *Toward Samson Agonistes: The Growth of Milton's Mind* (Princeton NJ: Princeton University Press), pp. 283–84.

26. Cf. Susan A. Handelman, *Slayers of Moses: The Emergence of Rabbinic Interpretation in Modern Literary Theory* (Albany: State University of New York Press, 1982), pp. 76–82.

27. Reported by Constance Naish and Gillian Story in *The Bible Translator,* 14 (1963), 91–92.

28. Bruns seems ready at times to include under the heading of 'midrash' Christian readings which would make Jesus the hero of the Old Testament narratives, see art. cit. pp. 635, 643.

29. Ibid., p. 632.

30. This would be a special example of what Stanley E. Fish in a different context calls an "interpretive community." See, *Is There a Text in This Class?* (Cambridge, MA: Harvard University Press, 1980), p. 11.

31. *Areopagitica* in Milton, *Works,* 4, 340.

32. Bruns (art. cit. p. 637) basing himself on notions drawn from W. V. O. Quine's *Word and Object* and Donald Davidson's *Inquiries into Truth and Interpretation.*

Theoretical Perspectives

CHAPTER 2

Biblical Covenants as Performative Language

Gerda Alster-Elata and Rachel Salmon

If we attempt to examine the covenantal language of the Torah, we find that the same language which functions referentially to describe a certain kind of agreement—either between God and human beings or between human parties—also has a performative function. This performative aspect of language has been brought to the fore and studied by contemporary Speech Act Theory.[1] However, even the biblical scholars who have not restricted themselves to a description of the referential meaning of the biblical narrative, have limited their application of Speech Act Theory to a description of the conventions which allow language to produce social effects.[2] Our own interest in the workings of covenantal language has led us to use the categories of Speech Act Theory in the opposite direction. Instead of describing how preexisting social conventions empower language, we wish to examine how the biblical language works to establish extra-linguistic conventions and institutions. In this paper, we shall focus upon how the language, which itself narrates the making of covenants in the Hebrew Bible, brings these covenants about.

According to Searle, covenants, along with promises, should be classified as commissives, that is, as speech acts which commit the speaker to the performance of a future action.[3] In our study of the covenants in the Torah, we find Searle's classification inadequate. First of all, in contradistinction to promises which are pronounced unilaterally, covenants always involve mutuality as a necessary condition.[4] Only if both parties maintain the speech act can the covenant be said to be in place. Furthermore, while Searle does not differentiate explicitly between divine-human and human-human covenants, we find a significant disparity between them in the Hebrew Bible, although the same term—ברית—is used for both.[5] Whereas the covenants between people bind both parties equally, God and human beings covenant with each other through two incongruent Speech Acts. In both kinds of covenants, although a person commits him or herself to keeping that commitment in the future, the pledge can be broken. In a human covenant, a broader covenant is null and void and the speech act has lost its efficacy. In the biblical covenants between God and humans, however, human defection does not simply vitiate the covenant; God's words are not nullified by any human act.[6] It appears that God's covenantal speech has made a permanent change in the world order.

God's part in the covenant thus approximates Searle's category of a declarative speech act. Unlike other sorts of speech acts which never fully succeed in making the word fit the world (assertives), or the world fit the word (directives and commissives), declarations actually do close the gap between language and a state of affairs in the world. They can do this, because a closed system of extra-linguistic constituitive rules guarantees a world in which they function by definition. For instance, the court is indeed open once the properly appointed official pronounces the words designated by the judiciary institution.[7]

According to Searle, extralinguistic support can be dispensed with only in metalinguistic and supernatural declarations. In the former, the relationship between word and thing is defined by the linguistic expression itself. From Searle's examples, we learn that the supernatural declarations he has in mind are those world creating pronouncements which open the book of Genesis.[8] Such declarations can conform neither to a preexisting state of affairs (nothing yet exists), nor to linguistic conventions (the utterance is the coming into being of language). That is to say, supernatural declarations make reality happen in a most radical way. The divine declarations involved in the act of covenanting do not, at first, seem to have such dramatic force, but an examination of divine-human covenants, in the Hebrew Bible, reveals that they do change the nature of the world.

We must, however, ask how the human participation in the act of biblical covenanting is similar to God's, and how it differs. How can a human commissive meet a supernatural declaration in the act of covenanting? What sort of speech act could we call this merging of divine and human language? We may address these questions by attending to the condition of mutuality involved in all covenants, a condition which Searle fails to analyze.

In the Torah, the requests of the foreigners to make a covenant—in the scenes between Avimelech and Avraham, Avimelech and Yitzchak, and Yaakov and Lavan—all reflect a perceived asymmetry or lack, and a sense of change. Something has occurred, in the existing balance of forces, to the disadvantage of the one who makes the request. In each case, the party which feels threatened initiates the covenantal process.[9] Examining the problem of mutuality in the context of divine-human covenants, we are not surprised that an asymmetry exists between God and human beings in the Torah. What is, however, surprising is that all the covenants are initiated by God—that is, God occupies the structural position which belongs to the weaker party in the human-with-human covenants.[10] Is it possible to say that God becomes aware of some sort of change or lack in His relation to humankind, which could motivate such an initiative?

The first divine-human covenant, that which God makes with Noah, opens with an unusually explicit and elaborate description of divine reasoning. Since the conventional English translations do not represent the verbal echoes of the Hebrew, we have translated in such a way as to make them obvious, so that we can study the sort of language work that is taking place.

> And the Lord saw that the wickedness of man was great on earth, and that all the inclinations of the thoughts of his heart were only evil all the day. And the Lord *changed* His mind (וינחם) about having *made* (עשה) man on earth and it *troubled* Him (ויתעצב) in His heart. And the Lord said, "I will wipe out man whom I have created from the face of the *land* (האדמה), from man to beast, to creeping thing, and to fowl of the heaven, for I have *changed* My mind (נחמתי) about having *made* them (עשיתם)." And *Noah* (נח) found grace (חן) in the eyes of the Lord. (Gen. 6:5–8)

Pondering, within the framework of true/false statements (referential readings) upon God's regret, we cannot help but ask how His perception could change—that is, be time-determined. How did God not know that "the inclinations" of His creature would be "only evil all the day"? Looking at the sequence of this narrative, we find ourselves involved in logical and chronological contradictions: despite God's omniscience, He learns something new about His creature, and despite His omnipotence, He must nevertheless wait upon the human creature. Any referential reading of a divine-human covenantal narrative ends in a paradoxical statement of the logically impossible relationship between divine omnipotence and human freedom. Why would God represent himself as one who is perturbed enough to think of destroying His own work, and as one who can maintain His creation only through the establishment of a covenant? What could be the illocutionary point of such a ploy? And how are we to understand this sudden discovery of Noah, who "found grace in the eyes of the Lord," thus giving a rather gratuitous motive for God to revoke his decision "to blot out" the world he created, through a further declaration. The incongruity of this narrative sequence brings to the reader's consciousness another incongruity: in a text so sparse, why did the previous chapter elaborate upon Lemech's naming of his son Noah?

> And he [Lemech] called his son *Noah* (נח) saying, this one will make us a *change* for the better (ינחמנו), in our *works* (ממעשנו—*that which we have made*), and the *troubles* (ומעצבון) of our handwork in the *land* (האדמה), which the Lord has cursed. (Gen. 5:29)

Initially, we would most likely read Lemech's speech as a metalinguistic speech act of naming conjoined with an expressive; Lemech expresses his desire for a better future through naming his son to be the one who will appease God's anger. In such a reading, the pun by which Lemech subverts his language system—semantically relating נח to נחם in order to connect the concept of change with that of comfort, rather than that of desolation—would seem to be mere wishful thinking, and to bear no necessary relationship to the future course of history. It is only in the light of his success—the grace (חן) which God "finds" in Noah (נח), seems to be the grace which his father designated in him—that we begin to wonder about the nature of Lemech's speech act. Although the text is silent here about Noah's merits, the words which record God's change of mind (such as נח, עצב, אדם, נחם, and עשה) are reverberations of Lemech's words, and thus seem to endow them, in retrospect, with the authority of prophecy. We must ask how

Lemech's human speech act took on the potency of making the world fit his words.

A possible way for understanding the relationship between Lemech's naming of Noah and God's speech is to look at it as the effect of *Nachträglichkeit:* much like the infantile traumatic experience, Lemech's naming of his son gains its power to produce a symptom only in retrospect, when a second event, carrying some of the same elements, takes place. At the time of Noah's birth, there is no reason to think that his father could pronounce anything beyond human speech acts. Only when God brings the natural disaster ("symptom") of the Flood, through a repetition of Lemech's words, can those words take on the property of causality. Lemech's original metalinguistic declaration can be said neither to have been determined by God (as would be the case in prophecy), nor can it be said to have determined God's supernatural declaration of destruction. Yet, when the elements of his speech recur in God's language, Lemech's words appear to wield an inordinate amount of power. Indeed, they cause an additional return to a previous, and especially potent, act of naming: Adam's naming of the animals.

The naming of Noah seems both to emerge from and differentiate itself from that original act of naming. Whereas Adam is told by God to name the animals, Lemech appears to act upon his own initiative. In trying to describe the nature of Adam's speech act, we may either say that the names which Adam gives conform perfectly to the animals' function in creation (word to world fit), or else that they establish that function (world to word fit). In the timeless world of Eden, where there is no gap between language and referent, these alternatives could, in fact, be seen as coextensive. In this way, Adam's speech act bears some resemblance to God's supernatural declarations. Lemech, however, is born into a world in which language and reality have already been drifting apart for the ten generations since the expulsion from the Garden of Eden. Lemech can perform a metalinguistic speech act, but he cannot, himself, make his words operative in the world.

This diminished capacity of language results directly from the sin of Adam and Eve in the Garden of Eden, which was both brought about by and punished through language. God gave Adam a negative command: whereas man may eat from "all the trees in the Garden," he must not eat "from the Tree of the Knowledge of

Good and Evil" (Gen. 2:16–17). The question arises, why the first pair's disobedience is brought about through the intervention of the snake. Could it be that they, themselves, were not able to perceive such a possibility? Indeed, in view of the fact that creation involved a process of separating out oppositions through supernatural declarations, we must assume that Adam understood the negative command as a statement about the essential nature of trees. Since no language had as yet been provided for differentiating between a supernatural declaration and a command, Adam had no reason to perceive any distance at all between God's words and reality.

The snake, however, loosens the bonds between word and meaning, by introducing the possibility of interpretation. First, by suggesting to Eve that the prohibition applies to all of the trees, the snake undoes God's linguistic distinction; then he disrupts referentiality by proclaiming that the threat of death will not be carried out, and, finally, he introduces linguistic ambiguity by suggesting an unstated motive—"for God knows that in the day you eat thereof, then your eyes shall be opened, and you shall be as God, knowing good and evil." (Gen. 3:5) What Eve *hears* makes her *see* differently; the Tree now appears not only edible, but desirable and potent. The space that this lesson in rhetoric opens up between what a thing (or word) is, and what can be done with it, enables her to make the deliberate choice to disobey. The snake's linguistic manipulations make it possible for its assertions to be simultaneously true and false: death is not immediately coextensive with disobedience, but humans become mortal. The world, too, becomes accursed through an additional supernatural declaration (Gen. 2:17–18). As the generations of humankind proceed, the original distinctions of creation are blurred. Finally, we find "the sons of God" (whoever they may be) mating with "the daughters of man," in an act which transgresses the boundaries of heaven and earth (Gen. 6:1–2, 4).

By the time Lemech names Noah, we would expect his words to have no more power than that of rhetoric. Yet, Lemech presumes to make a speech act directed not only towards changing language internally, but towards making a change in the world by undoing the curse. Not only does he exercise the metalinguistic declarative power to subvert his language system—by punning the root נח with the root נחם, and thus connecting the concept of change with that of comfort rather than desolation—but he tries to declare, through a repetition of the words God used when expelling Adam and Eve from the Garden of Eden, that the curse will be lifted from the land. For Lemech, there were only two possible language acts: supernatural declarations in which word and thing are one, or the purely rhetorical language introduced by the snake, in which word has no necessary connection with its referent. However, when God repeats Lemech's words, He performs neither of these language acts. Lemech had wished for the restoration of Eden, but the irreversibility of time introduced with the expulsion made such a "straightbackward" solution impossible. The path to the Tree of Life has been permanently cut off, but God will now provide a language through which man can choose to participate in God's world creating acts through choosing to obey.[12]

Just as the interplay of language in the scene in the Garden of Eden made deliberate disobedience possible by opening a space for interpretation, the sort of gap introduced between word and meaning in the naming of Lemech makes possible the choice of obedience. God takes up Lemech's pun and reverses it—whereas Lemech connected נחם with נח (ease or comfort), God uses נחם to indicate an unpropitious change of mind: a regret that He created humans in the first place, and a resolve to undo creation through a further supernatural declaration. Humans, by perpetuating disobedience, have blurred the distinctions of creation, and God will now wipe out those distinctions entirely. However by metathesizing נח with חן, which leads to the building of the Ark, God introduces space into his supernatural declaration of destruction, just as He introduced time into the death sentence proclaimed in the Garden of Eden. The statement that "Noah found grace in the eyes of the Lord," while affirming the positive connotations of the name Lemech had given his son, does not restore the Garden of Eden, where humans either obeyed because of the nature of things, or chose to disobey. The puns which can be made on Noah's name open the possibility of a new sort of language act.

The positive command is the sign that "Noah found grace in the eyes of the Lord." Noah is instructed to build an Ark, and to bring into it all of the animals according to the already established distinction of male and female, and the newly introduced one of pure and impure. The differentiations created in the Garden of Eden, and soon to be eradicated in the Flood, will be preserved through Noah's choice to obey God's minute instructions. Unlike Adam, whose natural function was "to tend and preserve" the Garden of Eden, (Gen. 2:15), Noah must deliberately decide to fulfill the will of God. Noah, whose very name figures alternatives, choses "to walk with the Lord" (Gen. 6:9) by carrying out His commandment. It is Noah's freedom to do otherwise—granted him by the multi-functionality of his language—that enables Noah to become a partner with God in the establishment of a new world.

Without the cooperation of Noah, God could either have reestablished the Garden of Eden (which would lead to the replaying of the scenario of the sin), or He could have blotted out creation. Once again, the concept of *Nachträglichkeit* can be brought into play, this time as a way of understanding God's position in the initiation of covenantal relations. On the one hand, God proposes the covenant, on the other, Lemech's speech act seems to have opened the human possibility of freely choosing to cooperate with God. The narrative of the Flood and its aftermath shows how this speech potential is realized.

After Noah has left the Ark, in obedience to God's command, he builds an altar upon which he sacrifices pure animals (Gen. 8:20). Upon smelling the pleasant odor of the offering, God once again speaks to Himself about the fate of the world, but this time, although He uses similar words, He reverses His decision. He resolves that He will never again curse the world because of man (Gen. 8:21). We would have expected, from the sequence of narration, that God's decision resulted from Noah's pious act. It seems, therefore, incongruous that God gives as His reason for clemency the observation that "man's inclination is evil from his youth onwards" (ibid.). This would seem to be a good reason for destroying the world, rather than for guaranteeing the future maintenance of its proper distinctions and order.

God, however, repronounces supernatural declarations of the sort which established man's nature in the Garden of Eden, but He now pronounces them with a difference. First, God makes a change in respect to the human relationship to the animals. Whereas people previously reigned over them, but, like them, ate only vegetarian food, they are now declared omnivore, but certain limitations are imposed on their consumption of meat (Gen. 9:4). On the one hand, this change in human nature will provide the ground for further distinctions—such as kosher and non-kosher—and for the laws pertaining to participation in sacrificial meals. On the other hand, eating again becomes—like in the Garden of Eden, when the Tree of the Knowledge of Good and Evil was prohibited—not fully a matter of complying automatically with one's nature, but also a matter of choosing to obey negative divine commands.

Next, the blessing "be fruitful and multiply" (Gen. 1:28) which determined humankind's nature in the Garden of Eden, and which is repeated as soon as Noah leaves the Ark (Gen. 8:17), is transformed from a supernatural declaration into a positive commandment.[13] This speech act opens the possibility of choice even in the way that so natural an act as procreation is performed.

The first covenant follows immediately; God declares that He is establishing a covenant (as He promised when He sent Noah into the Ark in Gen. 6:18). Initially, the covenant has the form of a supernatural declaration: God says that He will never again destroy all living creatures and never again blot out the distinctions of creation. The performative difference between a covenant and a divine promise, however, is not yet clear. The establishment of the "sign of the covenant" (Gen. 9:12–17)—the rainbow—seems to mark such a distinction.[14] By declaring the rainbow to be a sign, in addition to its function as a natural phenomenon, God gives it a historical role. We would, then, expect that sign to function vis-à-vis human beings—as a guarantee of God's promise—but we are told that it will be functional for God: "And it shall come to pass, when I bring clouds over the earth, and the bow is seen in the cloud, that I will remember my covenant" (Gen. 9:14–15). God's "remembrance" of the covenant, through seeing the rainbow, seems to attribute to God the human characteristic of forgetting. We could, perhaps, say that the sign of the covenant works as a language in time; the Hebrew word for sign (אות) also designates a character of the alphabet. Through the sign, God addresses human beings in temporal terms, so that people who has lost the eternity of the Garden of Eden can nevertheless converse with Him. In this first covenant, however, humans are only recipient, not active participants.

We soon see the outcome of God's pledge to maintain the distinctions of language and reality. Whereas before the Flood human beings, by transgressing and blurring distinctions in the world, had in effect made language purely rhetorical, in the story of the Tower of Babel, we find them exploiting language in the opposite direction. The univocal correspondence between word and meaning which God guarantees, tempts humans to make "a name" for themselves, that is to attempt to regain access to an essential language. Such a language would enable them to give material form to their most outrageous ambitions. Possessing "one language" and "one speech" (Gen. 11:1), all the peoples of the earth sought to coordinate their efforts to reach heaven. In a manner similar to that of the expulsion from the Garden of Eden—which prevented Adam and Even from achieving immortality—God confuses the language of humans so that they cannot become the master of space. (Gen. 11:1–9)

The next divine-human covenant—that between God and Avraham—takes place in two parts separated by at least fourteen years. It begins with a positive command to Avram[15] to separate himself from his country, the place of his birth, and his family. He also receives a series of promises: he will become the forefather of a great nation and be blessed, his *name* shall be made great, and, most significant, other nations shall be blessed through him (Gen. 12:1–3). Avram obeys the command, God reiterates the promise, and Avram builds two altars (Gen. 12:7–8). After Avram's separation from Lot, the sequence of promise and altar is again repeated (Gen. 13:14–18). When God finally says (Gen. 15:7), I am the Lord that brought thee out of Ur of the Chaldees, to give thee this land to inherit it," His words seem to be a summary. However, Avram, who has, so far, believed everything God told him, now asks: "whereby shall I know that I shall inherit it" (Gen. 15:8). The scene that follows this question transforms a unilateral promise into a covenant.

God does not answer Avram's question; instead, he commands him to bring a specific sacrifice. Avram brings the specified animals and cuts them in half, placing "each half over against the other." (Gen. 15:10) It is not clear how Avram knows to do this, but the verb ("ויבתר") which he uses is a metathesis of ברית. His act is opaque, much in the manner of Lemech's naming of Noah. Like Lemech's naming, Avram's offering does not lend itself to immediate interpretation, but becomes accessible as time passes. We have no way of deciding whether Avram and Lemech possess some sort of foreknowledge which enables them to act as they do, or whether it is the way their acts make an earlier scene suddenly appear meaningful that makes what follows seem plausible. This effect of *Nachträglichkeit,* which makes it impossible to attribute responsibility or trace causality unidirectionally, again appears at the initiation of the second covenant.

Once the sacrifice is in place, Avram enters into some sort of trance, in which he learns the future history of a people as yet unborn, and also—as he perceives "a smoking torch and a flaming torch which passed between the pieces" (Gen. 15:17)—what guarantees that knowledge. In retrospect, the narration tells us that "In that day the Lord made a covenant with Avram, saying: 'Unto thy seed have I given this land'" (Gen. 15:18). How, we may ask, does this covenant differ from the divine promises about this subject which have already been made?

Although Avram here appears to be quite passive, it is his question, or perhaps challenge, which initiates the sequence—much as Lemech's naming of Noah initiated the first covenant. Then, Avram prepares the sacrifice in a way which makes a sign possible; He cuts the pieces between which the flame can pass. This covenant is, indeed, established through the Hebrew verb "כרת" (Gen. 15:18)—to cut—instead of the verb "מקים"—to establish. The term "כרת," which appears for the first time in the Torah in God's declaration that all flesh would not again be cut off ("יכרת") (Gen. 15:11) by the water of a Flood, bears no apparent reference to the idea of a covenant. We tend to think of a covenant, as a binding, not as a cutting asunder. However, the use of the word teaches us something about the performative, rather than the referential, aspect of the act of covenanting. In order for God and human beings to covenant with each other, God must limit (cut back) His supernatural declarations so that they can function within the dimensions of time and space, and intersect with human language. Humankind, on the other hand, must cut itself off from the contingent world in which has hithertofore constituted its identity, in order to covenant with God.

In the second covenantal scene between God and Avram, the distinction between a unilateral divine promise and a divine-human covenant becomes increasingly clear. What intervenes between the two covenantal scenes is the narration of Sarai's attempt to take matters into her own hands: to provide Avram, via Hagar, with offspring through whom the covenant could be fulfilled. God, however, speaks again to Avram, repeating the already familiar sequence of positive commandment and promise. While He had previously told Avram to walk away from his homeland and ancestors (Gen. 12:1), and then to "arise and walk through the land" (Gen. 13:17), God now commands Avram to "walk before Me, and be thou whole-hearted" (Gen. 17:1). He then reintroduces the covenant, but this time instead of using the verb "to establish" or "to cut," He says: "I will give [אתנה] my covenant" (Gen. 17:2); and instead of making the covenant *with* ["את"] Avram, He now says that He will make it "*between Myself and you*" ["ביני ובינך"] (ibid.). The expression "between" does not replace "with" (Gen. 17:14), but it adds a new linguistic feature to the making of covenants, which will become increasingly important. It provides a nearly visual image of mutuality, and recalls the severed halves of the sacrificial animals which are united by the divine fire.

Whereas Noah was a passive recipient of God's covenant, and even the appointed sign, the rainbow—which would be visible to Noah—appears to be functional mainly for God, Avram will be made a participant. The covenant opens, however, with a series of supernatural declarations. While God affirmed the name that Noah's father gave him, Avram is renamed directly by God. The letter "ה" added to his name (as, in Gen. 17:15, it will be added to Sarai's), which is a letter of the name of God, is read by Him as signifying the covenant: "the father of a multitude of nations have I made thee" (Gen. 17:5). The promises of fertility and the inheritance of the land are then repeated (Gen. 17:6). So far, all of the speech acts originate from God, and are guaranteed by God's word.

However, God then addresses Avraham in a way that makes him directly responsible: "and you, keep My covenant, you and your seed after you, for all generations: this is My covenant that you will keep, between Me and you and between your seed after you, each of your males shall be circumcised" (Gen. 17:9–10). Circumcision is called, here, the covenant itself; in the next verse (Gen. 17:11), it is called: "the sign of the covenant between Me and you (plural); and several verses later (Gen. 17:13), it is said that: "My covenant in your flesh will be a covenant forever. The verb "כרת" which is frequently used for the making of a covenant, is used here in reference to the breaking of the covenant: "And the uncircumcised male who is not circumcised in the flesh of his foreskin, that soul shall be cut off ["ונכרתה"] from his people; he hath broken My covenant" (Gen. 17:14). Avraham's part of the covenant is as essential as God's; the supernatural declaration must be cut into the flesh. Between God and the human, now stands a word and an act which are somehow identical: both covenant and sign of covenant.

Avraham and Sarah cannot carry out "פרו ורבו" either as an act pertaining to their nature, or by choosing to fulfill a positive commandment. They are set apart by the unnatural birth of the son who will carry on the covenant. After God has, Himself, changed the names of these old people, they are again promised a son. They do not name him by themselves, nor does God name him directly, but He charges them to name their son for the laughter which his birth has aroused: "and thou shalt call his name Yitzchak, and I will establish ["הקמותי"] my covenant with him ["אתו"], for an everlasting covenant for his seed after him" (Gen. 17:19). It is perhaps significant that the covenant will be made *with* Yitzchak, who is almost entirely passive, rather than *between* God and him, as with Avraham. We are told in retrospect that the covenant was made also with Yitzchak's son Yaacov, although the act itself is not explicitly reported.

Why, we may ask, did God need to make any additional covenants after the covenant with Noah, which guaranteed the preservation of creation? As we have seen, the covenant with Avraham begins by separating him from the human families which have been scattered over the earth since the incident of the Tower of Babel. The covenant God makes with him establishes a separated nation and a historical thread distinguishable from the flow of time in the world. Avraham and his descendents will bear a visible sign of differentiation, and the blessings of all the other nations are dependent upon its maintenance. At this point, the gap seems to close between the sign of the covenant and the covenant itself; both are centered on a human deed of obedience, the participation of humankind which makes the world worthy of blessing, rather than mere preservation.

The family of Yaacov goes down to Egypt in accordance with the prophecy Avraham received when he prepared the sacrifice of the parts (ברית בין הבתרים, Gen. 15:13–14). There, although enslaved, they become a nation which God, who remembers the covenant, will take out from the midst of another nation. The climactic covenant is the one that God makes with an entire nation which, possessed of its own language, can finally covenant with God through a proper speech act. At Mount Sinai, a massive act of covenanting takes place. It is not that a new covenant is made, but that the old covenant, which was established with a family, is renewed, now, with an entire people.

The nineteenth chapter of the Book of Exodus sets out this covenantal scene in detail. The enormous responsibility that the People of Israel takes upon itself in entering the covenant is clear in the message that God sends through Moses in order to prepare the people.

> Ye have seen what I did unto the Egyptians, and how I bore you on eagles' wings, and brought you unto Myself. Now, therefore, if ye will hearken unto My voice indeed, and keep My covenant, then ye shall be Mine own treasure from among all peoples; for all the earth is Mine; and ye shall be unto Me a kingdom of priests, and a holy nation. (Exod. 19:4–6)

The period of time leading up to the gathering by Mount Sinai is called "the three days of the setting of bounds." All of the commands which the people must carry out during these days—maintaining distance from the mountain, purifying themselves, refraining from sexual relations—concern separations and distinctions. These are acts to be done, but in addition, for the first time in an act of covenanting, the human party speaks: "And all of the people answered together, and said 'All that the Lord hath spoken we will do'" (Exod. 19:8).

However, when God speaks the Ten Commandments directly to the assembled nation, they are extremely frightened: "And they said to Moses: 'Speak thou with us, and we will hear; but let not God speak with us, lest we die'" (Exod. 20:16). Although they will speak three times with one voice, in order to pledge themselves to keeping the covenant, they do not speak directly to God. Perhaps, we may say that they are so fearful because, unlike the snake and Eve, they do not interpret God's words about death rhetorically. They try to make their own speech, during the act of covenanting, echo the supernatural declaration: they attempt, that is, to close the gap between what is said and what is done.

> And Moses came and told the people all the words of the Lord, and all the ordinances; and all the people answered with one voice, and said: "All the words which the Lord hath spoken we

> will do." And Moses wrote all the words of the Lord, and rose up early in the morning. . . . And he took the book of the covenant, and read in the hearing of the people; and they said: "All that the Lord hath spoken we will do and we will hear." And Moses took the blood, and sprinkled it on the people, and said: "Behold the blood of the covenant, which the Lord hath made with you, concerning all of these words." (Exod. 24:3–4, 7–8)

In this scene, many elements of the earlier covenants—positive and negative commands, altar and sacrifice, the marking of the body with a distinctive sign—are present. The Book of the Covenant is both sign of the covenant and the covenant itself, as is the Sabbath, which God appoints: "for a perpetual covenant. It is a sign between Me and the children of Israel for ever" (Exod. 31:16–17). But for the first time, human covenanting words answer those of God. As God has pledged to preserve creation, the people of Israel pledge to keep their word.

They do not succeed. The human speech act meets the supernatural declaration, but it is not its equivalent; it does not make reality. No sooner has the people of Israel bound itself to the covenant, than it breaks its bonds.[16] The punishment—after God shows Moses how to plead for his people, and thereby maintain the covenant—applies to individuals: "that soul shall be cut off ("כרת") from among his people" (Exod. 31:14). The distinction of the nation remains; it ensures that the whole world can one day be blessed.

Two semiotic systems figure forth the ability of covenants to hold the divine and the human word together. The first is linguistic. In the cutting of the covenant, the Hebrew term כרת means to sever, but, in effect, it joins. In addition, the two letter stem בר of ברית, is the common Semitic-Indoeuropean stem for breaking; a metathesis of ברית is בתר, which means to split in two. In ברית בין הבתרים (the Covenant Between the Parts) these roots are juxtaposed, indicating the dual nature of the covenantal relationship between God and human beings.

The second semiotic system is the sign of the covenant (אות ברית), in its various ramifications. God's appointment of the natural rainbow in the cloud to be a sign of the covenant, is a declarative act: the function of the sign in the world is made by God's words. Referentially, the sign is paradoxical. God says that when He looks at the rainbow He will remember the covenant, but it is absurd to think of God as forgetting. The sign of the covenant with Abraham is a declarative act mutual to God and man. God institutes the sign by naming it, but only man can carry out the nonverbal act of circumcision. At Sinai, the Torah is both the content and the sign of the covenant.

The signs of the covenants between human beings try to imitate the declarative force of the divine-human covenants, but always fall short. They cannot, themselves, effect a change in the world, but only represent an intention. If either party violates the terms of the covenant, the covenant is wiped out and its sign reverts to a state of nature. In a covenant between God and a human, the human may violate his or her speech act and abort its declarative power, but God's fully declarative word can never be wiped out, nor His sign erased.

Since the Torah is both the sign of the covenant of the Jewish people with God and the covenant itself, the reader who intends to repeat it, performs, in reading it, the declarative speech act of becoming a partner to the covenantal relationship with God. The performance of the commandments of the Torah—one of which is to read the Torah—makes a reality, which brings God's word closer to the human word. Thus humankind covenants with God through the performance of an act which can contain the paradoxical relationship between the infinite and the finite, but which does not attempt to define the nature of that relationship in referential terms.

NOTES

1. See especially: John L. Austin, *How To Do Things With Words* (Oxford: Oxford University Press, rev. 2nd ed., 1975), and *Philosophical Papers* (Oxford: Oxford University Press, 2nd ed., 1970), pp. 233–52; Mary Louise Pratt, *Toward a Speech Act Theory of Literary Discourse* (Bloomington: Indiana University Press, 1977); John R. Searle, *Expression and Meaning: Studies in the Theory of Speech Acts* (Cambridge: Cambridge University Press, 1979), and *Speech Acts: An Essay in the Philosophy of Language* (Cambridge: Cambridge University Press, 1969).

2. For examples, see some of the articles in *Theorie der Sprachhandlungen und heutige Ekklesiologie,* ed. Peter Hunermann and Richard Schaeffler (Freiburg im Breisgau: Herder, 1987), especially: Frank Lothar Hossfeld, "Geprägte Sprachformen im Leben der Glaubensge-

meinde. Die Wachstumsstufen von Ps 18 als Hinweis auf das Leben des Gottesvolkes im Wandel der Geschichte," pp. 75–97.

3. Searle, *Expression and Meaning,* p. 8. Searle, mentions covenants only in passing under the heading of commissives; other Speech Act theorists do not mention them at all. By contrast, Ballmer and Brennenstuhl's lexically oriented study, critical of the looseness and internal overlapping of Searles' taxonomy (all five categories can be collapsed into declaratives, p. 55), does include "making of treaties" and its cognates among their "English Activity Verbs." See Th. Ballmer and W. Brennenstuhl, *Speech Act Classification: A Study in the Lexical Analysis of English Speech Activity Verbs,* part 2 (Berlin: Springer-Verlag, 1981). On commissives and directives as "interactional," see Nira Reiss, *Speech Act Taxonomy as a Tool for Ethnographic Description: An Analysis based on Videotapes of Continuous Behavior in Two New York Households* (Amsterdam: John Benjamins Publishing Company, 1985), p. 31. The view of speech acts as unilateral has been challenged by Paul Ricoeur, from the perspective of moral philosophy in "Les implications de la théorie des actes de langage pour la théorie générale de l'éthique," in *Théorie des actes de langage: éthique et droit,* published under the direction of Paul Amselek (Paris: Presses Universitaires de France, 1986), pp. 89–105.

4. Some scholars try to demonstrate that covenants are strictly unilateral. In so doing, they attempt to reconcile the notion of covenant in the Hebrew Bible with the Christian concept of grace. See for example: Ernst Kutsch, *Verheissung und Gesetz: Untersuchungen zum sogenannten "Bund" im Alten Testament* (Berlin, New York: Walter de Gruyter, 1973); and his highly polemical: *Neues Testament—Neuer Bund? Eine Fehlübersetzung wird korrigiert* (Neukirchen-Vluyn: Neukirchen Verlag, 1978).

5. For Bible scholars who have pointed to the formal similarities between ancient human treaties and biblical covenants and who examine the etymology of the term *brit,* see Klaus Baltzer, *The Covenant Formulary in Old Testament Jewish and Early Christian Writings,* trans. David E. Green (Philadelphia: Fortress Press, 1971); J. Begrich, "Berit: Ein Beitrag zur Erfassung einer alttestamentlichen Denkform," (*ZAW,* NF 19, 1944), pp. 1–11; Joseph Blank, "Das Mysterium von Israel," in *Jüdische Hoffnungskraft und Christlicher Glauben,* Walter Strolz, ed., (Freiburg: Herder, 1971), pp. 134–190. Otto Eissfeldt, *The Old Testament: An Introduction,* trans. Peter R. Ackroyd (New York: Harper & Row, 1972), pp. 9–10; Gordon Freeman, *The Heavenly Kingdom: Aspects of Political Thought in the Talmud and Midrash,* New York: University Press of America, 1986), p. 43; Paul Kalluveettil, *Declaration and Covenant: A Comprehensive Review of Covenant Formulae from the Old Testament and the Ancient Near East,* Dissertation; Jon D. Levenson, *Sinai and*

Zion: an Entry into the Jewish Bible (Minneapolis: Winston Press, 1985), p. 27; Walter Vogels, *God's Universal Covenant,* (Ottawa: University of Ottawa Press, 1986), pp. 2–6.

For critics who do not consider the Form-Critical parallel of treaty and covenant to be a useful model, see George E. Mendenhall, *Law and Covenant in Israel and the Ancient Near East,* (Pittsburgh: The Biblical Colloquium, 1955), pp. 31–36; and E. Nielsen, *The Ten Commandments in New Perspective: Studies in Biblical Theology* (London), pp. 131, 143.

6. For scholars who note this aspect of biblical covenants, see Pierre Buis, *La notion d'alliance dans l'Ancien Testament* (Paris: Cerf, 1976), p. 126; Gordon M. Freeman, *The Heavenly Kingdom: Aspects of Political Thought in the Talmud and Midrash* (New York: University Press of America, 1986), p. 45.

7. Searle, *Expression and Meaning,* pp. 17–20.

8. Ibid., pp. 18–19, 26.

9. See: Anson Laytner, *Arguing with God: A Jewish Tradition,* Northvale, New Jersey: Jason Aronson Inc., 1990), p. xvi; Blank, p. 153; and Dennis J. McCarthy, Society of Jesus, *Old Testament Covenant: A Survey of Current Opinions* (Oxford: Basil Blackwell, 1972), pp. 1–4 and "Three Covenants in Genesis," in *Institutions and Narrative: Collected Essays* (Rome: Biblical Institute Press, 1985), p. 6.

10. Biblical scholars who assert that the stronger party (suzerain or king) generally initiates the covenant seem not to realize that the wish for a covenant springs from the ruler's awareness of potential vulnerability.

11. Freud developed the concept of *Nachträglichkeit* in his essay on the "Wolf Man" ("From the History of an Infantile Neurosis," Standard Edition, vol. 17) in order to account for the inexplicable detail of the memories of sexual scenes and excitement (*Urszene*) from early infancy. Whereas other analysts explained these memories as inherited (personally, or as part of a common archetypal memory), rather than part of the real life experience of the analysand, Freud proposed a different solution. He claimed that such memories are formed as the result of a second, sexually colored event, which repeats some of the visual components of the first scene. In a convoluted manner, the sexual potency of the second scene becomes effective only after it has—through the repetition—enabled the earlier scene to become the traumatic *Urszene*. Thus, the link between temporality and causality is convoluted by an earlier event gaining impact only through a later event.

12. For critics who stress the creativity of obedience, see: Daniel J. Elazar, "Covenant as the Basis of the Jewish Political Tradition," in *The Jewish Political Tradition and its Contemporary Uses,* ed. Daniel J. Elazar, (Washington D.C.: University Press of America, 1983), pp. 22–26; Gordon Freeman, "The Rabbinic Understanding of Covenant as a Politi-

cal Idea," in *The Jewish Political Tradition*, ed. Elazar, pp. 66–73; Jon D. Levenson, *Creation and the Persistence of Evil: the Jewish Drama of Divine Omnipotence,* San Francisco: Harper and Row, 1988.

13. Having created people, "God blessed them; and God said unto them: be fruitful and multiply, and replenish the earth, and subdue it" (Gen. 1:28). This blessing is repeated when Noah leaves the ark (Gen. 9:1). God then gives Noah a series of negative commands, which He concludes with the imperative formulation—"And you, be you fruitful, and multiply"—of the earlier blessing.

14. For discussions of the sign as an essential constituent of the covenant, see: Jean L'Hour, *La morale de l'alliance,* (Paris: Cerf, 1985), p. 9; Jon D. Levenson, *Sinai and Zion: An Entry into the Jewish Bible* (Minneapolis: Winston Press, 1985), p. 27; George E. Mendenhall, *Law and Covenant in Israel and the Ancient Near East* (Pittsburgh: The Biblical Colloquium, 1955), p. 36.

15. We use the name Avram until the scene of renaming in Genesis 17.

16. See the incident of the golden calf in Exodus 32.

CHAPTER 3

Facing the Other: Levinas, Perelman, and Rosenzweig

Susan Handelman

"Idealism completely carried out reduces all ethics to politics"
Levinas(*Totality and Infinity* 216)

"Otherness" or "alterity" have become very fashionable terms in recent literary theory. The most problematic question, however, is defining just what and who is the "other." In most post-structuralist theory, otherness is usually accompanied by the notion of a "radial rupture" which subverts closed identities and all-encompassing systems. Is otherness, then, an inchoate anonymous unknown reminding us of the limits of our knowledge and thus the fount of endless skepticism? Or is it the passage through which the Otherness of divine transcendence crosses? Is it the basis for nihilism, or for a political awareness of the relation of power to knowledge and the commitment to subvert oppression? Is it Derrida's "difference," Kristeva's feminine semiosis, Lacan's Unconscious, Foucault's marginalized discourses?

Moreover, can the relation to the human other as an individual other person have anything to do with epistemological alterity in general? And what do these notions of alterity have to do with the relation of philosophy and literary theory to Judaism? Can traditional Jewish notions of law and covenant be maintained when the solicitation of otherness and radical rupture seem to require the continuous subversion all binding and contractual relations?

In this essay, I want to examine the ways in which the contemporary French-Jewish philosopher Emmanuel Levinas addresses these issues, for they are at the heart of his work. Levinas is one of the few writers who is able to restore *ethical binding* in the face of the ruptures enacted in postmodern thought. His aim is to deconstruct the subject but retain it as responsible, lucid, awake, obligated. In fact, Levinas' work may be characterized as an extraordinary ethical critique of philosophy and as such bears directly on our theme of "Summoning." It is a "summoning" of philosophical reason in the sense that a summons is an urgent call or order to a trial. It is also a summons of "witnesses" whose testimony will enact a judgment on philosophy, and a summons to a prior obligation of both the philosophical "knowing subject," and the subject as the "contents" or object of philosophy.[1]

I will analyze Levinas' work in relation to both contemporary literary theory and modern Jewish philosophy by comparing it to two other important modern theorists of language and ethics whose work, like his, needs to be brought much more into contemporary debates about these issues: the rhetorical theorist Chaim Perelman and the great German-Jewish philosopher Franz Rosenzweig. Finally, I will discuss some of the relations between Levinas' work and the Holocaust, that catastrophic event which seems to have broken all covenants between God and humanity, human and human, language and ethics.

LEVINAS' BACKGROUND

Since Levinas' work is not as well known in America as in Europe, let me begin with some biographical facts. Though Levinas is commonly described as a "French" philosopher, he was actually born in Russia, in Kovno, in 1906, and left in 1923 for philosophical studies (especially in phenomenology) in France and Germany. He became a French citizen and was mobilized into the French army when World War II began; the French uniform saved him from deportation to the gas chambers when he was captured by the Germans. While he was held in a prisoner-of-war camp, however, all his family remaining in Russia were murdered by the Nazis. When he emerged from the camp after the war, Levinas wrote of his "profound need to leave the climate of that [Heidegger's] philosophy" (*Existence* 19). He proceeded with an extensive critique of phenomenological thought and the way it related consciousness to being.

The entire thrust of Levinas' work is to reverse the subordination of ethics to ontology (the study of Being) and the other branches of philosophy. Ethics is not something to be added on after we establish a metaphysics or logic or aesthetics or epistemology. Ethics, which he defines as the irreducible relation of obligation to the other, is prior. Prior here does not mean "coming before" in any linear chronological sense, but a realm which has not been thought and upon which thought nevertheless depends for its possibility.

This search for what philosophy has not or cannot think is an enterprise common to many modern French and German thinkers, from Heidegger to Derrida. In Deconstructionist literary theory influenced by Derrida, the focus on the non-knowledge which always conditions and eludes knowledge led to a recognition of the instability of linguistic meaning, and a practice of skeptical critique as the constant unsettling of all foundations. Those more inspired by Foucault examine the hidden links of knowledge and power, force and signification. These varying means of rupturing philosophical "totality" all involve a solicitation of what is other as what has been "marginalized, repressed, excluded" by philosophy and its modes of intelligibility. The "subject" defined as the individual perceiving self or transparent consciousness who makes meaning of the world has been put into question. Levinas, however, differs from most post-structuralist thinkers by asserting that *"l'absolument Autre, c'est Autrui"* (*Totality* 39). The word *autrui* signifies the other as personal other; in other words, absolute alterity passes or is traced through the personal human other.

But there is another sense in which what is other is the Jew, and there is this other side to Levinas the philosopher as well. In 1947 Levinas also became the Director of the Ecole Normale Israélite Orientale, a Jewish school which is part of the Alliance Israélite, an organization dedicated to spreading French and Jewish culture throughout Jewish communities in France and its former mediterranean empire. He held this position simultaneously with his posts teaching philosophy in French Universities and has written prolifically on Judaism and Jewish life.

He has also delivered for the past twenty years, the annual Talmudic lecture at the Colloquium of French-Jewish Intellectuals. In these lectures he has argued that what modern Judaism needs most of all is a renewed relation to the Talmud, that vast corpus of ancient and medieval rabbinic commentary on Jewish law and lore. His work is permeated with a distrust of religious mysticism; in his view, such attempts at ecstatic fusion or "direct experience of the sacred" destroy the lucidity of an ethical metaphysics.

One of the figures Levinas uses to describe alterity in both his philosophical and his Jewish writings is "face." But the "face of the other" is not for him a visual image; it is, rather, a facing *relation*. The other faces my own separate and narcissistic ego, interrupts, and shames it—a calling into question which is the call of conscience as both an appeal and an order. The connotations of the Hebrew word for face (*panim*) in biblical and rabbinic tradition are all important here. The verbal root *panah* in Hebrew connotes a "turning" towards something, and also a kind of personal presence.[2] In Levinas, facing is being confronted with, turned towards, facing up to, being judged and called to by the other. Facing is a disruption of that free, autonomous self which through its reasoning and consciousness thinks it can construct the world out *of* itself, or know the world *from* itself.

For both Levinas and Franz Rosenzweig (1886–1929), the great German-Jewish philosopher whose work deeply influenced Levinas, that presumption is the archetypal gesture of philosophy: idealism. Indeed, Richard Cohen has persuasively argued that the very notion of the face in Levinas may have its source in the culminating pages of Rosenzweig's great work *The Star of Redemption* wherein Rosenzweig describes the apotheosis of truth with the figure of a face.[3]

The facing relation in Levinas is not, however, a relation of free reciprocal exchange, and *not* a Buberian I-Thou dialogue. Instead, this facing traumatizes and empties the subject. It binds the self to the other despite the self's will in an obligation prior to freedom, a heteronomy or *difficile liberté,* to use the title of one of Levinas' books on Judaism. Identity comes not from the coincidence of self with self but from the recurrence of the call of obligation to the other. On the one hand, Levinas seeks within the philosophical tradition for moments of recognition of this ethical otherness (for example, in Plato's notion of the "Good beyond Being" and Descartes' "Idea of the Infinite"). On the other hand, I think he is also calling philosophy *to* this recognition in what I would characterize as a kind of prophetic and rhetorical appeal that coincides with Levinas' understanding of Judaism.

RHETORIC AND POLITICS IN RECENT LITERARY THEORY

The relations of Levinas' Jewish thought to his philosophical thought and to his personal biography are highly complex matters which I can only touch upon here. Levinas never directly mentions his own experience of World War II in his philosophical work, but it seems to me to be one reason why he "brings philosophy to trial" and part of the explanation for the kinds of witnesses he summons in that trial—and for his very notion of signification as a kind of witness, of language itself as summons, judgment, apology, and teaching. That devastating experience must also have been one motivation for his attempt to construct a philosophy which itself is not based on war (even as a game) but on justice and peace—peace defined as that very moment of renunciation, apology, welcome, and vulnerable exposure to the other.

It is not fortuitous that Levinas begins and ends both his great philosophical books *Totality and Infinity* and *Otherwise Than Being* with meditations on war and peace. The very first sentence in the preface to *Totality and Infinity* is "Are we duped by morality?" Isn't war the very "truth of the real" as Heraclitus long ago argued when he said "War is king of all"? If so, politics as the art of foreseeing and winning war would be the "very exercise of reason" and moral consciousness would have no recourse against "the mocking gaze of the political man" (21). Needless to say, that mocking gaze is found in much recent literary theory which has taken an intensely political turn through schools of criticism variously dubbed the New Historicism, cultural materialism, or cultural poetics.[4] What might be some of the relations of Levinasian ethics to this new literary politics?

Both right-wing pragmatists such as Stanley Fish and left-wing Marxists such as Terry Eagleton argue that truth is a variable social construct connected to the interests and ideologies of particular social groups. The key question, however, is, What is the sociality of this social relation? For the political critics it is at bottom a contest for power, a struggle between domination and subversion wherein different social forces endlessly vie for control of meaning. The aim of this kind of criticism is to reveal the "social constructedness" (or what some critics call the "rhetoricity") as opposed to the "ontological groundedness" of these historical and social versions of truth. This act of "demystification" is intended to empower other voices which have been muted or repressed to contest these accounts. Roland Barthes' "pleasure of the text" has been turned into the "war of discourse."

Yet for most of the cultural-political critics there is no space "outside" this realm of war and negotiation, or outside the mutual implications of discourse and power and the constraints of institutions on "cultural practices." Hence they call for what they term a "rhetorical" notion of truth, and associate rhetorical criticism with the detection and deployment of language in the assertion of power, or with "textual strategies" in the war of discourse. Or, rhetoric is used—as in deMan or Derrida—to denote a form of negative epistemology and antagonism to philosophy, a language of tropes that interferes with and undercuts the philosophical logos.[5]

In any case, this is a very distorted notion of rhetoric which severs it from one of its ancient roots—what Aristotle called "dialectic" or deliberative argument, a mode of reasoning which deals with theses that are not necessary but only probable. That is, where formal logical syllogisms cannot apply, where there are no absolute grounds for truth, but in which decisions and actions still need to be reasoned over and taken.

That is the aspect of rhetoric which Chaim Perelman revives in his masterwork *The New Rhetoric*. Rhetoric for Perelman involves a critique of modern forms of logical and mathematical rationalism which have their precursor in Descartes, but which have been overextended and misapplied as criteria for *all* argument. Perelman argues that there are many areas of human thought and endeavor—including questions of politics, ethics, religion, philosophy, and so on—which elude the methods of mathematical and natural sciences. If we restrict our notion of reason to the model of formal logic, and Cartesian intuitive self-evident truths, we create uncompromising and ineradicable dualisms such as "reason/imagination," "knowledge/opinion," "universal objectivity/incommunicable subjectivity," "judgments of reality/judgments of value," and "theory/practice" (510). These dualisms

> and the assertion that whatever is not objectively and indisputably valid belongs to the realm of the arbitrary and the subjective

> create an unbridgeable gulf between theoretical knowledge, which is rational, and action, for which motives would be wholly irrational. (512)

The consequence is that practice ceases to be reasonable, critical argument becomes incomprehensible, and philosophical reflection itself meaningless.

Why such a fear of an "end of philosophy" or of the irrational? I suspect that Perelman's *the New Rhetoric* (1958) was written, like much of Levinas' philosophy, in response to the catastrophes and violence of World War II. Perelman was a Belgian Jew and one of the leaders of Belgian resistance; he also had a distinguished career as a professor of philosophy and law.[6] Like Levinas, he had personally experienced the effects of a massive collapse of reasonable discourse in the violence of that war. Like Levinas, he is searching for a "third way" beyond these dualisms, and for a form of reason that is itself neither violent nor injurious to the other and to individual human responsibility. He shares the Levinasian impulse to modify the Enlightenment version of the universal light of reason rather than abandon it completely to a war of conflicting power interests and self-interested ideologies.

So like Levinas, Perelman instead redefines, extends, and amplifies reason to include forms of reasoning which do not involve what is conceptually *self*-evident, necessary, or autonomous, but which "require an other" and depend upon the relation of address and assent of the other person through discourse. (Rosenzweig makes a similar turn from what he perceived to be the violence of the Hegelian version of history and philosophy to what he called *Sprachdenken* or "speech-thinking.")

In sum, Levinas and Perelman are both in search of a reason-of-the-other, an other-reason which is not however arbitrary, violent, or willful, but rather a non-necessary form of imperative. And that for Perelman is found in the forms of reasoning and persuasion of the rhetorical tradition from the Greeks onward, forms of discourse which were denigrated and neglected by Cartesian logicians and philosophers—described as merely "ornamental," "literary," or "sophistic." From this tradition, Perelman constructs a "critical rationalism" that "transcends the duality 'judgments of reality/value judgments,' and makes both judgments of reality and value judgments dependent on the personality of the scientist or philosopher, who is responsible for his decisions in the field of knowledge as well as the field of action" (*New Rhetoric* 514).

In other words, for Perelman rhetoric is a form of social but noncoercive and non-violent reason which is required to deliberate in areas where there are no necessary or absolute truths. That is, a realm where there are no truths which have *coercive* power, such as the "coercions" of self-evident reason or deductive logic or nonrational faith. Formal Cartesian reason is founded on the solipsistic notion of self-evident truths, clear, distinct, and necessary—there is no need for deliberation with others, nor any question of varying intensities of adherence to these truths, nor the possibility of withholding one's assent from them. Such reason, like the theoretical reason of Kant, "imposes itself on every rational being" and "agreement is inevitable" (2). Rhetoric, by contrast, is defined by Perelman as that form of reason which involves the freely given and responsible commitment of a deliberating audience. Perelman's "new rhetoric" is then a third way between the compulsions of formal autonomous reason and the coercions of violence. To deliberate or argue with another

> implies that one has renounced resorting to forces alone, that value is attached to gaining the adherence of one's interlocutor by means of reasoned persuasion, and that one is not regarding him as an object, but appealing to his free judgement. Recourse to argumentation assumes the establishment of a community of minds, which, while it lasts, excludes the use of violence. (55)

This is a notion of rhetoric quite at odds with the way the term is used in much contemporary literary theory where rhetoric has often been used to denote the ineradicable political biases and ideologies involved in language use and interpretation. Rhetoric is then the deployment of "textual strategies" in the war-game of interpretation; and/or linguistic self-consciousness and self-reflexivity; and/or the critical self-consciousness of the interpreter who recognizes that there is no ontological or transcendent foundation to language or truth, that all truth is embodied in the social constructs of linguistic practice. To attain this critical self-consciousness is posited as an act of demystification which is a necessary part of a politically progressive practice, a kind of "postmodern ethic."

In fact, much of the recent epistemological skepticism and political criticism in literary theory justifies itself through an implicit stance of ethical and moral superiority: that is, it claims to resist by its demystifications and radical critiques the absolutism of tyrants and fanatics. But Perelman has a remarkable insight to add to the debate: the radical skeptic is often not the opposite, but the counterpart of the fanatic—for both equate *adherence to theses* with recognition of absolute truth. Both skeptic and fanatic thus foreclose deliberative argument about choice when no absolute ground exists. Writes Perelman:

> Since rhetorical proof is never completely necessary proof, the thinking person who gives his adherence to the conclusions of an argumentation does so by an act that commits him and for which he is responsible. The fanatic accepts the commitment, but as one bowing to an absolute and irrefragable truth; the skeptic refuses the commitment, but under the pretext that he does not find it sufficiently definitive. He refuses adherence because his idea of adherence is similar to that of the fanatic: both fail to appreciate that argumentation aims at a choice among possible theses; by proposing and justifying the hierarchy of these theses, argumentation seeks to make the decision a rational one. This role of argumentation in decision making is denied by the skeptic and fanatic. In the absence of compelling reason, they both are inclined to give violence a free hand, rejecting personal commitment. (62)

This passage might be used to gloss the painful political controversy that has so troubled many contemporary literary critics—the connection between Paul deMan's radical skepticism and his pro-fascist writings in World War II.[7] Many of deMan's defenders have argued that his deconstructive skepticism was an implicit repudiation and overcoming of his earlier ideological writings, a posture of critical self-reflexiveness whose notions about "undecidability" and the "impossibility of reading" are intended to guard against all violent engagements. But Perelman's analysis indicates that such radical skepticism, which denies the grounds for any choice between meanings, is overly restrictive in its definition of truth and knowledge. Foreclosing deliberation and choice in endless aporias and "undecidabilities" is an act as absolutist and open to violence as that of the fanatic who refuses to debate due to her or his conviction of possessing that absolute truth.[8]

The same criticism could be made of the "ideological" critic, who holds that all values are masks for self-interested power plays; or the relativist who is intent on constantly undermining any and every claim to a firm foundation for a given value or truth, and refuses to allow for any deliberative argument about the hierarchy of values or criteria for making choices among them. For as the jurist knows, regardless of the lack of any absolute, clear, or unambiguous ground, choices still must made and decisions rendered.

In Perelman's view, both the fanatic and skeptic relieve themselves of the burden of personal responsibility, action, and commitment to choices made. Rhetorical argumentation, though, is oriented towards decision and the future: "it sets out to bring about some action or prepare the way for it by acting, by discursive methods, on the minds of the hearers." (47) Argumentation, Perelman reminds us, is not merely an intellectual exercise divorced from practical preoccupations. "Language is not only a means of communication: it is also an instrument for acting on minds, a means of persuasion" (132). That is precisely why argumentation is a substitute for the violence which attempts to obtain an action by the use of force or compulsion. I would ague that there are many lessons here for literary criticism and theory. First, that restricting questions about meaning or the nature of the literary text to questions about the *epistemological status of language* is as artificial as the attempt to restrict all reasoning solely to formal logic. Nor is the only alternative an uncritical embrace of "politics" and the assertion that the way language acts on the world is essentially ideological and marked by relations of force, domination, and violence.

In sum, for both Perelman and Levinas, aesthetics and politics need to be subsumed to a critical rationalism which for Perelman is rhetoric and for Levinas ethics.[9] As philosopher, however, Levinas partakes of the ancient philosophical contempt for rhetoric, which he views as the approach to the neighbor through ruse, as a mode of sophistic manipulation and violence rather than search for truth. But Levinas' insistence on language as preeminently a call or command before it is exchange of information, is at bottom rhetorical.

ROSENZWEIG'S CRITIQUE OF PHILOSOPHY

In other words, ethics as the obligation and binding of the self to the other constitutes what Levinas describes as "the 'rationality' of a reason less hard on itself than the reasons of the philosophical tradition," not a decline of rationality, but a fuller rationality (*L'Au-Delà du Verset* 176). Levinas' critique of reason does not negate reason but tries to formulate a "second" type of reason, a reason which is not autonomous and imperialistic or slavish and mindless. The essential point is that when aesthetics or politics become their own autonomous realms, obliterating the prior realm of the ethics, they inevitably convert into forms of violence and tyranny. They deny the alterity and singularity of otherness, which for Levinas passes through the human other and is the essence of the ethical relation.

To explain this idea better and consider the relation of Levinasian ethics to Jewish thought, we need to examine Levinas' relation to Rosenzweig. Along with Rosenzweig, Levinas saw (long before Foucault) the complicity of power and knowledge, of philosophy and violence. Rosenzweig's work was a fierce attack on Hegelian philosophy and especially Hegel's assertion that "History is the judge of history," that is, that immanent history was the dialectical Life of the Spirit on its road to the consummation of self-knowledge. In Rosenzweig, there is a devastating critique of philosophical idealism, but also an attempt to reconstellate the shattered fragments of that idealism in a new way. And this way involved Rosenzweig in a new relation of philosophy to theology.

What World War II was for Levinas, World War I and its catastrophic slaughter had been for Rosenzweig. For both thinkers, it became imperative to judge the violence of that history and to give its victims voice. That meant locating an "elsewhere" or "beyond" or other which could enact a judgment upon immanent history, even while recognizing that there can be no recourse to traditional theology or traditional notions of transcendence to secure this judgment.

This project ultimately involves both Levinas and Rosenzweig in a kind of prophetic eschatology. And this search for such an elsewhere, or "otherwise than being," or time of the other, is central to the project of many other modern Jewish thinkers—even those who are highly secularized such as Walter Benjamin. One line could be traced that goes from Rosenzweig to Levinas, and from Levinas to Derrida on into post-structuralism; another line goes from Rosenzweig to the Frankfort School of Critical Theory through Benjamin and T. W. Adorno, both of whom were influenced by Rosenzweig's critique of totality.[10] Levinas mentions his profound debt to Rosenzweig in the very first pages of *Totality and Infinity:* "We were impressed by the opposition to the idea of totality in Franz Rosenzweig's *Stern der Erlösung*, a work too often present in this book to be cited" (28).

To briefly (and too simplistically) explain this reference: Rosenzweig's great undoing of totality in *The Star* was a critique of the pretensions of Western philosophy from, as he puts it, "the Ionean Islands to Iena" (that is from the Greeks to Hegel) to "know the All." This project, Rosenzweig argued, has roots in the fear of death. Philosophy flees this singular human mortal self by attempting to construct impersonal deathless systems. It tries to reduce the heterogeneity of reality into single, impersonal, explanatory principles (*Star* 1–15). The project culminates in Hegelian idealism where philosophy seeks to construct out of itself a completely autonomous totality, identifying the self-fulfillment of Thought with the consummation of world history, and with Hegel's claim that his own philosophy itself is the final union of Thought and Being wherein identity dialectically overcomes difference. Needless to say, Rosenzweig is only one of the countless philosophers and critics from Kierkegaard to Derrida who have devoted their energies to opposing that notion.

One of Levinas' special contributions, however, is the application of Rosenzweig's critique to contemporary forms of impersonal reason. For example, he writes, "Heideggerian ontology, which subordinates the relationship with the Other to the relation with Being in general, remains under obedience to the anonymous, and leads inevitably to another power, to imperialist domination, to tyranny" (*Totality* 47). Levinas' critique of Heidegger and his connection of Heideggerian philosophy to political violence may be applied, I would add, to deMan's linguistic theory, the key to which is the *impersonality* and *autonomy* of language. And this critique would shed another light on both Heidegger's and de-Man's own problematic relations to Nazism.

One could even say that in much literary theory of the 1970's and 80's, "Language" or "History" have taken up the role of impersonal term through which all is mediated or known. The alterity of the singular, personal human other is then defined only as a subordinate function or "site" of impersonal significations or ideologies. But Levinas' critique of impersonality is not made to defend the personal ego as some individual, unified, sovereign center of meaning—a notion which most post-structuralists have also vigorously attacked. As he puts it, "It is not I who resist the system, as Kierkegaard thought; it is the Other" (*Totality* 40).

The aim of Levinas' work is to show that reason and freedom are not autonomous but are founded on prior structures, and that freedom is justified not *of itself,* but *by and for the other.* In other words, what claims to be autonomous, independent "for and of itself" (classical reason, the dialectical march of History, reflexive self-consciousness, the impersonal world of art, the narcissistic ego, the play of the signifiers, institutional Discourse, etc.) in Levinas is *faced* with the other and this facing, as the very questioning and shattering or hollowing out of the subject becomes an extraversion into a *for-the-other.* Before the face of the other I am judged, brought to account, accused and so made responsible.

But one cannot *logically* or *deductively* prove that the other puts me in question; one cannot accomplish the break with totality through the very kind of philosophical consciousness which is by definition the attempt to grasp and master the All, or what Levinas calls an "ego-ology." His notion of the face is thus a rhetorical appeal, an attempt to create an outside of philosophical consciousness (or the totality) by which it can be judged and brought to account.

That is why he writes that the call to question is not a matter of turning around upon oneself and becoming *conscious of* the calling to question. The absolutely other is not reflected in consciousness. . . . We are concerned with questioning a consciousness, and not with the consciousness of questioning" ("Trail" 41). The exile of the self through the demand of the other is not the negative "consciousness of this exile." In Levinas, the exile of the self is a turning outward, an extraversion, a positivity, "precisely the welcome reception of the absolutely other" which summons me to reply. He redefines the subject as for-the-other, not as a consciousness bringing objects to representation "for *itself.*" Moral consciousness, then, is not "an experience of values" but an access to exteriority, to Being as other, and finally beyond ontology to the otherwise than being ("Signature" 183).

Subjectivity as for-the-other, in sum, involves a "plural reason" commanded not by the logic of identity which itself is the return of difference to the same—a for itself—but instead a reason commanded and penetrated by the other, heteronomous instead of autonomous.

FOR ITSELF AND FOR-THE-OTHER

The "extraversion" of the for-itself into the for-the-other is another key move one finds in Rosenzweig. Rosenzweig models for Levinas a path by which the totality of Idealist cognition of the All is shattered, and how the subsequent fragments (subject—object—universe, or God—humanity—world) each isolated in and for themselves can then be opened up to and for-the-other. In Levinas this opening constitutes the ethical move par excellence; in Rosenzweig it is the very meaning of Revelation. And for both Rosenzweig and Levinas, it is a fundamental characteristic of Judaism.

In an essay on Rosenzweig, Levinas makes the crucial comment that the conjunction "and" used to designate the reconnections made in *The Star* among God, humanity, and world as Creation, Revelation, and Redemption means "for": God for humanity, humanity for world, and so forth. The unity Rosenzweig constructs is not any formal unity of philosophical logic but "is in the sense that they are one for the other, when one is placed in these elements themselves" ("Entre" 128). "One for the other" is a "living" relation, not a philosophical category, or a Hegelian dialectical synthesis which empties the terms of their irreducible individuality, or perceives them from the outside in the all-seeing gaze of the philosopher.

For Rosenzweig, the I is drawn out of its mute and isolated self-enclosure, (which Rosenzweig identifies with the mythical, aesthetic, and pagan worlds) by God's emerging from God's concealment, questing for and turning to the individual human self (*Star* 156). That is how Rosenzweig understands God's question to Adam, "Where are You?" in Genesis. But as Rosenzweig notes, God receives no real response from Adam to this initial question; instead

Adam hides himself, and blames Eve and the serpent; Adam remains defiant and self-enclosed. Only when God calls out to Abraham in the story of the sacrifice of Isaac in Genesis 22:1—in the vocative, in direct address, not with an indefinite "you" but with his proper name "Abraham"—that is, in all his nonconceptual individuality, in love for his singularity

> now he answers, all unlocked, all spread-apart, all ready, all-soul: "Here I am." Here is the I, the individual human I, as yet wholly receptive, as yet only unlocked, only empty, without content, without nature, pure readiness, pure obedience, all ears. (176)

For Rosenzweig, this movement of turning and opening to the other is the essence of Revelation before Revelation signifies any propositional or doctrinal content. And this "turning towards the other," as we remember, is a prime meaning of the face (panah, panim) and also essential in Levinas.[11]

In Levinas' philosophical writings, a similar pattern emerges but it is derived without direct exegesis of the Bible or explicit reference to Jewish thought, although terms such as "election," "creation" and "here I am" are used. The subject is elected (the "chosen people"), called out of its narcissistic self-enclosure not by any traditional God of theology but by the "revelation of the face" of the other, the human other through whom the other than being "passes" or is traced. Levinas reverses, in a sense, the path of the *Star:* in the *Star,* God's immediate and pressing love as "shining countenance" (157; 164) opens up and awakens the human soul to both God and to the love of the neighbor; in Levinas, the immediate and pressing face of the other opens and awakens the ego, and traces the otherness of a divinity which is otherwise than being, otherwise than any theology, escaping the revelation of any logos.

It is important to emphasize here that like Rosenzweig, Levinas claims not to base his philosophical writings a priori on any traditional "theology." He firmly maintains that he does not use the Bible or theology as his starting point, nor does he rely on or intend any orthodox theology. His "other than being" is not intended to be theological—"of the logos," or any "ology"—that is, any identification of logos and being or assertion of a God who is the Being behind or beyond beings. Though the other "resembles

God," the relation to the other and the assignation from the Good survive the death of God (*Otherwise Than Being* 123).[12]

The face is not, he reiterates, the image of the God who has passed. "Being in the image of God does not signify being the icon of God but to find oneself in his trace":

> The God of Judaeo-Christian spirituality preserves all the infinity of his absence which is in the personal order itself [*illeity*]. He does not show himself except in his trace, as in the 33rd chapter of Exodus. To go toward Him is not to follow the trace, which itself is not a sign. To go toward him is to go towards the others who are in the trace. ("Trail" 46)

In other words, ontological absence becomes ethical presence; difference becomes my non-indifference to the other. Ethics as obligation and responsibility to and for the other is the relation and Revelation of Otherness.

THE HOLOCAUST WITNESS

Finally, I want briefly to examine how this notion of the self emptied out and bound over to the other is radicalized in Levinas' later work, and its possible connections to Levinas as a holocaust survivor.

The famous biblical phrase here I am with which Abraham answers God (*hineni* in Hebrew) is also, of course, the formulaic response given by many other biblical characters and prophets when called by God. In Levinas' later philosophical works, he uses this phrase to analyze and describe subjectivity as unlocked, wholly receptive, emptied and bound over to the other: "The word *I* means *here I am* [*me voici*] answering for everything and everyone" as a gratuitous sacrifice (*Otherwise* 114). He describes the here I am as the "I possessed by the other," a figure of inspiration and obsession, and a "reason" or "intelligibility" beyond the cogito. In effect, this analysis founds the "I think" of the rational Cartesian *cogito* (which itself founds modern philosophy) upon the biblical here I am of subjectivity and ethics.

Here I am is also a language of the accusative—both grammatically and as the language of "witness," of the "first person." But he emphasizes that here I am is a witness *before* any content or "truth of representation": "It is the meaning of language, before language scatters into words." This "bearing witness of itself to the other" (*Otherwise* 119) is the "sign bearing witness of the giving of signs"—an ultimate exposure and vulnerability which is the condition for all communication.

In other words, this one-for-the-other constitutes the very ability of a sign to be a sign, to stand for something else, and the very possibility for there even to be communication, shared meaning. Signs, that is, are given, offered to the other before they can even comprise a system, a code, a contract, a game. Speech is always said to someone before it has any particular content. There is a prior summoning in language—before the reciprocity of exchange of information, or code, or convention. There is a primordial donation in response to a primordial command, or what he calls an "election by the Good."[13]

And there is an ongoing and continuous oscillation between this prior content-less realm, which Levinas now calls "saying" or *le dire,* and the realm of codes, systems, concrete meanings, contracts, representations, or what he calls *le dit* (the "said"). This oscillation between "the saying and the said," he affirms, is necessary to guarantee that the contracts and codes, the politics and philosophies, do not obliterate the ethical and revert into violent tyrannies.

But in these later writings the terms he uses to describe subjectivity and responsibility often become disturbing: trauma, wounding, hostage, obsession, persecution, sacrifice without reserve, and so on. In a highly charged description Levinas writes: "signification is witness or martyrdom. It is intelligibility before the light" (*Otherwise* 77–78). Imagery of wounding now describes the way the other puts the self in question; it is a radical denuding and shattering of egoism, so that the self is now "like a stranger, hunted down even in one's home, contested in one's identity . . . it is always to empty oneself anew of oneself . . . like in a hemophiliac's hemorrhage" (92). I cannot help but hear in the voice behind this voice, and in these disturbing images of bleeding wounds the witness of the Holocaust survivor, even though that event is never explicitly evoked. And I would argue that in Levinas, the witness of the Holocaust enters into the "reason" of philosophy. At the same time, this rhetoric of witness is indirect for he does not explicitly invoke either his personal experiences or specific historical events within his philosophical work. The most profound signification of these events for him is not their specificity for any one nation or group. On a deeper level, this is consistent with his philosophy: witness is not "confession," a witness for and of the personal experiences of the self, but a testimony for-the-other.

So Levinas does "not make a graven image" or icon of these wounds as some kind of holy stigmata upon which we should fixate in horror. The task instead is to make these traumas revert into the foundation and guarantor of language and ethics. "Hebrew" reminds, calls to, founds "Greek" not by losing its specificity or being sublated (to use the Hegelian term) into the "universality" of Greek reason, but by being witness to the ethical relation to the other . . . in a prophetic call to all human beings.

But it is also almost as if this notion of signification as martyrdom is a kind of secular or philosophical equivalent of the Jewish notion of *kiddush ha-shem*—the "sanctification of the name of God" that Jewish tradition ascribes to the death of a Jew murdered for his or her faith. As if Levinas is attempting to sanctify and redeem the deaths of those murdered in the Holocaust, that event which above all expressed hatred and intolerance for the other.[14] And also as if he is making it impossible for the persecutors to escape responsibility, to forget, deny their involvement . . . and making it impossible for any one of us, any reader of Levinas to escape ours.

For he expands his notion of substitution to an extreme responsibility that makes even "the persecuted one liable to answer for the persecutor" (*Otherwise* 111). As if the very outrage of persecution itself inverted into a grounds of solidarity as expiation rather than violence. One can see why this becomes an almost "unsayable" position. It also has strong Christian echoes and moves beyond Jewish tradition.[15] In classical Jewish law, one is not to actively seek martyrdom; the only cases in which one must allow oneself to be killed are if one is ordered upon pain of death to commit adultery, idolatry, or murder. In these cases, one is required to choose death rather than commit any one of those three sins. In other cases, such as for self-defense, the Talmud says, "If one arises to kill you, arise and kill himself first." One does not always give one's life for the other.[16]

Yet for Levinas, finally, the subject so-called and elected finally signifies all human beings—not just the Jews. And so, on the concluding page of *Otherwise Than Being* there are the following words: each individual of all the peoples "is virtually a chosen one, called to leave in his turn, or without awaiting his turn . . . the concept of the ego . . . to respond with responsibility: *me,* that is, *here I am for the others,* to lose his place radically." (*Otherwise* 185).

NOTES

1. In a sense, Levinas' philosophy and language theory is a kind of phenomenological translation of the covenantal idea. Harold Fisch, whose work we honor by this collection, has similarly devoted much of his career to tracing the covenantal idea in Western literature. In chapter 4 of his recent book *Poetry With A Purpose: Biblical Poetics and Interpretation,* Professor Fisch eloquently describes the nature of the biblical prophetic call and contract which underlies the Scripture's notion of language as summons, bond, obligation, witness, judgment—and its model for the relational contract between reader and writer, text and interpreter, God and Israel. See also, especially here his gloss on the meaning of the *Shema,* "Hear O Israel: the Lord our God, the Lord is One" (Deut 6:4): "To accept the role of 'hearer' in the sense understood by 'Hear O Israel' is to accept an almost overpowering responsibility. It is not a simple act of response that is required of us as though we were readers of a novel called upon to assist in the creating of a fictional illusion; rather we are called upon to commit ourselves, to accept an obligation. For the word *shema* implies not only reading but also obeying; the text seizes us even against our will" (49).

There is a profound sense in which the lifework of Levinas in philosophy and the lifework of Harold Fisch in literary studies are inspired by the same source and directed to the same goals—to the "translation" of Hebrew into Greek and to the prophetic calling of Greek to Hebrew.

In fact, Professor Fisch was responsible for bringing Levinas to Israel in July, 1972 for a conference at Bar-Ilan University of the Institute for Judaism and Contemporary Jewish Thought of which he was the Chair. See Levinas' paper and the response by Abner Weiss in the collection of conference papers edited by Marvin Fox, *Modern Jewish Ethics.*

2. See, for example, Maimonides' discussion of the meaning of the trope face in *The Guide for the Perplexed,* part I, section 37. Among the biblical significations Maimonides enumerates for face (panim) are "the presence and existence of a person," "the hearing of a voice without seeing any similitude," that is, the inability to comprehend God's true existence as such; and "attention or regard" for the other person.

3. See Rosenzweig's *Star,* pp. 418–424, entitled "The Face of the Figure" and Cohen's explication of these passages in his essay "The Face of Truth in Rosenzweig, Levinas, and Jewish Mysticism."

4. A good introduction to these schools of criticism is Vesser's *The New Historicism.*

5. See, for example, the oft-cited essay by deMan "Semiology and Rhetoric" in *Textual Strategies,* ed. J. Harari, and Derrida's "White Metaphor: Metaphor in the Text of Philosophy" in *Margins of Philosophy.* Brian Vickers in the concluding chapter of his *In Defense of Rhetoric* lucidly explains the distortions in many of these contemporary invocations of rhetoric.

6. Foss and Trap write that Perelman's impetus for writing his masterwork were the problems he encountered in defining the nature of justice and reasoning about values, and the difficulty of resolving questions of value on rational grounds, that is, not being able to draw an "ought" from an "is." Along with his co-writer, Lucie Olbrechts-Tyteca, he decided to investigate the ways authors in different fields actually used arguments to reason about values—from literary to political to philosophical texts and daily speech. They "rediscovered" the neglected heritage of Aristotle's "dialectical" as opposed to "analytic" modes of reasoning, that is, rhetoric as informal, nondemonstrative reasoning (Foss and Trap 102–3).

This jurists' perspective has much to add, I would argue, to current questions about the nature of interpretation, the relation of the literary to the political, and recent literary interpretations of rabbinic texts. Most of these attempts to relate literary criticism to rabbinic texts have no satisfactory way of linking up their dual functions of *halakhic* that is, legalistic deliberation, and *aggadic* that is, nonlegal creative story telling.

This problem is due in part to the identification of "Law" with oppression in much French and German post-structuralist literary theory (e.g., Kristeva; Barthes et al.) an identification which often goes back to a Protestant antinomianism. It is also due to the separation of literary criticism and theory from the kind of rhetorical theory which Perelman is proposing . . . a "new" rhetoric because it returns rhetoric to its ancient rational deliberative functions and away from its demotion to a "merely literary" analysis of style and tropes. Perelman's juridical rhetoric is also close to Levinas' defense in his Jewish writings of the *halakha,* the Jewish legal tradition which for Levinas is the embodiment and guarantor of the ethical relation. Both Perelman and Levinas are also inspired by the Kantian notion of practical versus theoretical reason.

7. The debate over DeMan surfaced a few years after his death when, in 1987, a set of his writings from 1940–1942 for the collaborationist Belgian newspaper *Le Soir* were discovered. See the volume of these writings translated into English by Ortwin de Graef, *Wartime Journalism, 1939–1943,* ed. Werner Hamacher et al. (U of Nebraska P: Lincoln, NE, 1988) and the companion volume by the same editors, *Re-*

sponses: On Paul DeMan's Wartime Journalism (1989). For the extensive debate on this subject, see also the two special issues of *Critical Inquiry,* vol. 14 (Spring, 1988) and vol. 15 (Summer, 1989).

8. Perelman makes an important distinction between a "disinterested" or "objective spectator" and an "impartial" one when it comes to judging discussions that must lead to a decision. (One of the most frequently heard statements in current literary theory is that "everything is political" meaning that there is no possibility of disinterestedness, objectivity, or impartiality). Perelman writes that "interference in a controversy whose outcome will affect a specific group may be made only by one who is a member of, or closely bound up with, the group in question": "being *impartial* is not being *objective,* it consists of belonging to the same group one is judging, without having previously decided in favor of any one of them" (60). Like Levinas, Perelman wants to preserve the possibility of "dissociating our beliefs from our interests and passions" (61).

9. This "critical rationalism" is also a feature of many other major modern Jewish philosophers who stressed the rational and ethical character of Judaism (Hermann Cohen is the most outstanding example). Nathan Rotenstreich attributes this trend in part to the influence of Kant. Ethics could remain a realm unchallenged by Kant's critique of metaphysics and religion. But also, "The ethical interpretation of Judaism makes possible a further, more radical interpretation, that the ethical teaching of Judaism may be meaningful and binding apart from religious attachment. Thus the ethical interpretation can be placed historically on the borderline of the religious attitude and the secular transformation of Judaism" (Rotenstreich, *Jewish Philosophy* 3–4).

10. When asked by Richard Kearney whether his search for a non-site or *u-topos* other than that of Western metaphysics can be construed as a prophetic utopianism, Derrida answers by affirming a positive moment in deconstruction as a response to the call of alterity, and says that although he interrogates the classical ideas of *eschaton* or *telos,* "that does not mean I dismiss all forms of Messianic or prophetic eschatology. I think that all genuine questioning is summoned by a certain type of eschatology." Though he does not feel the kind of "hope" that would allow deconstruction to have a prophetic function—as "exodus and dissemination in the desert" it does have, he admits, certain "prophetic resonances," but as a search without hope for hope (*Dialogues* 118–119).

11. For Rosenzweig, God's turn towards humanity is an opening up and act of love which simultaneously is the command to the human person to turn and open up to the other—to love the neighbor. The neighbor to whom this love is also commanded is the turning of the

human toward something else, to the world, and that is redemption. Rosenzweig also connects this receptive "Here I am" and the moment of revelation with Jewish law whose foundation is love as command. That is, this summons to hear is itself the preface to every commandment, and especially of the commandment which for Rosenzweig is the essence and highest of all the other commandments, to "love God with all your heart, soul, and might."

12. See Levinas' important essay "God and Philosophy" (1973) in his *Collected Philosophical Papers*. Here he attempts to clarify the relationship between philosophy and religion, and define his notion of a religion that exceeds not only theology but also is not even founded on "religious experience" or faith and the loss of faith.

13. For Levinas, the election or calling or displacement of the subject (as Abraham was elected, called, displaced) to undeclinable responsibility and sacrifice for the other means that the subject is "unique" not because of any particular attributes of the ego, nor because it is loved by God, but by very virtue of this undeclinable assignation. (*Otherwise* 115) These terms, nevertheless, again seem not only to echo but be founded on classical Jewish descriptions of the covenantal call.

14. In an epigraph, Levinas dedicates *Otherwise Than Being* to the memory of those killed by Nazis, both those "closest" among the six million Jews, and the "millions of all confessions and all nations, victims of the same hatred of the other man, the same anti-semitism."

15. Andrius Valevicius is quite right to point out in these Dosteveskian and Tolstoyan accents, Levinas' Russian background and the connection of even his most mature philosophy to slavic as well as Jewish thought. See his chapter 12, "From East to West: Levinas and Russian Thought" (1988): 146–155.

16. There is another similar famous passage from a Talmudic discussion about the meaning of Lev 25:36, the directive not to take interest when one lends money to sustain "your brother who has become poor" but "fear your God; that thy brother may live with you." What is the meaning of "that thy brother may live with you?

> That is what Ben-Patura expounded: Two men are journeying through the desert, and one of them has a single pitcher of water. If one of them drinks it, he (alone) will get back to civilization. But if both of them drink it, both of them will die. Ben Patura taught that they should both drink and die, as it said "That your brother may live with you." Said Rabbi Akiba to him: "That thy brother may *live with you.*" Your own life comes before the life of your fellow-man. (*Sifra, Behar* 5:3; p. 109c (ed. Weiss); cf. *B. Metzia* 62a)

This is the same R. Akiba who also propounded that the fundamental principle of the Torah was "You shall love your neighbor as yourself." See discussion of these issues in relation to Levinas by Abner Weiss in Fox, *Modern Jewish Ethics* 139–152. See also David Roskies' compendium of Jewish responses to catastrophe, martyrology, and the like, *The Literature of Destruction* and his *Against the Apocalypse* for the typology of the historical Jewish responses to suffering.

REFERENCES

Cohen, Richard A. "The Face of Truth in Rosenzweig, Levinas, and Jewish Mysticism." *Phenomenology of the Truth Proper to Religion*. Ed. Daniel Guerrière. Albany: State University of New York Press, 1990.

DeMan, Paul. "Semiology and Rhetoric." *Textual Strategies: Perspectives in Post-Structuralist Criticism*. Ed. Josué Harari. Ithaca: Cornell University Press, 1979. 121–40.

Fisch, Harold. *Poetry with a Purpose: Biblical Poetics and Interpretation*. Bloomington: Indiana University Press, 1988.

Foss, Sonja K., Robert Foss, and Robert Trapp. *Contemporary Perspectives on Rhetoric*. Illinois: Waveland Press, 1985.

Fox, Marvin, ed. *Modern Jewish Ethics: Theory and Practice*. Columbus: Ohio State University Press, 1975.

Glatzer, Nahum. *Franz Rosenzweig: His Life and Thought*. 1953; New York: Schocken, 1961.

Handelman, Susan A. *The Slayers of Moses: The Emergence of Rabbinic Interpretation in Modern Literary Theory*. Albany: State University of New York Press, 1982.

Kearney, Richard. "Jacques Derrida." *Dialogues with Contemporary Continental Thinkers: The Phenomenological Heritage*. Manchester: Manchester University Press, 1984. 105–26.

Levinas, Emmanuel. *Collected Philosophical Papers*. Trans. Alphonso Lingis. Dordrecht: Martinus Nijhoff, 1987.

———. *Difficile liberté: Essais sur le judaisme*. Paris: Editions Albin Michel, 1963.

———. "Entre Deux Mondes (biographie spirituelle de Franz Rosenzweig)." *La Conscience Juive données et débats (textes des trois premières Colloques d'Intellectuels Juifs de Langue Française)*. Ed. Amado Lévy-Valensi and Jean Halperin. Paris: Presses Universitaires de France, 1963. 121–49.

———. *Ethics and Infinity: Conversations with Philippe Nemo*. Trans. Richard A. Cohen. Pittsburgh: Duquesne UP, 1985.

———. *Existence and Existents*. Trans. Alphonso Lingis. 1947; The Hague: Martinus Nijhoff, 1978.

———. "Franz Rosenzweig: une pensée juive moderne." *Revue de Théologie et de Philosophie* 98 (1965): 208–21.

———. *L'Au-delá du verset: Lectures et discours talmudiques.* Paris: Editions de Minuit, 1982.

———. "Martin Buber and the Theory of Knowledge." *The Philosophy of Martin Buber.* Eds. Paul Schilpp and Maurice Friedman. La Salle, IL: Open Court Pub., 1967. 133–50.

———. "On The Trail of the Other." Trans. Daniel Hoy. *Philosophy Today* 10 (1966): 34–46.

———. *Otherwise Than Being Or Beyond Essence.* Trans. Alphonso Lingis. 1974; The Hague: Martinus Nijhoff, 1981.

———. *Quatre lectures talmudiques.* Paris: Editions de Minuit, 1968.

———. "Signature." Ed. and trans. Adrian Peperzak. *Research in Phenomenology* 8 (1978): 175–89.

———. *Totality and Infinity: An Essay on Exteriority.* Trans. Alphonso Lingis. 1961; Pittsburgh: Duquesne University Press, 1969.

Maimonides, Moses. *The Guide for the Perplexed.* Trans. M. Friedlander. 2nd ed. New York: Dover, 1956.

Perelman, Chaim. "The New Rhetoric: A Theory of Practical Reasoning." *The Rhetoric of Western Thought.* Ed. J. Golden. Dubuque: Kendall Hunt, 1976. 298–317.

Perelman, Chaim, and L. Olbrechts-Tyteca. *The New Rhetoric: A Treatise on Argumentation.* Trans. J. Wilkinson and P. Weaver. 1958; Notre Dame: University of Notre Dame Press, 1969.

Rosenzweig, Franz. *On Jewish Learning.* Ed. Nahum Glatzer. 1955; New York: Schocken, 1965.

———. *The Star of Redemption.* Trans. William Hallo. 2nd ed. 1930. Notre Dame: University of Notre Dame Press, 1985.

Rotenstreich, Nathan. *Jewish Philosophy in Modern Times: From Mendelssohn to Rosenzweig.* New York: Holt Rinehart, 1968.

Valevicius, Anarius. *From the Other to the Totally Other: The Religious Philosophy of Emmanuel Levinas.* New York: Peter Lang, 1988.

Veeser, H. Aram, ed. *The New Historicism.* New York: Routledge, 1989.

Vickers, Brian. *In Defense of Rhetoric.* Oxford: Clarendon Press, 1988.

CHAPTER 4

The Difficulty of Finding a Moral Basis for Accepting the Covenant

Daniel Statman

Is there a moral basis for accepting the Divine Covenant? Theologians have argued that it is not only unwise but immoral not to do so. Moral reasons, however, do not exhaust the practical domain, and one could have good reasons which are not moral ones for doing something. From a religious point of view, the absence of a moral obligation might even be considered desirable; one should obey God, so it is sometimes argued, not for moral reasons, certainly not for prudential reasons, but solely because He is God. The believer ought to obey God regardless of the moral value of what is commanded, and even when there is a conflict between God's commandment and morality. In cases of conflict the believer is required to "suspend the ethical", as Kierkegaard put it, for the sake of total obedience to God.

For purposes of discussion here, I assume what is widely called the "Judeo-Christian tradition." According to this tradition, God, all-wise, all-good, all-powerful, creator and sustainer of the world, in a mysterious act of revelation granted the people of Israel the Torah, which is "the book of covenant" between God and the children of Israel. Throughout this chapter I shall use the terms "God's law" and "God's covenant" interchangeably. If anybody objects to this usage, I believe it makes no significant difference with regard to the problem I shall be exploring here.

An essential part of the thesis I develop here is methodological. It concerns the method by which our problem ought to be understood, and accordingly the way by which an answer may be approached. This methodological suggestion is independent of my own particular application of it. Even if my application is incomplete and unsuccessful, the method might still be useful and fruitful, and others might develop it better. My suggestion is thus the following: I suggest we approach the question of the moral obligation towards God's law through an analogous one, namely, the question of the moral obligation which citizens allegedly have towards the law of their countries. This latter question has received very much attention in the last two decades in moral philosophy, as well as in legal and political philosophy. In fact, this is a good example of the unity of these different fields, which are really only different aspects of one philosophical field, namely, practical philosophy. We shall try to examine whether the arguments that have been put down as a moral basis for obeying a country's laws (I shall refer to them sometimes as "earthly laws") are applicable and valid in the case of obeying Divine law. Since the arguments for obeying the law are numerous, or, more precisely, the different versions of these arguments are numerous, my paper must be seen only as a sketch and as an invitation for discussion. I do not presume to cover *all* of these arguments, but only those that seem to me especially relevant and interesting. In fact I shall concentrate mainly on two arguments, and comment briefly on two others.

A moral obligation to obey the law means an obligation to do certain things solely because the law requires them. Often, there are other good reasons for doing these things. In these cases a second reason, the obligation to obey the law, is added. When there are no other reasons, this obligation might by itself suffice to establish one's moral obligation to do what the law requires. It is important to notice that the existence of a moral duty to obey the law implies nothing regarding the *strength* of this duty. To use David Ross's famous terminology, the duty to obey the law (if there is such a duty) is only a prima facie duty that can be overridden by a stronger duty. In other words, such a duty would constitute only *one* reason for action, which might be outweighed by other reasons.[1]

Let us now apply this brief analysis to the obligation to obey God. This notion means firstly that the mere fact that God has commanded something is a reason, a moral reason, for doing it. That is, by commanding, God creates moral obligations.[2] Secondly, this obligation need not be one's actual duty, what one ought to do all things considered. There might be other moral reasons which explain why one should *not* obey God, either in general,[3] or in some particular cases. I shall not go into such reasons here. However, one illustration might be helpful. If one has a moral obligation to obey God, then Abraham faced a *moral* dilemma in the story of the sacrifice of Isaac. On the one hand, he had a moral obligation to sacrifice Isaac merely by virtue of the fact that God required him to do so: on the other hand he had an obvious moral duty not to kill his beloved son.

If one has a moral obligation towards God, then God, or, more precisely, the relation of human beings to God, is not beyond morality but falls under the same moral rules that govern the relations between human beings. God is seen as another member of the moral community, a member to whom we have obligations similar to those we have towards other members of the community. Thus the obligation to obey God would be merely an instance of the application of some general moral rule which applies similarly to many other instances concerning the relations between humans. It is worth noting that in making God a member of the moral community the gap between God and human beings is reduced, and a more immanent conception of God is suggested. Hence, religious views which emphasize the gap between God and humanity, and see God as essentially transcendent, would object to the idea of grounding obedience to Him in moral considerations.

THE ARGUMENT FROM COVENANT

The natural candidate for any attempt to justify adherence to the words of the Torah is the Torah itself since the Torah is considered a covenant, that is, a sort of contract between God and human beings. Covenants, like agreements in general, must be kept. So if a covenant exists between humankind and God, then surely people have a clear obligation to adhere to it. I shall refer to this argument as 'the argument from covenant.'

There is a well-known long tradition which tries to ground the human obligation to earthly laws in a similar consideration. It is assumed that citizens undertook, or have undertaken, some kind of promise to keep the law, that they have consented to obey the law. As a consequence, so it is argued, they have a moral obligation to obey the law. This argument has different versions and it stands at the basis of the contractual tradition in political philosophy. Most contemporary critics reject it.[4] The general form of the criticism runs as follows: The alleged consent is either an historical one, or not. If it is historical, the argument is evidently false. It is very hard, if not impossible, to find any time in history where citizens explicitly undertook a commitment to obey the country's law. Furthermore, even if we could find such an historical act of consent, it could not obligate *us*. Surely one could not be put under an obligation merely by the promises of one's ancestors. If the consent is not historical, then it is either explicit or, in some way, implicit. Since it is hard to point to any explicit consent, philosophers have tried to point to some "weaker" consent, be it what they have called tacit consent,[5] implied consent,[6] or hypothetical consent,[7] that is supposed to obligate the citizen. We cannot go into these different theories here, theories that have been rejected by most critics. In short, it can be shown that these theories are either false, or really abandon the argument from consent in favour of some other argument.

Let us consider now the relevance of all this to the Divine covenant. The Bible tells us that the people of Israel undertook this covenant voluntarily. Exodus 24:7, reads as follows: "And he [Moses] took the book of the covenant, and read it in the hearing of the people, and they said: All that the Lord has said we will do, and obey." [*naase venishma*]. The Talmud (Shabbat 88a) says that though this commitment was forced upon the people of Israel, they re-undertook it voluntarily in the time of Ahasverus. Thus, the first objection against the idea of an historical consent does not apply here; such consent *did* take place according to traditional belief. However, this does not counter the second objection, that is, how could the consent of our ancestors obligate us? Who gave them the right to include me in their covenant? One of the basic elements in the law of contracts is that one cannot make a commitment for another without the latter's explicit authorization and, certainly, this should apply to any kind of covenant.

Can any actual and express act of self-commitment be pointed out? One possibility that I can think of are some prayers, where the believer explicitly declares an undertaking of God's law. But these utterances are better interpreted as part of a religious ritual than as a genuine promise. They do not express acceptance *of* the demands of religion, but rather constitute part of religious practice itself.

They are not a *promise* to obey God; they *are* obeying God. Another possibility I can think of, which applies only to a small number of believers, is the declaration required from the gentile who wishes to convert to Judaism (the *Ger*), affirming acceptance of the commandments (*qabalat mitzvot*). This has an analogy in the law of a few countries, where a new citizen has to declare allegiance to the country's laws. However, this kind of argument would apply only to a very small group, the group of converts. Secondly, and this applies to most versions of the argument from covenant, I have doubts, following Rolf Sartorius (1981: 13) whether such a sweeping promise is indeed binding. I doubt whether one can reasonably be held to such a general and committing promise, to obey each and every law of the state or of God. I tend to believe that such a promise cannot and should not be taken too seriously, and thus, that it does not have the same moral force as other promises.

Different arguments have been construed to overcome these problems in the domain of earthly laws. It has been argued, for instance, that not leaving one's country could count as a consent to its laws,[8] that voting in elections could count as such a consent,[9] and so on. Without entering into these arguments I would only note that none of them seems relevant with regard to the Divine covenant. If we take the idea of such a covenant seriously, it is hard to see when and how each of us has knowingly and voluntarily entered into it. I thus conclude, that the argument from covenant does not seem to be very helpful for our purposes.[10] I shall turn now to examine the more popular traditional argument for obeying God, the argument from gratitude.

THE ARGUMENT FROM GRATITUDE

According to the argument from gratitude the human obligation towards God does not rest on any prior commitment undertaken sometime in the past, but on the tremendous benefits people have received, and constantly receive, from God. While the previous argument assumes that one's obligation to keep God's covenant depends on a voluntary agreement to this covenant, the latter presupposes that such an obligation can be incurred, at least to some extent, even non-voluntarily (though not involuntarily). This fact might provoke some objection from the outset, that is, it raises the question of how one could be under an moral obligation—indeed, a very serious one—without voluntarily committing oneself to it. The objection is misplaced and exhibits a basic misunderstanding of morality. It is just not true that all, or even most, moral duties depend on one's prior agreement. We often find ourselves in situations where we must (morally) do something we never consented (nor would ever consent) to do. Furthermore, sometimes this thing we must do might have a crucial effect on our entire life, such as in some tragic dilemmas. But even in these cases one is not free to opt out, so to say, and stop playing the moral game. Just as one cannot escape God's commands to carry out certain actions, as we learn from the story of Jonah, one cannot escape moral requirements, including those one did not accept voluntarily. Hence, the mere fact that the obligation to keep the Divine covenant is incurred non-voluntarily cannot count as a reason against the argument from gratitude.

It is important to clarify the relation between this argument and the argument from covenant. Firstly, while the argument from gratitude is based on the superiority of one of the sides, the benefactor, over the other, the beneficiary, the argument from covenant is based on the equality of both sides, each entering into the covenant voluntarily. This equality does not exclude the possibility of one of the sides being stronger or wiser or richer than the other. The point is that these inequalities are irrelevant to the existence and to the validity of a covenant, which depends on a self-commitment freely made by each side. Secondly, while in a covenant each side owes the other something, in gratitude only one side has such a debt. This might explain the religious attractiveness of the argument from gratitude throughout history, as expressing the inferior position of humankind in respect to God. The idea of God being under an obligation towards people has seemed blasphemous to many theologians. Thirdly, these arguments seem to exclude each other, or, at least, to weaken each other. The reason for this is simple. If one gives benefit to another as part of an obligation (e.g., one promised to do so), one is entitled to less gratitude than one who benefits a stranger, towards whom one lacks any previous duty, as in the behavior of The Good Samaritan in the well-known parable. Some philosophers believe that doing one's duty can never count as a source of real gratitude.[11] Even if we do not go so far, it seems hard to deny that, other things being equal, fulfilling one's duty entitles one to less gratitude than acting voluntarily, above and beyond the call of one's duty. That being so, it would seem that if there is a mutual commitment, expressed in the form of a covenant, between God and humankind then God is entitled to less gratitude that He would have been entitled to if such a covenant had not existed. If God's providence is, so to speak, a fulfillment of a promise or of a vow He made (see Deut. 7:12), and thus a fulfillment of an obligation, then Divine providence is less entitled to gratitude. That means that if the argument from covenant is valid then the argument from gratitude loses at least some of its force. However, since I believe it is invalid, everything is open in regard to the argument from gratitude.

What is, then, the argument from gratitude? In short the argument states: (a) that one owes a debt of gratitude to God, and/or to one's country, and (b) that the only way, or the best way, to pay this debt is by strictly obeying God's (or the country's) law.[12]

The argument from gratitude concerning obedience to earthly laws was first phrased by Socrates in a famous passage in the Crito (50d–51d). Let me quote the words of "the Laws":

> Are you not grateful to those of us which were instituted for this end, for requiring your father to give you a cultural and physical education? . . . Then since you have been born and brought up and educated, can you deny . . . that you were our child and servant, both you and your ancestors? . . . We have brought you into the world and reared you and educated you, and given you and all your fellow citizens a share in all the good things at our disposal.

The argument from gratitude concerning obedience to Divine Law is in fact to be found in the Bible. Before his death Moses reproaches the people of Israel saying: "Do you thus requite the Lord, / O foolish people and unwise? / is not He thy father who bought thee? / has He not made thee, and established thee?" (Deut. 32:6). Following in his spirit, the prophets complain again and again that the children of Israel do not pay their debt of gratitude to their benefactor. So Isaiah cries: "Hear, O heavens, and give ear, O earth, for the Lord has spoken: I have reared and brought up children, and they have rebelled against me. The ox knows his owner, and the ass his master's crib: but Israel does not know, my people does not consider." (1:2–3)[13] In medieval philosophy the argument from gratitude has been the standard argument in favour of obeying God's commands.[14] In modern philosophy it has been defended by Richard Swinburne in his *The Coherence of Theism* (1977), Ch. 11.

It seems reasonable to suppose, with John Simmons (p. 165), that the central role played by the argument from gratitude in the justification of religion helps to explain the tremendous importance assigned to gratitude in earlier generations. Hume, for instance, says that "Of all crimes that human creatures are capable, the most horrid and unnatural is ingratitude, especially when it is committed against parents."[15] And for Kant, ingratitude was one of the vices which are "the essence of vileness and wickedness" (Kant 1963, p. 218). These very serious condemnations of ingratitude seem more understandable given the above religious background.

It is time to enter the essence of the matter. I shall approach the argument from gratitude through points (a) and (b) mentioned above in turn. In the first place I seek to examine whether indeed one owes a debt of gratitude to God or to one's government. In the second place I seek to examine whether this debt must be expressed in the form of obedience. It is quite obvious that a negative answer to the first question implies a negative answer to the second one too. More precisely, it implies that the second question does not arise at all; if one has no debt to pay, the question of *how* to pay it cannot arise. On the other hand, a positive answer to the first question leaves everything open to the second; Even if one owes a debt of gratitude, it is not at all clear that obedience, not to say *total* obedience, is the way, the *only* way, to pay this debt.

When, then, does an agent A have a duty of gratitude towards a benefactor B? What are the relevant factors in determining the size of this duty? One necessary condition, agreed upon by most philosophers who have analyzed the concept of gratitude, is what I shall call "the altruistic condition." A has a duty of gratitude towards B only if B has brought him some benefit voluntarily and intentionally, and did what was done *for the sake of* A. In contrast, if one brings benefit to another merely by pursuing one's own business, no gratitude is required. If, for instance, my neighbours make a party in their garden, then even if I enjoy the music played there very much, I owe my neighbors no debt of gratitude. This required altruistic motivation need not be "pure," that is, B's *only* motive in bringing benefit to A, but nonetheless, it must constitute a significant part of B's motivation.

A second condition seems to be, what I shall call, "the effort condition." According to John Simmons:

> It seems quite clear that where an obligation of gratitude is owed to the benefactor, he must have made some special effort or sacrifice, or incurred some loss, in providing the benefit in question. (p. 170)

This condition implies that the greater the effort, the greater the debt of gratitude, and where no effort at all is involved, only a small gesture of gratitude (if at all) is fitting. The question which bothers me about the effort condition is whether it is indeed an independent condition, or merely an expression of the altruistic condition. Let me explain these two alternatives. According to the latter view the importance of the benefactor's effort derives from its being indicative of an altruistic motivation towards the beneficiary. Naturally, the stronger one is motivated to bring benefit to another, the greater the sacrifice one is willing to make for his or her sake. Thus, contrary to Simmons, the benefactor's sacrifice has no intrinsic value in determining the debt of gratitude; it has value only because of the valuable motivation behind it. In contrast, according to the first view I mentioned, the benefactor's effort is intrinsically important in determining the debt of gratitude. The logic of this view is simple. If the benefactor has made no sacrifice and no special effort, then no *real* gratitude seems to be in order. If the beneficiary nevertheless offered any act of gratitude the natural response of the benefactor should be—"forget it; it was nothing." In a sense this response would be absolutely correct; *ex hypothesis* it indeed cost the benefactor nothing.

What seems to be at stake here is a very fundamental question concerning gratitude, that is, what exactly is supposed to be *done* in an act of gratitude. According to the view which emphasizes the independent necessity of the effort condition, the essence of gratitude is "something which is thought to repay, or make up for, the effort or loss of the benefactor." (Simmons, 171). Gratitude is thus viewed in terms of justice; one has been paid, and so justice demands one pays back. According to the second view, the essence of gratitude is not some kind of a repayment but rather an expression of appreciation for the benefactor's good will, and for the benefit bestowed upon the beneficiary. The focus here turns on the grateful *feelings* or *attitude* of the beneficiary, rather than on any specific acts owed to the benefactor. Though these feelings tend naturally to express themselves in the practical domain, there is no particular act or set of acts to which the beneficiary is obliged or committed.[16] Furthermore, according to this view, the very concept of owing is inconsistent with the notion of gratitude. Gratitude is based on the idea of a truly free gift on the part of the benefactor. Now, a truly free gift cannot, and should not, be paid for. I cannot be said to *owe* any debt for a true gift given to me.[17]

Deciding between these two concepts of gratitude is not easy, and it requires the formulation of a complete theory of gratitude. As we shall see later, there is no necessity for us to make this decision here. For the time being I would like to emphasize that even if the effort condition is not a necessary condition, it still seems to *increase* the debt of gratitude.

The altruistic condition highlights the personal nature of gratitude. Gratitude is owed to a specific person who acted out of a special motivation to benefit *me*. I would like to note two results of this observation. Firstly, just as the benefit that deserves gratitude must be carried out intentionally and personally, so must the act of gratitude. It cannot be done unintentionally or non-voluntarily. It must stem from a sincere motive to express gratitude towards a specific person, namely the benefactor, and this motive must reveal itself in the form which the gratitude must take. Secondly, it seems that one can have duties of gratitude only towards beings who are capable of intentional altruistic behavior, and not towards natural things such as springs or lands, or artificial things such as buildings, institutions, or cars. Speaking of gratitude in these latter cases should be taken only metaphorically; one cannot seriously have a duty of gratitude towards a spring whose waters one drinks. That is not to say one doesn't have a duty to preserve the spring, not to exploit too much of its water, and so forth. The point is that these duties cannot sensibly be taken as duties (of gratitude) towards the *spring*.[18]

This last remark about the personal nature of gratitude is directly relevant to the application of the argument from gratitude to earthly laws. Furthermore, it seems to suffice to reject this argument. The reason for this is very simple. We must ask ourselves, who is the benefactor to whom we allegedly owe the debt of obeying the country's laws, and to whom an altruistic motivation can be assigned? Chaim Gans has argued conclusively that there are three ways to identify this alleged benefactor, none of which is very promising. The first, suggested by Socrates in the *Crito*, anthropomorphizes the laws, viewing them as a person. This sounds very mysterious metaphysically; laws seem to be an entity of the kind that cannot have intentions at all, neither benevolent nor malevolent. The second way of interpreting this benefactor could be grounded in a Hobbesian, or later, an Austinian conception of law, according to which the source of the law's validity is personal; the Leviathan, the sovereign. But this theory of law is very problematic as contemporary philosophers of law have shown.[19] Furthermore, even if it were correct, it would be hard to assign to this sovereign altruistic motivations—especially in Hobbes's own view, according to which the sovereign is egoistic just like any other human being. The third and last way of identifying the benefactor, a way which has received some attention recently, assumes that the persons to whom we owe gratitude are the government officials who operate the laws and enforce them.[20] But it seems that most of these officials do not act out of altruistic motivation, and those who do surely deserve a more personal expression of gratitude than merely having citizens obey the country's laws.

I find this criticism decisive. The argument from gratitude cannot establish the required moral obligation to obey the law. Leaving all other difficulties aside, without an identifiable personal benefactor, no duty of gratitude can arise.[21]

Turning now to one's obligation towards God, we can start our discussion noting that the above criticism clearly does *not* apply here. In the case of Divine law there is an obvious personal benefactor, namely, God. *If* one owes a debt of gratitude here, it is clear to *whom* one owes it. Furthermore, on the face of it, there are good reasons for supposing that a weighty debt of gratitude is indeed appropriate here. According to traditional religious doctrines, God is not only our benevolent creator but He also sheds His providence upon us, a providence without which we could not exist even for one moment. Everything in the world depends upon God. So, if one has a duty of gratitude towards one's parents for producing one and raising one, all the more so does one have a debt of gratitude towards God, on whom the existence of the parents also depends.[22] Secondly, as God is supposed to be all-good, there seems to be no problem in ascribing to Him the most purely altruistic motivation. Saadia Gaon presents a simple argument for this statement; Since God is perfect, He needs nothing. Hence, creating the world could not have been executed for *His* own sake but only for the sake of humankind out of pure love and benevolence (Saadia, ibid.). Taking into account all these facts about the nature of God and his relation to human beings, it seems reasonable to conclude that humans do have a duty of gratitude towards God. I believe that given the traditional beliefs about God, this conclusion, in general, can hardly be denied.

Nevertheless, this conclusion is far from ending our discussion. We must ask how great, so to speak, this debt is, which we owe God. This question takes us back to our brief comments on the effort condition. If gratitude amounts to compensating the benefactor for his or her loss and effort, God surely needs none of it; we cost Him nothing and so there is nothing to pay back to Him. Although bringing us into existence and sustaining us is no doubt a very great benefit for us, still, for *God* it is no trouble at all. That means, firstly, that there is nothing to repay *for,* and secondly, that there is nothing to repay *by;* It cost God nothing to bring us benefit, and there is nothing we can give Him in repayment that He does not already have.

Saadia saw this last point clearly and that is why he characterizes the general duty of gratitude as follows:

> I maintain that reason bids us respond to every benefactor either by returning his kindness if he is in need of it, or by offering thanks if he is not in need of recompense. (*Beliefs and Opinions,* Ibid.)

Not surprisingly, the same notion of gratitude was adopted by the contemporary philosopher Richard Swinburne too. Concerning one's obligation to one's parents Swinburne emphasizes:

> It is not that children have a duty to pay something back to the parent, but that because in an important respect the parent is the source of their being he is entitled to their *consideration.* (p. 206, italics added.)

The idea of gratitude as a repayment suggests that the gratitude should correspond, at least in some degree, to the benefactor's payment. This implies that the bigger the payment, that is, the benefactor's loss and sacrifice, the bigger the repayment owed. But if God needs no repayment, only thanks and consideration, that "can lead," as Robert Nozick put it, only "to a limited obligation to our creator and sustainer—there is no arriving at Abraham by this route." (1981, p. 746, n. 10). One's duty to express gratitude in this case does not seem sufficient to establish the very demanding requirement that one obeys every and any command one receives from God. Of course, God may have the *right* to command us and to punish us for disobedience, but that is not the issue here. The question that interests us here is not whether God has the right to command people, nor whether people ought to obey these commands, but rather whether the reason they ought to obey could be founded in their duty of gratitude. I believe the answer to this question is negative.

The fact that the gratitude owed to God is better understood as an expression of thanks and not as a repayment has another important result regarding the *form* of this gratitude. An act which expresses thanks should, by its very nature, be more personal than an act which repays a debt. *Saying* to the benefactor how grateful one is, for instance, is a good illustration of such a personal gesture of gratitude. Hence, it seems one should express one's gratitude towards God in similar ways, prayer for example. This remark takes us back to the beginning of our discussion. We argued that even if one has a duty of gratitude, it is not necessarily true that obeying the benefactor's commands is the only way, or the best way, to discharge it. In regard to one's feelings of gratitude towards God, I believe the best way to express them is by prayer, and the like, and not by strict obedience. While such obedience can well express one's feelings of awe and humility towards God, it is not the best way, certainly not the *only* way, to express gratitude.[23]

To conclude our discussion on the argument from gratitude we can return now to the problem we raised above concerning the essence of gratitude. The question was whether gratitude should be construed in terms of justice, focusing on some more or less specific *acts* which one *owes* to one's benefactor, or whether the essence of gratitude lies in certain *feelings* one is expected to have, which do not imply any specific acts, though, quite naturally, they are usually expressed in some kind of activity. It seems that neither of these notions of gratitude is strong enough to found the obligation to obey God's law. Gratitude as a repayment does imply specific acts, but, unfortunately, this tenet cannot be applied successfully towards God. On the other hand, gratitude, in the sense of feeling grateful, is no doubt relevant here, but it does not commit us to any specific acts, certainly not to obeying all of God's commands.

OTHER ARGUMENTS

The failure of the argument from gratitude concerning obedience to earthly laws often gives rise to a different argument, known as the argument from fair play, which has been developed in the last decades by Hart (1955), Rawls (1964), and others. According to this argument, the duty to obey does not flow from the mere receipt of benefits but from the unfairness of enjoying them without contributing, along with the other citizens, to their production; in being a "free-rider." One's obligation is thus not towards the government, the ruler, or the government officials, but towards the other citizens, one's partners in the joint enterprise of the state.[24] On the face of it, this argument seems irrelevant in the case of God's law. One's duty to comply with Divine precepts is usually considered a duty towards *God* and not towards one's fellow believers. However, on reflection, this is not so simple. According to the Bible, Divine providence depends not only on the behavior of individuals, but also on the behavior of groups of people, such as cities (Sodom), nations (especially Israel), and even all of humankind (at the time of the Flood). This means, that one's behavior affects not only one's own fate but also the fate of many others. If the nation as a whole keeps its part in the covenant then God will shed His providence on it—and that will cover violators of the covenant too. Hence, these violators might be considered as free-riders; they enjoy the benefits resulting from the efforts of others, while not contributing their part to these efforts.

However, this speculation, which I find quite interesting, seems incompatible with Divine justice. If God's providence is perfectly just, and if in the end everybody gets exactly what he or she deserves, then the above free-riding must be only apparent; if someone seems to be riding freely, you can be sure he or she will pay full price for it, either here or in the next world. Hence, no real free-riders exist.

The same approach seems to apply to another possible argument, one that seeks to derive one's duty to keep the covenant from the harmful results that violating the covenant has on other innocent human beings; possibly wars, hunger, and death. This argument corresponds to a consequential, or a utilitarian, justification to obey the law, according to which obeying the law is a moral duty because disobeying it has harmful results. But, again, in the case of obedience to Divine law, this is not so simple. If, ultimately, everybody gets what he or she deserves, then ultimately no one could be the cause of any misfortune which was not due to happen anyway. Hence, to conclude these last two points, the obligation to obey God cannot be justified by an appeal to one's obligation to other human beings, be it an obligation of fairness or an obligation to prevent harm and misery.

It is time to sum up. The question of the existence of a moral obligation to obey the laws of a country has received much attention in the last ten to twenty years. Most of the philosophers who have discussed this question have reached a negative conclusion. They have argued that one does not have a moral obligation to obey the law as such, that is, there is no moral obligation to do things just because the law requires it.[25] In this essay I have tried to show that this skeptical attitude towards obeying earthly laws is also appropriate to the question of whether one should obey Divine law. If I am right then one's obligation towards God is not a moral one.

Could there be any different kind of obligation towards God? Is the term 'obligation' at all appropriate to express the human relation to God? The answer to these questions lies beyond the concerns of this essay.[26]

NOTES

1. For such an understanding of the concept of a moral obligation to obey the law, see Smith 1973, pp. 950–951.

2. The term 'creates' should not be taken too literally. The above argument does not presuppose a Divine command theory of ethics according to which God creates the property of moral wrongness itself, or that He makes it the case that x is wrong (e.g., Wierenga 1983). Our thesis assumes that though the general moral duties do not depend on God, their specific application might still depend on Him. Any specific

moral requirement can be seen as a conclusion of an argument containing a major premise, namely, some general moral rule, and a minor premise, namely, a statement to the effect that some instance x falls under that rule. Now, according to the thesis discussed above, this minor premise might be a theological one, that is, a premise that has 'God' as its subject ('God is the owner of the world,' 'God is man's benefactor,' etc.). In this sense God can be said to determine the minor premise, and thus create a moral obligation.

3. The main general moral reason which has been put forward against obedience to God is based on the idea of the moral worth of autonomy. It has been supposed that worshipping God and obeying Him are incompatible with man's moral autonomy. This alleged incompatibility has been strongly expressed by Rachels (1971). The tension between autonomy and obedience, or autonomy and authority is relevant to obeying earthly laws too. A clear and well-known argument for the incompatibility of autonomy with the state's authority can be found in Wolff 1971.

4. See Simmons 1979, ch. 4; Greenawalt 1987, ch. 5; Gans 1988, sec. 3.

5. This kind of consent was probably John Locke's intention, see Simmons, pp. 79–84.

6. This possibility is discussed in Greenawalt, pp. 64–68; Gans, 363–366.

7. See Rawls 1973 and note 10 below.

8. See Crito, 50–51.

9. See: Plamenatz 1968; Singer 1973.

10. I have ignored a modern version of the argument from covenant developed by John Rawls (1973) and others, which bases the argument on the citizens' hypothetical consent to the law. This version is different from the "standard" argument which is based on the citizens' *actual* consent. To say that one ought to do x because one, after reflection, would have consented to x, is really to say no more than one ought to do x because x is rational. This still leaves us with the necessity of explaining why it is rational. The same applies to religious duties too. It is one thing to say that one ought to do x because one has committed oneself to doing so by accepting the Divine covenant, and quite another thing to say that one ought to do x because one ought to accept (or reaccept) this covenant.

11. See Lyons 1969.

12. The argument from gratitude should be clearly distinguished from an argument based on the *respect* one owes to God (see Swinburne 1977, Ch. 15), or to one's government (see Raz 1979, pp. 250–261). The

obligation to respect x does not depend on any benefits bestowed by x, but on the character of x which merits respect, while in gratitude these benefits are essential.

13. These sentences can also be interpreted as expressing a different argument, according to which man has a duty towards God because God is man's owner. This 'argument from ownership' is developed in Swinburne 1977, p. 207, and Brody 1974. However since it has no serious parallel in the domain of obedience to earthly laws, I shall not elaborate on it here.

14. See, for example, Saadia Gaon, *Beliefs and Opinions,* Bk. 3, ch. 1; Bahya Ibn Pakuda, *Duties of the Heart,* 3.

15. *A Treatise of Human Nature,* Bk. 3, pt. 1, sec. 1.

16. On the general indeterminateness of the duty of gratitude, see Weiss, p. 498; Simmons, p. 167–8; Greenawalt, pp. 152–3; Smith, p. 950. This indeterminateness makes it hard to prove that any *specific* act is required by a duty of gratitude.

17. Cf. Weiss 1985.

18. Walker (1980) argues that "gratefulness need not always be 'focused' upon another person, does not always have to be gratefulness to *someone*" (p. 45). This might indeed be true. It only shows that the concept of gratefulness is distinct from the concept of gratitude (not merely "wider" than, as Walker believes, ibid.), and is based on different considerations.

19. See Hart 1961; Raz 1971.

20. See Soper 1987; Greenawalt, pp. 152–153; Simmons, pp. 189.

21. In confronting this crucial problem one might argue that duties of gratitude can arise not only towards persons, but towards institutions too (see Walker 1988). In view of my comments on the personal nature of gratitude I find this idea quite dubious. Cf. Simmons's criticism of it, pp. 187–190.

22. The relation children-parents is usually considered as a paradigm of the appropriateness of gratitude. See, for example, the citations above from the Bible and from *Crito*. But see Simmons's objection to this paradigm, pp. 182–3.

23. See also note 16 above.

24. Rawls, (ibid, p. 9–10) suggested that the duty of fair play arises only in cooperative schemes. This assumption has been criticised by Simmons, pp. 109–14; Greenawalt, pp. 129–33.

25. See, for example, Smith 1973; Simmons 1979; Raz 1979, pp. 234–49; Lyons 1976, pp. 208–14.

26. I owe a debt of gratitude to David Heyd and David Widerker who kindly commented on an earlier version of this essay.

REFERENCES

Brody, B. 1974. "Morality and Religion Reconsidered," in B. Brody, ed., *Readings in the Philosophy of Religion.* (Englewood Cliffs NJ: Prentice-Hall), pp. 592–604.

Gans, Ch. 1988. "Grounds for Obeying the Law" [in Hebrew]. *Mishpatim* (published by Tel-Aviv University) 17:353–391.

Greenawalt, Kent. 1987. *Conflicts of Law and Morality.* Oxford: Clarendon Press.

Hart, H. L. A. 1955. "Are There Any Natural Rights?" *Philosophical Review* 64:175–232.

_____. 1961. *The Concept of Law.* Oxford: Clarendon Press.

Kant, Immanuel. 1963. *Lectures on Ethics.* New York: Harper & Row.

Lyons, Daniel. 1969. "The Odd Debt of Gratitude." *Analysis* 29:92–6.

Lyons, David. 1976. *Ethics and the Rule of Law.* Cambridge University Press.

Nozick, Richard. 1981. *Philosophical Explanations.* Oxford University Press.

Plamenatz, J. 1968. *Consent, Freedom and Political Obligation.* Oxford.

Rachels, James. 1971. "God and Human Attitudes." *Religious Studies* 7:325–37.

Rawls, John. 1964. "Legal Obligations and the Duty of Fair Play," in S. Hook, ed., *Law and Philosophy.* New York University Press.

_____. 1973. *A Theory of Justice.* Oxford University Press.

Raz, Joseph. 1971. *The Concept of a Legal System.* Oxford: Clarendon Press.

_____. 1979. *The Authority of Law.* Oxford: Clarendon Press.

Sartorius, Rolf. 1981. "Political Authority and Political Obligation." *Virginia Law Review* 67:3–17.

Simmons, John. 1979. *Moral Principles and Political Obligations.* Princeton University Press.

Singer, Peter. 1973. *Democracy and Disobedience.* Oxford.

Smith, M. B. E. 1973. "Is There a Prima Facie Obligation to Obey the Law?" *Yale Law Journal* 82:950–76.

Soper, P. 1987. "The Obligation to Obey the Law," in R. Gavison, ed., *Issues in Contemporary Legal Philosophy—The Influence of H. L. A. Hart.* Oxford: Clarendon Press.

Swinburne, Richard. 1977. *The Coherence of Theism.* Oxford University Press.

Walker, A. D. M. 1980–1981. "Gratefulness and Gratitude." *Proceedings of the Aristotelian Society* 81:39–55.

_____. 1988. "Political Obligation and the Argument from Gratitude." *Philosophy and Public Affairs* 17:191–211.

Weiss, Roslyn. 1985. "The Moral and Social Dimensions of Gratitude." *The Southern Journal of Philosophy* 23:491–501.

Wierenga, Edward. 1983. "A Defensible Divine Command Theory." *Nous* 17:387–407.

Wolff, Robert P. 1971. *In Defense of Anarchism*. New-York: Harper & Row.

CHAPTER 5

The Perpetual Covenant of Jewish Learning

Menachem Fisch

In conscious defiance of the well-known prohibition against ever committing the Oral Torah to writing, the Judaic sages of late antiquity compiled lengthy records of their learning. Commencing with the Mishna (c.200 A.D.), followed by the Tosephta (c.250), the Tannaitic midrashim of the third century (the Sifra [to Leviticus]), the Sifre (to Numbers and Deuteronomy), the talmud of the Land of Israel (c.400), and the Amoraic midrashim of the fifth century (Genesis and Leviticus Rabbah), and culminating in the talmud of Babylonia (c.500), the process of documentation inaugurated by R. Yehudah Ha-Nasi yielded the vast and unique canon of rabbinical Judaism. What, we might enquire, was the object of the exercise? What was it that the rabbis sought to accomplish by compiling and passing down the texts they produced? Given both the initial audacity of their decision to do so and the sheer enormity of their undertaking, the question is central to any understanding of the talmudic era.

To say that, following Hillel the Elder,[1] the rabbis (reluctantly) sought to document their halakhic and exegetical conclusions for fear of a possible disruption of the traditional process of oral transmission will not suffice. Had that been the case the texts they produced would have been very different, resembling much more than they do such systematic and definitive law codes as the *Mishne Torah* or the *Shulkhan Arukh*. The talmuds and *midrashim* bear no such resemblance. Halakhic rulings, it is true, are normally stated when reached, but even with regard to halakha proper it is the process of deliberation rather than the conclusions it eventually yielded that by far occupy the main bulk of the texts. But on the wide range of non-halakhic issues treated throughout the canon—theological, metaphysical, exegetical—the texts, though equally rigorous and polemic, remain as a rule pluralistic and above all open.[2] The rabbis, it seems, deliberately avoided closure except when absolutely necessary—namely, on matters of ritual and law.

All this seems to point to the conclusion that the over-all aim of the texts was didactical (if it is at all reasonable to speak of texts compiled over a period of two and a half centuries as having a common objective). What the authorships of the *talmudim* and the midrashic compilations seem to have wished to convey to future generations was first and foremost their way of learning. For the pharisees and their successors *talmud Torah*—Torah-study—was deemed the very highest of works. Torah-study, they urged, in being a prerequisite to all deeds, outweighs all deeds.[3] So much so that in the eyes of the Mishna (with the sadducee dissenters very much in mind) a bastard sage is rated higher in rank than an ignorant High-Priest.[4] In the canonical texts of Judaism Torah-study undoubtedly forms a class of its own among humanity's obligations and responsibilities. And yet there exists no tractate talmud Torah among the writings of the talmudic sages. Central as it had become, the rabbis had apparently decided that Torah-study is best learnt by example. To this end they produced a record and recapitulation of their learning unparalleled in the history of Western culture. No community of learners known to me ever invested so much time and effort systematically to recapitulate the process of their own deliberations on such vast a scale. Read thus, as a sustained attempt to convey a theory of human learning and human knowledge, the texts demand the attention of the epistemologist. How, he or she might ask, did the rabbis conceive of humanly possible intellectual achievement? What was considered by them a step forward in Torah-study? What did they deem the most efficient ways of achieving progress thus construed? And to what extent do the texts under consideration pertain to a single epistemological program? Do they speak in one voice on such matters, or do the texts imply that the very nature of talmud Torah remained for them an open question?

To state my case at the outset, the aim of this paper is to argue that these questions were debated and decisively resolved close to

100 A.D., and that the texts that emerged as a result not only documented, but sought to establish a tradition of learning pertaining to a theory of knowledge and to standards of rationality and intellectual progress intriguingly similar to those characteristic of modern sciences as we have only recently come to understand it. Moreover, that, unlike scientists of the past, the rabbis had at their disposal, and eventually canonized, a text in which those very standards were explicitly argued for in full philosophical idiom.[5] But in order to substantiate these claims a little more needs to be said both of science and of rabbinical learning.

First to science.

The dramatic upheavals in the physical sciences at the turn of the century generated a philosophical crisis. Until then superseded theories, as prominent even as Ptolemaic astronomy, Descartes' vortices, Newton's corpuscular theory of light, phlogiston theory or Lamarckian evolution, had simply been dismissed as bad science; as the unfortunate and evidently avoidable consequences of methodological shortsightedness. But to describe Newtonian physics as bad science was unthinkable despite it having been refuted. For one thing, although relativity theory and quantum mechanics could not be portrayed as further developments of classical physics, since they clearly contradicted it, only in the context of a body of theory similar to that of classical physics could the problems to which the two new theories were presented as solutions be formulated. The motivation to innovate and rethink old beliefs (scientific or other) depends on how pressing the problems that they give rise to are felt to be, which in turn depends on how compelling and fruitful they had seemed to have been in the first place. In this respect classical physics was a supreme scientific achievement even from the vantage point of the theories that eventually replaced it. However, to appreciate it as such a totally new approach to the philosophy of science was called for. Science could no longer be portrayed as a gradual accumulation of truths. During the heyday of Newtonianism, the uncontested truth, and astonishing predictive power, of mechanics, parts of optics and physical astronomy had to be explained. It was no longer regarded, as in the works of Francis Bacon or René Descartes, a question of deliberating theoretically whether or not science could in principle achieve its ultimate goals, but a question of explaining how in fact it had evidently done so already! But with the downfall of Newtonian physics, and with it the refutation of all enlightenment accumulatory theories of science, the question was again rendered theoretical.

Theoretically, argued Karl Popper in his 1934 classic *Logik der Forschung,* all forms of justificationism ultimately rest on a logical fallacy, since the argument-schema, characteristic of all such reasoning is obviously invalid. From the fact that theory **T** logically implies the eventuation of **E**, and the fact that **E** is known to occur, *nothing* follows regarding the truth value of **T**, simply because **E** may have been eventuated by any number of things. In other words, Popper argued, to the embarrassment of his positivist contemporaries, the very concept of the empirical confirmation of general hypotheses, let alone their actual verification, is in principle wrong-headed.

The inevitable and revolutionary conclusion is that, regardless of what generations of researchers thought they could and indeed had achieved, science is incapable in principle of securing truth at all. But if science cannot be said to progress by accumulating demonstrably true, or at least well-confirmed theories, in what sense can it be said to have progressed at all? If not truth, what are the aims of scientific enquiry, and how, if not by seeking to validate our hypotheses, can they be achieved?

Popper's well-known answer rests on the following: although we have no way of ever knowing whether a conjecture has found its mark, by prudently criticizing our efforts we are sometimes capable of *knowing that we are mistaken.* If the occurrence of **E** follows logically from theory **T**, and if **E** is found convincingly *not to* occur, logic permits confidently to conclude that **T** is in some respect false. (Due to the logically valid argument-schema known as the *modus tollens:* if **p** implies **q**, and **not-q**, then **not-p**). But how can such an *epistemologia negativa* form the basis for a theory of *progress?* In what sense can knowledge be said to *grow* if all we can ever confidently know is that we are wrong? The answer, Popper suggests, is that although we can never verify our knowledge claims, by consulting the phenomena, we can to an extent assess the worth of an hypothesis relative to the performance of its problematic predecessors. Although Young and Fresnesl's undulatory theory of light, for instance, could not be validated by any amount of empirical evidence (despite the fact that at the time all agreed that it was), the fact that it withstood tests in which former emission theories had failed, testifies to its relative superiority. Progress in science is a matter of problem seeking and problem solving, no more and no less.

Science, in Popper's view, progresses not by accumulating well-confirmed knowledge gleaned off compilations of data, but by constant troubleshooting; by repeated cycles of imaginative conjecture and keen refutation; by seeking constantly to expose the shortcomings of its current theories, and willing, if necessary, to rethink and radically modify even its most cherished convictions.

Science is a rational activity, we now realize, not because it is capable of producing uncontested truth, but, quite to the contrary, because it prudently treats each and every theory it produces as potentially flawed; as either totally wrong or at least as only partially correct. More generally, the very essence of rational action is to constantly test the means we employ to eventuate desired goals in the hope of exposing their shortcomings in order to attempt to put them right.[6] Scientific knowledge is passed on from one generation of researchers to the next, to be carefully studied, constantly tried and criticized, and hopefully to be modified and further expanded. But in order to be in a position effectively to criticize or to test a theory one needs first thoroughly to understand it. Hence, as Popper himself has stressed,[7] two different yet complementary traditions are required to ensure and sustain an ongoing rational enquiry. First, and obviously, the theories themselves need effectively to be transmitted from one generation of researchers to the next, otherwise scientific work would be trivially terminated. To serve this purpose institutions of learning are required in which current theories are taught and understood as thoroughly as possible. But to avoid mere indoctrination, a second tradition—a critical tradition—is equally pertinent. Scientific theories are typically handed on, accompanied, as Popper puts it, by "a silent . . . text of a second-order character" which says in effect: 'this is the very best we have, study it carefully, and if possible improve it.'" The two traditions that nourish the logic of scientific discourse thus combine to toe the delicate line between dogma and mere fancy. Scientific theories need to be taught as tentative though not frivolous; to be taken in all seriousness yet not as infallible; as the very best we have though not as the best possible.

Bearing this in mind, let us now turn to the rabbis.

The distinctive feature of rabbinic Judaism is the distinction between the Written and the Oral Torah; that is to say between Scripture and its interpretation, between Text and exegesis. With regard to the former—the Written Torah, the *Torah shebikhtav*—namely, the bare and uninterpreted text of the Hebrew Scriptures,[8] Judaism grants the human being no say whatsoever. The written word of the Scriptures is held to lie entirely beyond the reach of human discretion. Once given on Sinai, "engraved upon the tablets," it is not within human power to authorize the amendment of even a single letter. The written Torah, the text itself, is regarded univocally by the rabbis as unchanged and unchangeable, invariant to the passage of time. It came into being, one early midrash tells us, prior to the creation of the world together with God's throne (the *kise hakavod*).[9] Echoing Plato's *Timaeus* perhaps, another well-known midrash depicts the Creator God as having "consulted the Torah and created the world".[10] With regard to the transcendental and a-temporal nature of the Written Torah, I repeat, the rabbis were fully agreed.

But what of the Oral Torah, of the interpretation of the Text? Again, in seemingly Platonic fashion the Bavli *Nidah*, 30b, explains that since there are no days in which one enjoys more happiness and tranquility than in the bowels of one's mother (crouching hands on its temples, eyes closed and mouth open, feeding directly to the stomach), the fetus is then taught the whole Torah. However, "as soon as it sees the light [of day], an angel approaches, slaps its mouth and causes it to forget all the Torah completely." One is henceforth required to approach the prime task of Torah-study devoid of privileged Platonic "re-cognition." The Platonic or Cartesian or enlightenment idea that one is somehow sufficiently endowed to seek, arrive at and fathom the one Truth unassisted from without has no rabbinic equivalent. Hence one of two: either we are in possession of the Truth by virtue of Divine revelation, or we are not, in which case, lacking the capacity to discover it unassisted, the human interpreter is doomed to conjecture as best he or she can, ruling when necessary by majority vote and constantly revising past decisions.

Both these positions—the *traditionalist* approach predicated on reception and meticulous transmission of the initially revealed Truth, and the nontraditionalist, reformist, or *progressivist* approach that views the Oral Torah as the context dependent tentative product of ongoing debate—were forcefully represented, and fiercely debated by R. Yohanan b. Zakkai's direct disciples at Jabne, the first of the great talmudic academies. Moreover, and this is perhaps the main point I wish to convey, unlike perhaps any other non-halakhic issue raised in the talmudic literature, this debate seems to have been decisively resolved.

For the traditionalist, then, Torah-study is a matter of meticulous reception and transmission of the one Truth. Consequently, the content of a transmitted legacy will itself not be debated. The only issue open to question will be the credentials and credibility of the transmitter, especially in cases of conflicting teachings. No person, however, is a perfect transmitter. The process of Torah-study, for the traditionalist, is therefore necessarily degenerative. Much knowledge will normally be lost en route, and until prophecy is restored, will be in principle irretrievable. Time, or history, as in premodern Western thought is for the traditionalist a *decaying and corrupting* factor. "Much Torah have I studied from my masters, and much Torah have I taught," complained the arch-traditionalist R. Eliezer b. Horqanos "the great",[11] "but I succeeded in taking from my teachers no more than a dog lapping at the sea. And my students from me, no more than a quill dipped in an ink pot".[12] Finally, traditionalist institutions of learning will be necessarily elitist and highly selective. Only a select and small group of devoted initiates will be admitted into the inner circle to be charged with holy task of passing on the Truth.

Contrary perhaps to R. Yohanan's own views, such seems to have been the situation in the newly established center of learning at Jabne, led at the time by the stern and uncompromising Rabban Gamliel, head of the academy, and his above mentioned brother-in-law R. Eliezer. Under Rabban Gamliel's leadership, we are told,[13] the new center of learning was highly selective. A guard was actually employed, and the doors were kept shut in order to exclude all but the very best. After a series of clashes with his adversary R. Joshua b. Hananyia—the hero of the present account—a revolt apparently broke out. As a result Rabban Gamliel was (temporarily) removed from office and R. Joshua's disciple and follower, the young R. Elazar b. Azariah was offered the job. Upon assuming office, we are told, Elazar did two things. He threw the doors of the academy open for all who wished to study—never to be shut again. And, on the very same day, he summoned all bearers of tradition, and proceeded to take a majority vote on each and every one of them—a procedure unheard of in traditionalist circles! The controversies related in Mishna *Eduyoth* are reputed to have been resolved on that famous "same day."

This brings us to perhaps the most dramatic moment described in the entire talmudic literature: the oft-quoted dispute between R. Eliezer b. Horkanus and R. Joshua b. Hanania and its conclusive resolution related in the Bavli *Baba Metzia* 59b:

"*Tanna*" [we know from Tannaitic Sources] "[that] on that day R. Eliezer settled all matters (*heshiv kol teshuvot shebaolam*) but his opinions were not accepted." The question is to what day does the story refer? Most commentators are of the opinion that the day in question is the day in which the susceptibility to ritual uncleanness of a certain type of oven (the so called oven of Akhnai) was debated—a debate described in the previous paragraph.[14] However, the beginning of a new paragraph indicated by the word "*tanna*," and the depiction of R. Eliezer as having on that particular day "settled all matters" (or in literal translation "provided all the answers in the world") rather than those specifically related to the issue of the oven, seem to indicate that perhaps the day in question was of greater significance. "That day," I suggest, refers to the day R. Elazar b. Azariah took office at Jabne. There also, in the story of the removal of Rabban Gamliel related in *Berakhot* 27b, the description of the removal of the guard and that of the voting of *Eduyot* are each introduced by the word "*tanna*." To which the Bavli adds: "And each time it is said 'on that very day' (*bo bayom*) it is meant that day (the day of Rabban Gamliel's removal from office)." In any event, despite the slightly different wording (in *Baba Metzia* it is not *bo bayom* but *be-oto ha-yom*), according to Mishna *Eduyot* 7:7, the debate concerning the oven of Akhnai was indeed resolved on that very day. Read thus the great debate between R. Eliezer and R. Joshua that followed is of extraordinary significance.

On that day, we recall, R. Elazar, the newly appointed head of the academy, called upon all bearers of tradition to present their learning. Among the first to appear would have been the great traditionalist R. Eliezer, who attempted to "settle all matters" but to his utter amazement was voted down. Reluctant to accept the ruling of the majority (a procedure of no significance to the traditionalist concept of Torah-study), R. Eliezer characteristically then turned to seek supernatural 'proofs' of his position, probably assuming that his credibility as a reliable transmitter was at stake.

> He said to them: 'let the carob tree prove that I am right,' thereupon the carob tree was torn a hundred cubits out of its place. . . . They said to him: 'from a carob no proof can be brought.' Again he said to them: 'let the water duct prove that I am right,' whereupon the water in the duct flowed backwards. They said to him: 'from a water duct no proof can be brought.'

Finally, having further failed to convince his audience by causing the walls of the academy to collapse, Eliezer turned to the ultimate traditionalist proof, calling upon no less than the heavens themselves to vouch for his "answers":

> He then said to them: 'let the heavens prove that I am right!,' whereupon a heavenly voice declared: 'what have you against R. Eliezer? The *halakha* is always in accord with his view.' At this R. Joshua stood up and declared: 'It is not in heaven' (Deut, 30:12) . . . 'Since the Torah was given from Sinai, *we pay no attention to a heavenly voice.* For already at Sinai you wrote in the Torah: by a majority you are to decide.[15]

Eliezer, as perhaps expected, still stubbornly refused to accept the ruling of the majority, whereupon he was excommunicated and was refused the right to teach—a move without parallel in the talmudic texts, certainly with respect to so eminent a sage as Eliezer.

Second generation Jabne, it seems, had made a clear and decisive choice with regard to Torah study. In doing so R. Joshua and his followers declared the covenant of learning, of Torah-study, as founded upon a sharp demarcation of divine and human authority. Where the dividing line runs between word and meaning, between text and understanding, between *interpretandum* and *interpretans*. The development of the Oral Torah, they ruled, is given exclusively to the mundane thisworldly sensibilities of humanhood. And within the hermeneutic space allocated to humanity, the Almighty himself is restrained from interfering.[16] Within it, human knowledge is in principle devoid of external warrant, where it remains forever conjectural, open to question, and necessarily context dependent.

However, the texts produced thereafter contain several seemingly traditionalist pronouncements that might be taken to indicate that R. Joshua's victory was not as decisive as I have tried to make out.[17] A closer look at these declarations that seem to impart a Divine origin to later rabbinical rulings, reveals, however, a picture of talmud Torah considerably more subtle than that of simple mouth-to-ear transmission. Commenting on the verse: "and the Lord delivered to me two tablets of stone written with the finger of God; and on them was written according to *all the words the Lord spoke . . .*" (*Deut.* 9:10), the talmud (Yerushalmi *Peah* 2:6) and midrash (e.g., Lev. Rabbah 22:1, and *Eccl. Rabbah* 1:10 and 5:8) state that "the Scriptures, the Mishna, halakha, talmud, *Tosephtoth*, the *Agadoth and even everything a seasoned student is eventually to proclaim in the presence of his teacher* (*atid lehorot liphne rabo*), were all originally declared at Sinai." Which cannot be taken to mean that the opinions voiced by future students are therefore all *true,* since the saying also obviously applies to conflicting opinions. The midrash also clearly indicates that it is not the case that future *talmidei khakhamim* will proclaim only those opinions they happened *to know* were first given at Sinai. Rather, what the saying seems to convey is a license to put forward any opinion a serious student of Torah sees fit on the grounds that *eilu va-eilu divre Elohim haim.* (This point is further strengthened by the importantly different and probably earlier version of this same midrash in Bavli *Megillah* 19b, that talks not of what future students will learn in the presence of their teachers, but of "what future scribes will eventually *innovate.*") Even Maimonides, who might seem to have subscribed (at least in his introduction to the Mishna) to traditionalist point of view, depicts no more than thirty one *halakhic* rulings as *halakha le-Moshe me-Sinai* that are, in his opinion, indeducable from the Scriptures by means of accepted rabbinical modes of learning.

Taken as a whole (their different structures and agendas notwithstanding) the talmudic texts, as Neusner argues, by no means record "a process of sedimentary order, accumulation and conglomeration." The epistemological commitment evidenced by the process of learning and system building they reconstruct is not premised, even in part on authoritative preknowledge.

> The authorship of the Bavli does not take over, rework, and repeat what it has received out of prior writings but makes its own statement, on its own program, in its own terms, and for its own purposes. And . . . it does whatever it wishes with whatever it has received out of the past.[18]

But even more than by the statement the Bavli eventually makes, it is the meticulously recorded *process of learning* by which it is made that attests most vividly to the nontraditionalist nature of the talmudic enterprise. It is through and through a pluralistic process of deliberation and debate, the disputative nature of which is all pervading. And although some final rulings are described as given to Moses at Sinai, the process by which even they are arrived at is, in most cases, hardly one geared towards their authentication as such, but by and large one of rational deliberation.[19] Perhaps more importantly, as noted at the outset, large portions of the texts in hand, perhaps their greater part, do not strive to achieve final rulings at all. In matters of metaphysics, biblical exegesis, general conduct, and even theology proper, debates are reconstructed and are set before the reader in all detail, but, as a matter of course, not decided. The reader is presented with a plethora of opinions of equal footing, some mutually exclusive, as if the objective was to exemplify ways of learning rather than to dictate one consistent and coherent doctrinal system of thought. All of which attests compellingly to the nontraditionalist view.

The analogy to science is striking. In science too one confronts a given and, in itself, uninterpreted corpus of phenomena or 'text.' One then attempts to render the 'book of nature' meaningful by constructing systems of theory that are likewise lacking of external verification. There exists no court of appeal, we now realize, higher than one's own self-criticism, which, again, ultimately rests on one's own conjectures. In science a heavenly voice is no longer acknowledged, in the writings of the rabbis it is, but is rejected.[20] There are, of course, fundamental differences. Science, at least today, is in no way regarded as a covenantal enterprise. Neither is science viewed as a binding obligation, as something one is in any way *required* to perform. Torah-study certainly is. Indeed it is viewed by the rabbis as the very highest of charges. But, and this is the crucial point, the unquestioned omnipresence of a covenantal God, the divine origin ascribed to the subject matter of enquiry, and the deep and solemn sense of religious obligation that motivates the enquirer, have little if any bearing on the *epistemology* of Torah-study. In *this* sense the analogy to science is valid. If the warrant of the heavenly voice is rejected, there is nothing to vouch for the truth claims and the normative rulings of the Oral Torah other than human rationality. And if that is case, we are in the realm of Popper's thorough yet constructive skepticism.

There is, however, little if any explicit epistemological reflection in the talmudic and midrashic texts themselves. "The talmud liberates the intellect," as David Hartman puts it, viewing God as "making His human covenantal partners [exclusively] responsible for intellectually developing the Torah".[21] But, to the best of my knowledge, the philosophical problem of what warrants the claims of the thus liberated intellect, is not discussed systematically in the rabbinical texts themselves. One finds in them no *theory of knowledge,* and subsequently, little if any systematic discussion of talmud Torah.

Could it be then that halakhic truth was simply regarded by the rabbis as truth by convention? That the total exegetical freedom they declared really meant that they were inventing the norm as they went along? That, in their opinion, there was really nothing that their interpretations and rulings could be said to be true *of*?[22]

The rabbis, I believe, would have been appalled by such a proposal. Regardless of the interpretive autonomy granted to human beings in their efforts to discern the Word of God, the idea that the ultimate goal of Torah-study is to discover the true meaning of the written Word is all pervading. To deny this would be to conflate two very different issues, one might loosely term ontological and epistemological. On the ontological claim, if I may call it so, that the Written Torah is thoroughly meaningful, that there exists in the Mind of God one comprehensive and true interpretation of the Text, all were of agreement. The issue in question is epistemological; namely, how, in the absence of an accessible higher authority, can human hermeneutic conjectures be warranted? How can we know that we know? The answer implicit in the writings of the rabbis is that we cannot. As noted, the talmud and midrash do not address the question directly, but the interpretive procedures they exhibit clearly attest to the type of "Popperian" theory of rationality outlined above.[23] What one finds are countless debates and disputes in which different interpretive schemes are suggested, energetically criticized and constantly modified in the light of criticism.[24] (And all this is done far more markedly than in pre-Popperian science, where, for centuries, the accepted view had been that scientific enquiries could be finalized, and that scientific knowledge could be verified once and for all.) The fact that the talmudic corpus on all issues, other than ritual and law, disputes were left open as a matter of course, together with the fact that committing the Oral Torah to writing was strictly prohibited, both strongly indicate that the rabbis consciously viewed their covenantal charge as a perpetual and essentially open-ended one; one in which they were liable to be only partly right and at times even wholly mistaken.

All this, however, is still largely circumstantial. The talmudic and midrashic literature contains no systematic discussion of these questions. And we have so far made our point, to paraphrase Einstein, not by listening to what the rabbis said on such matters, so much as by examining what they were actually doing. There exists one text, however, which not without debate was canonized by the rabbis as part of the Written Torah, in which, I submit, the epistemological questions bearing on the Jewish covenant of learning are both raised and resolved in detail. I am referring to the book of *Qohelet—Ecclesiastes.*

As Harold Fisch and others have noted:

> Nowhere in *Ecclesiastes* is the I/Thou relationship evoked. God is referred to in the third person, and only as *'El* or *'Elohim,* never as YHWH, the God of intimacy and dialogue. *Ecclesiastes* is indeed the nearest the Hebrew Bible gets to pure monologue.[25]

He is undoubtedly right. Hence one of two: either the book is written from an essentially Jewish perspective about regions of endeavor in which the I/Thou relation does not obtain, or else the implied narrator adopts a position that assumes no such relationship. Harold Fisch clearly opts for the latter, concluding, as his chapter heading indicates, that *Qohelet* is essentially an ironical text intended to "show us what happens when man withdraws himself into the inwardness of his own consciousness and distances himself from God." *Ecclesiastes,* according to this view, amounts, in its philosophical claim, to a *reductio ad absurdum* of the very possibility of an anthropocentric and self-sufficient theory of knowledge, driving in the form of a keen *disputatio* towards the final and inevitable conclusion: "The end of the matter, when all is said and done: Fear God and keep his commandments, for *that* is the whole . . . of Man" (12:13).

I find such an overall assessment of *Qohelet* as a total negation of human wisdom unduly exaggerated. In the course of the book certain rival viewpoints are clearly dismissed by *Qohelet* by reducing them to absurdity.[26] But not all is reduced to "nothingness and futility," as Harold Fisch and many others[27] tend to interpret the term *hebel*. In fact the meaning of *hebel,* I would suggest, is far less harsh. It denotes not "nothingness and futility," but tentativity and temporality. Something substantial but of a fleeting and momentary existence as (literally) the mist of our breath.[28] Something which may hold today but be found not to hold tomorrow. I would suggest that in the sober eyes of *Qohelet,* stating his own rather than an imaginary humanist's opinion, such is the nature of all humanly possible knowledge. What is indeed futile in the eyes of *Qohelet* (*reut ruakh,* i.e., grasping at the wind) is not the attempt to know, but the pretension to accomplish atemporal certitude. *Qohelet*'s conclusions are indeed a far cry from classical humanism, but, I submit, they are by no means a dismissal of *hokhma* as such, only of human *hokhma* as final and permanent knowledge.

Expounding upon the tentativity and essential open-endedness of all humanly possible knowledge, *Qohelet* is written, I believe, not from without but from squarely within the Jewish covenantal world view. It is not a study of the unbearable consequences of distancing oneself from God, as Harold Fisch maintains, but a profound, troubled, and candid assessment of what man can meaningfully hope to achieve in his covenantal relationship with an omnipotent and omniscient God Creator *given* that everything one can be said to know or to do is *hebel.*

Acknowledging the all-pervading temporality of human existence and human understanding, argues *Qohelet,* all we may claim to know must be assessed in historical perspective. Whereas in reality—from the Creator's omniscient perspective—"there is nothing new under the sun," a human being, he soberly realizes, has no hope of achieving omniscience: "He (God) has set the world in their heart" but in a manner "that no man can find out the work that God has made from beginning to end" (3:11). Reality, as revealed to human eyes, is thoroughly context dependent, and regulated by everchanging circumstances. "Under the heaven" in the mundane realm of human existence and human endeavor, "To everything there is a season, and a time to every purpose" (3:1). Whereas it may be proper for one generation to plant, in different circumstances the thing to do might very well be to uproot the planted; there are circumstances in which it is best to break down, in others to build up, and so forth. But an objective, a-temporal, and timelessly valid ruling with regard to planting or building appropriate in all circumstances is beyond human reach. The upshot of course is that it is for each and every generation to do its best to assess anew the rulings of former generations in the light of the particularities of its situation and rule accordingly, and subsequently to refrain from committing future generations to its tentative and temporary conclusions. "Wisdom is good with an inheritance" (7:11), writes *Qohelet,* and yet "Do not say, How was it that the former days were better than these? For thou dost not inquire wisely concerning this" (7:10). Seek always to expose your views to the criticisms of the wise rather than to the praise of the foolish, *Qohelet* urges, "It is better to hear the rebuke of the wise, than for a man to hear the song of fools" (7:5). And above all my son, he concludes (12:12) "be admonished: of making many books." Where humans are left alone to their wits, true *hokhma,* aware of its tentativity, should remain forever oral, and as such as open as possible to further criticism and amelioration.[29]

If *Qohelet* is read, as I propose, as solemnly (rather than ironically) deliberating the prospects of leading a meaningful and God-fearing life "under the sun" (1:3) in an orderly and regulated world (1:5–7,9), but one so vast and complex that within the confinements of his temporary existence (1:4,11) we have no hope of fully comprehending (1:8); and if, as I suggest, rather than despair of rationality and surrender to paralyzing skepticism, righteous apathy or carefree hedonism, *Qohelet* presents us with a view of autonomous self-correcting *hokhma* constantly seeking truth yet forever aware of its own limitations, we are dealing with a profound and extraordinary modern text. For *Qohelet,* quite unlike contemporary Greek and later Arabic and early modern European philosophy, truth, the desired goal of wisdom, is ultimately regarded as a regulative concept rather than as an obtainable objective. Progress (*yitaron takhat ha-shemesh*) is achievable only by insistently treating our present conclusions critically, and by being willing to modify them accordingly. Even when we seem capable of formulating self-evident principles of conduct, such as always to steer wide of the company of women "whose heart is snares and nets, and [whose] hands are fetters" (7:26), *Qohelet* keenly observes that the application of such principles to concrete situations is always problematical. Here and there, says *Qohelet,* I can claim fully to have assessed one man in a thousand (perhaps since I am myself a man), but never a woman (7:28).[30] Hence, although we may confidently claim to know in theory the type of woman to avoid, it is impossible ever to know whether any one particular woman is indeed of the type to be avoided.[31]

The philosophical concerns of *Qohelet* are squarely epistemological: What kind of knowledge is humanly possible, he asks, and how is it best acquired? The setting of his queries, however, is markedly covenantal. *Qohelet* is driven not by detached philosophical curiosity. There is a deeply troubled note of urgency to his deliberations far removed from the calm, cool and calculated style normally encountered in philosophical discussions of such topics. For it is as deeply a religious book as it is philosophical. The problem of the book is not merely how to make the best of our tentative existence, but how to do so *in the eyes of God*. The ever present omnipotent and omniscient God of *Qohelet* is not only the object of awe and admiration, but first and foremost the object of fear.

> What profit (advantage) has the worker from his toil? I have seen (understood) the task which God has given to the sons of men to be exercised in it. . . . He has set the mystery of the world in their heart, so that no man can find out the work which God has made from the beginning to the end. . . . I know that, whatever God does it shall be forever: nothing can be added to it, nor anything taken from it: and God does it, so that men should fear before him. (3:9–14)

However, it is wrong to conclude that since we lack the capacity fully to comprehend the will and work of God we are therefore to remain piously passive, and rely on God "to avenge the prosecuted" (3:15). This will inevitably lead to chaos (16). Limited as we are, it is up to us to do justice under the sun to the extent to which we are capable. For tentative as our knowledge may be, we are accountable for our deeds: "I said in my heart, God shall judge the righteous and the wicked: for there is a time there for every purpose and for every work" (17). It is as barren to be overly pious, writes *Qohelet* elsewhere, as it is to be "overwise."[32] It is not merely that we would like to know, we are *obliged* to try to know even though we can never fully succeed.

The setting is thus similar to that of Torah-study. There too we are obliged to reach an understanding lacking external confirmation of our efforts[33] and we are likewise prohibited from resorting to mere passive piety. Needless to say the fundamental epistemological problem is one and the same: to what extent can we ever claim to have understood "the work which God has made." And the 'Popperian' solution to it, implicit in the rabbis' writings, is, if my reading is correct, fully elaborated in *Qohelet*.

In one of the concluding verses (12:11), *Qohelet* states that "The words of the wise are like spurs, and like nails well driven in are the sayings of the masters of collections; they are given by one shepherd." The ascription of wisdom to the "one shepherd" is taken by the rabbis to refer to the Oral Torah. Elazar b. Azaria, significantly a student of R. Joshua, interpreted it as follows: "the masters of collections" are the sages who congregate to study Torah in small groups (collections), whereby some will rule a thing pure and some impure, some will forbid whilst others allow, some will declare a matter unfit and some fit. And in case a person should say 'how am I then to study the Torah?' we should tell him 'they are given from one shepherd.' Therefore listen closely and attempt to understand both those who rule it pure and those who rule it impure; those who allow and those who forbid; those who declare it unfit and those fit (Bavli *Hagigah* 3a and Tosephta *Sottah,* 7). In short, Torah-study, R. Elazar takes *Qohelet* to claim, is a perpetual, open-ended and pluralistic enterprise. Most interestingly, it was no other than Elazar b. Azaria himself who made the final decision, significantly, also on "that very day," to rule in favor of the House of Hillel and include *Qohelet* in the Biblical canon—a question formerly debated but never resolved (Mishna *Yadaim* 3:5).

NOTES

1. Cf. Tosephta *Berakhot* 6:24 and Yerushalmi, *Berakhot* 63a.

2. A good example of the type of a-halakhical pluralism I have in mind is the following from *Genesis Rabbah* (c.f. also Bavli *Sanhedrin* 108b) Commenting on Gen. 6:18: "and thou shalt come into the ark, thou and thy sons, and thy wife, and thy son's wives with thee", R. Yehuda b. R. Simon and R. Yohanan in the name of R. Samuel b. R. Isaac conclude (parasha 34:7) that "from the time Noah entered the ark copulation was forbidden" (hence "thou and thy sons to themselves, and thy wife and thy son's wives to themselves"). And Noah apparently obeyed (Gen. 7:7). By the same token, upon leaving the ark, family life was presumably allowed to return to normal: "Go out of the ark, thou, and thy wife, and thy sons, and thy son's wives with thee" (Gen. 8:16). This time, however, Noah apparently decided not to comply, and chose, on his own initiative, "to extend the commandment" (ibid., 18). Whereby (apropos Gen. 9:8) the following unresolved debate between R. Yehuda and R. Nehemiah is recorded (parasha 35:1): the former is of the opinion that since Noah disobeyed he was disgraced (and is no longer singled out, and is addressed thereon by God together with his sons), whereas the latter concludes that "since Noah extended the commandment and conducted himself in holiness, he and his sons were rewarded by God's word." The controversy is fundamental. Is sanctification achieved by suppressing the flesh, or by appropriately acknowledging our earthly and bodily needs? The two conflicting interpretations are stated, pitted against each other, but no attempt is made to decide the issue.

3. See Mishna *Peah* 1:1, and the Bavli *Kidushin* 127b, where Torah study is deemed superior to all deeds "the fruit of which man may enjoy in this world and still their capital is invested in the next." Maimonides, however, rules that: "No commandment equals that of Torah study, rather Torah study is comparable to all other commandments put together, since study leads to deeds, and therefore has precedence over deeds everywhere" (*Mishne Torah,* Talmud Torah, chap. 3:3). See also op.cit. chap. 1:4.

4. Mishna *Horayot,* 3:8.

5. The argument proposed in what follows hence directly contradicts Jacob Neusner's claim that scientific and talmudic reasoning attest to "logics" so different as to render students of the latter incapable of adequately participating in the former. C.f. J. Neusner, *The Making of the Mind of Judaism: The Formative Age,* Brown Judaic Studies, no. 133, Scholars Press, Atlanta Georgia, 1987.

6. For further details see my "Towards a Rational Theory of Progress," forthcoming in *Synthese.*

7. "Towards a Rational Theory of Tradition," *Conjectures and Refutations,* Harper & Row, New York and London, 1965, chap. 4.

8. Not only is the bare Text meaningless in itself, but lacking both vowel notations and punctuation marks (whose insertion in the Torah scroll is prohibited) it is actually unreadable. A point made forcefully in J. Faur, *Golden Doves with Silver Dots: Semiotics and Textuality in Rabbinic Tradition,* Indiana University Press, 1986, chap. 4.

9. *Genesis Rabbah:* parasha 1.

10. Op.cit. Not all agree that this particular midrash represents a Platonic viewpoint. See, for example, E. E. Urbach, *The Sages, Their Concepts and their Beliefs* (Hebrew), The Magnus Press, The Hebrew University, Jerusalem, 6th printing 1986, pp. 176–77.

11. R. Eliezer, who was described by his master R. Yohanan b. Zakkai as a "lime-coated (water) hole that leaks not a drop" (Mishne *Abhot,* 2:8) is reputed to have declared "If all the seas were ink, all the reeds quills and all men scribes, they [still] could not have written all that I have learnt and studied" (*Abhot de-Rabbi Nathan,* 25), and to have added: "And I never said a word I had not heard first from my master" (Bavli *Sukah* 28b).

12. Bavli *Sanhedrin* 68a.

13. Bavli *Berakhot* 27b–28a.

14. For a recent example of such a reading see J. P. Rosenblatt and J. C. Sitterson, eds., *"Not in Heaven": Coherence and Complexity in Biblical Narrative,* Indiana University Press, Bloomington & Indianapolis, 1991:1–5.

15. Interestingly, in its original, and very different context from that of R. Joshua's claim, the phrase seems to mean quite the opposite: "Thou shalt not follow a multitude to do evil; neither shalt thou speak in a cause to incline after a multitude to pervert justice" (Exod. 23:2)—namely, as a warning *to refrain from* deciding by a majority in all matters! In other words, R. Joshua's claim for discretion, even when opposed by a heavenly voice, is itself warranted by an act of bold interpretation!

16. The rejection of the heavenly voice bears distinctly halakhic implications. Maimonides thus rules as follows: "It says in the Torah: 'It is not in heaven' from which we learn that a prophet is incapable of halakhic innovation. If a prophet claims to have been sent by God to add or cancel commandments, or even to interpret existing commandments anew, even if he produces signs and demonstrations—he is therefore a false prophet" (*Mishne Torah,* Yesodei ha-Torah, chap. 9:1).

17. The most conspicuous perhaps being the opening paragraph of tractate *Abhot* (c.250 A.D.): "Moses received Torah from Sinai and handed it on to Joshua, and Joshua to the elders, and the elders handed it on to the prophets . . . ," which, as Neusner puts it, bears the implication

of "a process . . . of transmission of received materials, refined and corrected but handed on not only unimpaired, but essentially intact" (*The Making of the Mind of Judaism,* p. 142), "[t]hough", he adds, "self-evidently, the remainder of the chapter hardly illustrates the type of process alleged at the outset."

18. Op.cit., pp. 142–43.

19. This point is brought out vividly in a story related by R. Yehuda in the name of Rav (Bavli *Menahot* 29b) in which Moses is described as taking his place in the back rows of R. Akiva's academy, and becoming thoroughly distraught by not understanding a word. Finally, one of the students enquired of the grounds of one of Akiva's rulings, Akiva answered that it is *halakha le-Moshe me-Sinai,* upon which, even though still not understanding, Moses is reputed to have regained his calm.

20. Or rather, it is for the human to decide whether or not to accept its rulings. Thus the heavenly voice that passed a ruling in favor of the House of Hillel in its three year long dispute with that of Shammai was accepted (Bavli *Erubin* 13b), though not without it adding that both conflicting positions are equally to be regarded "the words of the living God" (*eilu va-eilu divre Elohim haim*). From which follows, as noted above, that it was not the *truth* of their positions which was at stake (since it is impossible for both conflicting systems to have been equally true *simpliciter*). Indeed, the heavenly voice's unsuccessful attempt to settle the dispute between R. Eliezer and R. Joshua in favor of the former, further attests to the dialectic, since R. Eliezer, though a disciple of the Hillelite R. Yohanan b. Zakkai, is frequently described as a Shammaite (e.g., Mishna *Terumot* 5:4). Add to that the fact that alongside the heavenly voice's ruling in favor of the house of Hillel and R. Joshua's defeat of R. Eliezer's Shammaite approach, there exists a firm tradition that in the days of the Messiah the halakha will be according to Shammai!

21. D. Hartman, *A Living Covenant: The Innovative Spirit in Traditional Judaism,* The Free Press, a Division of Macmillan, Inc. (1985), New York & London, pp. 32–33. The "spirit of intellectual autonomy" (p. 38) and "enormous interpretive freedom" (p. 37) conveyed in the rabbinical texts reaches a dramatic climax in midrashic accounts of the Heavenly Academy, the *yeshiva shel ma'ala.* In one case (Bavli *Baba Metzia* 86a) it is told of a dispute concerning the ritual impurity of a certain type of leprosy. God is reputed to have ruled it ritually pure, while all other members of the Academy (?) maintained that it was impure. "Who should decide the issue?" they asked, "Rabbah bar Nahmani" they answered, the leading authority on such matters. The sage was thereby summoned to the Heavenly Academy (not without difficulty since the angel of death was unable to take his soul while he was still learning), where he declared God to be right. And if that is not enough, the final

halakhic ruling on the matter goes against both Rabbah and God (Maimonides, *Mishne Torah,* Tumat Tzara'at 2:9)!

22. The scientific equivalent of such a position is the doctrine that John Dewey dubbed instrumentalism or conventionalism, according to which scientific theories involving nonobservables are not ascribed truth values at all, but are meant to function merely as convenient 'pigeon-hole systems' efficiently to store experiential knowledge. For an eloquent presentation of such a theory see Pierre Duhem, *La Théorie Physique: Son Objet, Sa Structure,* (2nd ed.) Marcel Rivière & Cie, Paris, 1914.

23. Popper too is an outspoken realist, although, as he admits, it is impossible conclusively to prove the existence of an orderly external reality. "I propose," he writes, "To accept realism as the only sensible hypothesis—as a conjecture to which no sensible alternative has ever been offered":

> there are excellent reasons for saying that *what we attempt in science is to describe and (so far as possible) explain reality.* We do so with the help of conjectural theories; that is, theories which we hope are true (or near the truth), but which we cannot establish as certain or even as probable (in the sense of the probability calculus), even though they are the best theories which we are able to produce . . . (*Objective Knowledge: An Evolutionary Approach,* The Clarendon Press, Oxford, 1975, pp. 40–42)

In order to render Popper's theory of rationality as criticism applicable to rabbinic hermeneutics, however, one needs to go a step beyond Popper. Popper's analysis of problems and solutions to problems is limited to the type of difficulty a scientist would typically run in to, and a realist at that. Problems in other domains, however, are normally not contradictions between theory and supposed fact. The problems involved in interpreting a text or testing an appliance are quite different. Hence a far more general analysis of problems and problem solving is required. I have attempted to further generalize Popper's approach in my "Towards a Rational Theory of Progress" (see note 5 above).

24. The story related in Bavli *Baba Metzia* 84a, of the unique friendship and collaboration between R. Yohanan and his adversary Resh Laqish makes this point forcefully. As the story goes, at one point during a rather heated halakhic debate between the two sages, R. Yohanan tactlessly referred to Resh Laqish's criminal past. As a result the latter fell into a deep depression from which he failed to recover, and eventually died. Yohanan was grief-stricken and began also to show signs of deep depression. His students, we are told then got together to seek out a suitable study-partner for their disturbed master, and a bright young scholar was selected. Whereby, the Bavli tells us, each time Yohanan voiced an opinion, his new young colleague would produce a multitude of confirming

evidence—*tana de-mesayea.* "Are you supposed to replace Resh Laqish?!," fumed Yohanan, "Why do I need confirmations? Do I not know that my opinions are sound? Whenever I pronounced a ruling or voiced an opinion in the past, Resh Laqish would produce four and twenty questions and criticism, for which I was required to sweat out four and twenty new arguments! That is how halakha *expands*. Confirmations are useless!" Whereupon Yohanan began to scream "Where art thou Resh Laqish? Where art thou Resh Laqish?" So much so that out of sheer pity for their master his students prayed for his speedy death. This story, I think, speaks for itself.

25. H. Fisch, *Poetry With a Purpose: Biblical Poetics and Interpretation,* Indiana University Press, Bloomington & Indianapolis, 1988, chap. 9, p. 158.

26. One salient example is *Qohelet*'s analysis, in the latter part of chapter 3, of the view that since "whatever God does, it shall be forever: nothing can be added to it, nor anything taken from it" (3:14), and since we are incapable of fully understanding "the work which God has made" (11), the task of doing justice should be left to God [15]. If that were the case, concludes *Qohelet,* if all life "under the sun" conducts itself as a predetermined clockwork we are incapable of comprehending, if for lack of total knowledge one cannot be made morally responsible, the inevitable, absurd, and wholly unacceptable conclusion is that a human "has no preeminence over a beast!" (19).

27. See, for example, M. V. Fox, "The Meaning of *hebel* for Qohelet," *JBL,* 105/3, 1986:409–27, who surveys the relevant literature concluding not unlike Fisch that:

> For *Qohelet* the reliability of the causal nexus fails, leaving only fragmented sequences of events which, though divinely determined, must be judged random from the human perspective. . . . The belief in a reliable causal order fails, and with it human reason and self-confidence. But this failure is what God intends, for after it comes fear. And fear is the only emotion that *Qohelet* explicitly wants God to arouse. (427)

28. Unlike Fisch and Fox, R. B. Y. Scott (*The Anchor Bible,* vol. 18) translates *hebel* more literally as "vapor" or alternatively "empty breath," but even Scott takes the term to mean unsubstantiality (2:1) and futility (2:15, 23, 26 and passim).

29. The extent to which *Qohelet*'s (and for that matter the talmud's) original notion of wisdom as ongoing critical self-correction later underwent radical changes as a result of exposure to the philosophies of late antiquity, is evident from Sa'adia Gaon's very different interpretation of this verse. Sa'adia takes it not as a warning against wrongly finalizing current tentative knowledge, but, on the contrary, as an urging to publish

as many scientific books possible in order "that they may be preserved for future generations to learn from, and remain available for all time [!]"; not as "be admonished: of making," but as "be careful to make many books." (*The Five Megiloth,* edited and translated by R. Joseph Kappah, *Ha-Aguda lehatzalat ginze Taiman,* Jerusalem, 1962, p. 163.) Sa'adia obviously regarded scientific truth as both humanly obtainable and final.

30. "One man among a thousand I have found (*matzati*); but a woman among all those I have not found." It is easy to show that in the context of Chapter 7 the verb 'to find' (limtzo) does not mean merely to locate, but to find out, to understand or to discern, as in finding an answer to a question—i.e. perceiving its adequacy as such. Compare verses 24, 26 and 29. See also (3:11) and (7:14).

31. See also Chapter 7 verses 5–7: In general "It is better to hear the rebuke of the wise, than for a man to hear the song of fools", however, Qohelet adds immediately, "this also is hebel" for "Surely oppression makes a wise man mad; and a bribe destroys [his] heart". In other words, although seeking the rebuke of the wise is always advisable, we can never be sure that the judgment of the seemingly wise man whom we approach was not led astray by such ulterior motives.

The perpetual uncertainty of humanly possible knowledge even of the facts of a particular case, in relation even to fully ascertained legislation, seems to be at the very heart of the Talmudic laws of evidence. According to the *halakha,* court hearings are preceded by an interrogation of the witnesses in order to establish the *viability* of their testimony; where viability is equated with precision (e.g. the ability of the witnesses to state precisely the date, time, place, etc. of the events testified). Since, as the Talmud puts it: *irrefutable evidence is no evidence at all* (Bavli Sanhedrin, 41a)! In other words, the reliability of a testimony is seen by the rabbis to turn on the fact that though refutable in principle, it was not in fact refuted. That is as close to the truth one can get! As far as I know such a Popperian principle of testimony remains unique to the Talmud to this very day. See also Y. and H. Ben-Menahem, "Popper's Criterion of Refutability in the Legal Context", in A. Peczenik et. al. (eds.) *Theory of Legal Science,* D. Reidel, Dordrecht, 1984; pp. 425–35.

32. The term *tzadik,* I believe, is used by *Qohelet* literally to denote simple-minded justification (*hatzdakah, tziduk*). It is therefore a degrading term when taken to the extreme. His position being, that we are required to understand to the best of our ability, and to fall back on justificationary piety only beyond the tested limits of our knowledge. To remain totally passive, even out of piety, is mere folly (4:5). And yet although it is clear to *Qohelet* "that wisdom excels folly, as far as light excels darkness" (2:13), to be wise is first and foremost to be aware of the boundaries of wisdom. And where wisdom fails us, and only there, is

piety required: "Wisdom is good with an inheritance: and by it there is profit to them that see the sun. For wisdom is a defence . . . the excellency of knowledge is, that wisdom gives life to those who have it." And yet "Consider the work of God: for who can make that straight, which he has made crooked? In the day of prosperity be joyful, but in the day of adversity consider: God has made the one as well as the other, to the end that man should find (fully understand) nothing after him" (7:11–14). And elsewhere: "For this comes from the multitude of dreams and vanities, and many words: but fear thou God. If you seest the oppression of the poor, and the violent perverting of judgment and justice in a province, do not marvel at the matter: for there is a high one who watches over him that is high, and there are yet higher ones over them" (5:6–7).

33. There is a sense, argues *Qohelet* at one point, in which one could perhaps claim to have access to Divine confirmation. Since "surely I know that it shall be well with those who fear God, . . . but it shall not be well with the wicked, and, like the shadow, he will not prolong his days; because he does not fear before God" (8:12–13). All we need to do, it could be argued, is to observe the well-abouts and the sufferers, and, assuming Divine justice, try our best to imitate the deeds of the former on the grounds that their favorable circumstances attest to their righteousness. However, he is quick in answering, such a Calvinistic ethic is of no avail since God's time scale is at times prolonged beyond human comprehension. "There is a vanity (*hebel* i.e. temporary situations) which is done upon the earth; that there are just men, to whom it happens according to the deeds of the wicked; again, there are wicked men, to whom it happens according to the deeds of the righteous" (8:14), "Because sentence against an evil work is not executed speedily, therefore the heart of the sons of men is fully set in them to do evil" (11).

CHAPTER 6

The Sign of the Covenant

Betty Rojtman

The covenant God proposes to Israel is the very largesse of a liege lord, disproportionately generous. It contains the gratuitous promise of a never-to-be-taken-away favor, one which underscores the futility of any condition. At the same time, however, this covenant involves the legal mediation of a contract in which Israel pledges allegiance in a binding relationship. The covenantal links between God and Israel would, thus, reveal a particular register of relationship lying halfway between the poles of an incommensurable gift from the infinite to the finite, and the mutuality of a contract. This relationship derives from the former its one-sided nature but retains from the latter a freedom and responsibility grounded in the sign. The fidelity stipulated in this undertaking would no longer be an integral part of the contract, but linked in a deeper fashion to the sign which it calls for. Borne by human beings, the sign paradoxically functions to liberate humans from the covenant in the sense of a legal necessity and from the necessity of the sign; it frees them into the realm of responsibility.

In biblical history, the beginnings of the covenant are apparent first in the threat, and eventually in the actuality of the flood. Noah is saved from the deluge together with his entire family. On leaving the ark, he offers up a sacrifice of thanks to God. We are told, then, that "Noah found favor in the eyes of the Lord" (Gen. 6:8), a turn of phrase in which the disproportion of merit and reward is evident. Here the tolerance of the Creator is made explicit: He bows

---

Translated from the French by Jay Shir.

before the evidence of human wickedness in order to recognize their predisposition to evil which His will, from now on, must take into account.

> And Noah built an altar to the Lord; and took of every clean beast, and of every clean bird, and offered burnt offerings on the altar. And the Lord smelled the sweet savour; and the Lord said in his heart, I will not again curse the ground any more for man's sake; for the impulse of man's heart is evil from his youth; neither will I again smite any more everything living, as I have done. While the earth remains, seed time and harvest, and cold and heat, and summer and winter, and day and night shall not cease. (Gen. 8:20–22)

This first divine movement thus clearly takes the form of indulgence and a renunciation of an overly strict insistence on conformity to the good. And without any more compensation, softening the previous absoluteness of the demand which until now had put man on trial before the Idea of Man, God now swears never again to destroy all life as He had done. In the next verse God gives his blessing to Noah, as he had to Adam: "And God blessed Noah and his sons, and said to them, Be fruitful, and multiply, and replenish the earth." (Gen. 9:1) God's shift, as well as His blessing, seems to be free and spontaneous; both are presented as unconditional. Nevertheless, they follow upon Noah's offering to God and immediately precede the enunciation of the Noachic laws. This is the first instance of a relationship in which God's gift and man's are exchanged.

Note that it is not the "proof" Noah offers in his sacrifice which calls down divine favor in an act of reciprocity. On the contrary, verse 22 seems to say it is his very pleasure with Noah's sacrifice that provokes God's meditation on the evil nature of humankind. Noah's gift, rather, succeeds in annulling a more demanding contractual relation and in restoring, as it were, an unconditional order in which the free grace of God for his creation may operate, beyond any question of merit. For Noah's sake, God relaxes, to some degree, the contractual mechanism of retaliation as He recognizes man's sovereignty, even in the matter of evil: for this, it seems, is the necessary leaven for life and liberty. God's promise, however, is made irreversible in His repeated word of undertaking, according to the ritual of taking a spouse.[1] The commandments which follow (be fruitful, etc.) are not in any way needed to ensure or guarantee it. When God bestows his prodigality upon Noah and his family, He blesses their descendants, telling them to be fruitful and multiply. (Gen. 9:1) The joyful tidings of the blessing are repeated in the commandment to fertility. (Gen. 9:7) (cf. As the commandment of fertility echoes the promise),[2] the possibility is now opened to the human being to rise in response to the entirely gratuitous blessing, and thus to match the already vouchsafed grace. It is in this context of double obligation (both God and humankind are bound) and yet non-reciprocality (God's undertakings are not conditional on human performance) that the first formal covenant is established:

> And God spoke to Noah, and his sons with him, saying, And behold, I establish my covenant with you, and with your seed after you; and with every living creature that is with you. . . . I will establish my covenant with you; neither shall all flesh be cut off any more by the waters of the flood, neither shall there any more be a flood to destroy the earth. (Gen. 9:8–11)

What is the meaning of the covenant at this late stage of the dialogue, after the divine oath, and after the divine blessing? The commentators tell us that Noah, who had received the promise and taken on the law, was distressed. Having entrusted himself to God, he requested from Him tokens of proof. To respond to the commandment to be fruitful and multiply meant to take part, to assume a risk in the promise, to commit himself to action. Noah hesitates: what if the flood, in spite of the Creator's kindly gesture, were to . . . ?[3] At that point God takes it upon himself to confirm the irreversibility of the oath: the world shall never revert to chaos, beyond all consideration of a human capability of rendering it livable. In the text this confirmation, this solemn undertaking, is given the name of a covenant which strengthens the faint heart of the believer and withdraws from him a portion of his responsibility for the cosmic future. This, in any case, will be: Noah may live; his future is assured. This conventional form of the covenant is sealed by the sign as a lasting pledge:

> And God said, This is the token of the covenant which I make between me and you and every living creature that is with you, for perpetual generations. I have set my bow in the cloud, and it shall be for a token of a covenant between me and the earth. And it shall come to pass, when I bring a cloud over the earth, that the bow shall be seen in the cloud: and I will remember my covenant,

> which is between me and you and every living creature of all flesh and the waters shall no more become a flood to destroy all flesh. (Gen. 9:12–15)

The bow-in-heaven is a sign for man, a concrete representation still needed by Noah and his generation.[4]

The covenant, guaranteed by the sign, thus occupies a position midway between promise and contract. In its legal shape, it ratifies, to the benefit of humanity and in confirmation of his faith, an exchange in which the stakes are actually won at the moment the game is begun.

Ten generations later we encounter the same scenario when the covenant is renewed with Abraham. The patriarch has already left his native land for Canaan (reported in Gen. 11:31) when God speaks to him in the twofold language of commandment and promise:[5]

> Now the Lord said to Abram, Get thee out of thy country, and from thy kindred and from thy father's house to the land that I will show thee: and I will make of thee a great nation, and I will bless thee; and make thy name great; and thou shalt be a blessing. (Gen. 12:1–2)

The instinct which impelled Abraham to leave Ur of the Chaldees fortunately coincides with the divine will. God discovers in Abraham this identity in process of being born, an identity in natural accord with His will and revealed in His commandment. As He had blessed Noah, God blesses Abraham, even before his new departure, prior to his act of obedience, which then is perceived more as a logical consequence of the blessing than as a precondition for it. It is as if there were a fundamental harmony between this suspended blessing and the conduct which calls it down. This equilibrium is maintained until chapter 15 where Abraham suddenly questions himself and his worth,[6] and questions at the same time the blessing to come. In a sorrowful dialogue we see the Father of believers grappling with the promise and demanding proof:

> After these things, the word of the Lord came to Abram in a vision, saying, "Fear not, Abram, I am thy shield; thy reward will be very great. And Abram said, Lord God, what wilt thou give me, seeing I shall go childless, and the steward of my house is Eliezer of Damascus?" (Gen. 15:1–2)

But God persists in promising to Abraham that there shall be issue of his loins, as many as the stars in heaven; He soothes his servant's worry that he has exhausted his capital of good will, that he has already received too much without meriting the gift. Still, doubt grips Abraham again at the moment of the promise of the land: "By what shall I know that I shall inherit it?" (Gen. 15:8) It is then that the necessity of the covenant arises for the second time. The "covenant between the parts" is contracted in the midst of Abram's sleep and terror when God announces to him the Egyptian exile and enslavement. This strange episode is concluded in the text by the ratification—as it were, the institutional ratification—of the previous accord:

> In the same day the Lord made a covenant with Abram, saying, To thy seed have I given this land, from the river of Egypt to the great river, the river Euphrates." (Gen. 15:18)

The commentators are astonished at Abram's insistence on being comforted on this point. Surely, they understand, Abram's faith in the world to come is not in question here.[7] Rather, he stumbles over his future in this world; he distrusts a promise inserted into matter and time. It is on this point that Abram grows weak: may God's freely given gift persist in the exile of this world? The answer comes in the form of a reprimand together with the news of an effective exile in which a proof will be given of a grace inherent even in exile and operating through exile itself.

Here again the covenant plays the role of a confirmation, of a bridge erected over an expanse of time from the basis of a grace made manifest in the present. The covenant needs, apparently, to be in the form of an agreement, an exchange of obligations and merits; it thus makes concrete a relationship felt from the beginning to be a dizzying thing which could not otherwise stand because of its own gratuitiousness. It is the means by which the promise may be effectuated; it gives the promise boundaries, a logical and contractual foundation and a means of being received, with the requirements of merit only legitimating that which was already freely granted.

The sign which guarantees the covenant is delivered, as it were, to a man in yet a third context, in Gen. 17, when Abraham receives the commandment of circumcision. Here, too, the dialogue between Abraham and God recalls those of the preceding episodes: God reveals Himself to Abraham as El Shaddai, the God of sufficiency, of limits, and of law who uses His power to ensure protection to His creature within the boundaries of natural coherence.[8] This is a screened-away presence which keeps watch behind phenomenal reality. This God of guardianship requires loyalty and trust, despite the prior evidence of physical law, of statistics, or reason. "Walk in My ways and be blameless [lit. 'entire']" (Gen. 17:1).[9] God reveals Himself and makes promises; but since their accomplishment is, as before, deferred to future generations, the temporal gap raises doubts. Thus God offers the covenant virtually inscribed, as it were, in Abraham's flesh, calls up in him a visible sign. The circumcision is both this sign and the condition of the covenant: the founding sign of the covenant.

> And God said to Abraham, Thou shalt keep my covenant therefore, thou and thy seed after thee in their generations. This is my covenant which you shall keep between me and you and thy seed after thee; every manchild among you shall be circumcised. And you shall circumcise the flesh of your foreskin, and it shall be a token of the covenant between me and you." (Gen. 17:9–11)

Until now, God has offered signs at Noah's and at Abraham's request. Here, the human sign functions as a counterpart to those divine signs in an inversely proportional relation. God draws Abraham's attention to the responsibility of the sign as a replacement for His own, which disappears and becomes void. It would seem, then, that in an authentic covenant the human sign furnishes the guarantee of identity and at the same time neutralizes the complementary necessity of the divine sign. It is as though the human capability of producing a sign in the alliance were itself sufficient to guarantee the covenant; as if man has here provided himself with the means toward his own confirmation and won his independence in relation to the rainbow, promised to the wavering generations. In this logic, God's commandment to keep the covenant is first and foremost a commandment about the sign; it is the possibility of transcending the contractual nature of the alliance while restoring its natural basis of mutual recognition.

Thus the first commandments given to Israel are appeals to a human "revelation" which finds within itself its own confirmation; they are appeals to the sign: circumcision, the Sabbath, blood on the lintels. Does God need this mark in order to pass over the houses?[10] But it is the Hebrew, certainly, who by the sacrifice of the Passover lamb bears witness, in his own eyes, to his irrevocable participation.

These elements recur in the supreme covenant of alliance between God and Israel which was established in the desert of Sinai: the whole of the Torah is a covenant contracted *before* being the imposition of a Law. The nature of this accord, furthermore, is determined by Israel's response. According to the Mishna, the people spontaneously engage with the covenant before familiarizing themselves with its precise terms, and without demanding any sign other than their own enthusiasm. (Exod. 19:8)

On this point the commentators diverge: the people's solemn undertaking of the covenant is in fact recalled in Exod. 24, in other words, after the Revelation of the Torah and the enunciation of its laws. Nevertheless, certain traditions[11] indicate here a chronological reversal of the texts (congruent, moreover, to one of the great principles of exegesis),[12] a reversal which locates the people's oath of allegiance in a time before the stipulation of the obligations it entails:

> And Moses came and told the people all the words of the Lord; and all the judgments, and all the people answered with one voice, and said, All the words which the Lord has said we will do. . . . And he took the book of the covenant, and read it in the hearing of the people: and they said, All that the Lord has said we will do and obey. And Moses took the blood and sprinkled it on the people, and said, Behold the blood of the covenant, which the Lord has made with you concerning all these words. (Exod. 24:3–8)

The theory of the inversion of sequence[13] presents Israel as pushed forward by a blind impulse of confident submission. This interpretive choice considerably alters the covenant's meaning, obscuring its legal force and emphasizing instead its value as an exchange, as an affective response. It is, then, the relationship of human beings with the covenant which permits the measurement of the degree of its institutionalization. Here the agreement of the people to fulfil the commandments takes the place of the missing sign: there is no need for any more tangible one. Their agreement is the sign which renounces the intelligible sign (na'ase ve'nishma).

This resubmission of the covenant to the human will indicates something of its uncertain character. It instantiates the essence of all Hebraic spirituality: the inscription of the Word in the future of the world, and the relation between the absolute and the contingent. This basic relation fluctuates in its necessary historicity. The bond of the covenant is inalienable; yet its form is a sign, in its conditioned human responsibility. Abraham recognizes himself as saved in terms of his soul: The question he asks has to do with the "crossing of the desert," a promise linked to flesh and to time. Thus the sign *for* man is the proof of the promise, fired by history. The sign *of* man is the proof of the sign, which restores the covenant in its atemporal validity. The breach by which the covenant is made is the indication of this risk and vulnerability.

In this way the gap separating divine speech from the event which verifies it may be explained. The approximate character of the promise within the concrete is a function of its visibility and of the human expectation of that visibility. The instance of the "covenant between the parts" made with Abraham is striking in this respect:

> And he said to Abram, Know surely that thy seed shall be a stranger in a land that is not theirs, and shall serve them: and they shall afflict them four hundred years. . . . But in the fourth generation they shall come back here. (Gen. 15:13, 16)

So much for the scriptures. The exegetical tradition based upon allusions in the text tells us that the Egyptian exile lasted no more than 210 years while the Bible itself speaks elsewhere of 430 years.[14] What are we to understand? A remission of sentence for good conduct? Has disorder appeared within the unforeseeable flow of history?

This fuzziness in the existential experience of the covenant seems to be the price paid for freedom, a margin of uncertainty which that freedom conserves. The shift from one number to the other thus signals the agreement between Word and circumstantiality—the accommodation of the Word to human understanding. If there is indeed room in the traditional interpretation for the notion of an "emergency plan" to bring Israel out of Egypt,[15] the commentators nonetheless are careful to maintain the equivocal character of a fundamentally ambiguous text. The numbering of the generations is reexamined and comes out exactly: the four hundred years began with the birth of Isaac, and the exile with Abraham's wanderings. Borne upon the promise, a secret number thus passes through History like a watermark on paper, printed in reverse in rebus fashion, absolute beneath the shifting, self-modifying sign, subjected to the risks of every representation.

This phenomenon recurs with the news and narrative of the second exile, the Babylonian one. Through the same voice that prophesied destruction the Lord predicts the Return:

> For thus says the Lord: that after seventy years are accomplished at Babylon, I will take heed of you and perform my good word[16] towards you, in causing you to return to this place. (Jer.29:10)

The number seventy is traditionally so symbolic that one senses from the very prophetic utterance, an irreducible distance from the event. Commentators seek within history the unyielding accomplishment of the Word in the flux of time. Kings as well, succeeding one another on the throne of Babylon or Persia, watch out for omens and recalculate the divine prophecies. The Talmud tells us that first Balthazar, then Ahasuerus, believed they were witnessing the breakdown of the prophecy and the refutation of the Hebraic expectation.[17] The prophet Daniel himself gave in to the obscurity of the signs: should the seventy years begin with the accession of King Nebuchadnezzar, the capture of Judaea or the destruction of the Temple of Jerusalem? Has God been disappointed by the feeble response of the Jews in exile to Cyrus's proclamation of the reconstruction? Has the plan of redemption been altered—cancelled, perhaps—in its historical realization? Or has the Word perhaps been misunderstood, even though it had been made exact from the beginning in the prophet's mouth, precise in its essential ambiguity?

In exile the Presence is hidden; it underscores the text of the sign: a misleading sign of this modified Word where the believer's faith loses its sight. But the divine gift is in no way cancellable, and it is thus accepted in the midst of silence. It delivers up its meaning in an unpredictable casting of the dice after the Israelites have already chosen to undertake responsibility for it. In the exchange of signs it must be a human being who wades first into the sea for the surface to be broken; at the same time he unveils a certitude which remains impenetrable to anyone who is not liberated from the necessity of that certitude. It is as if the ultimate confirmation of the covenant were achieved through the enactment of its renunciation. Thus Isaac bound on the altar and Abraham on the way to Moriah question the logic of events on the grounds of divine logic. "You stay here with the ass. The boy and I will go *up there*" (Gen. 22:5). Up there, says Rashi, to the place of the promise, destroyed by the order to sacrifice. Consider also Pharaoh's decree to throw the newborn children into the Nile at the very moment when Miriam was prophesying the coming of the savior. She followed the cradle of her brother Moses on its journey through the rushes "to learn what would befall" her prophecy (Exod. 2:4; cf. Tractate Sota, 13a) and to find out by which unsuspecting turnings the flouted Word would be accomplished from within despite its apparent denial.

This play of shadows sustains the tale of Esther, the tale of double silence—God's and Esther's—through which God announces that he shall hide His Face.[18] We remember that at no point in that narrative is the divine Name spoken, nor is His Providence evoked. In the pure contingency of events it is demanded of Israel that they decipher the enigma.

Esther's generation is an especially appropriate one to make such an effort of elucidation. The queen is descended from Saul, whose own ancestress was Rachel, Leah's nocturnal sister.[19] Rachel silently handed over to her older sister the signs of her identity, signs which would enable her to be recognized by Jacob. She is the sister of exile who died on the way while awaiting the Return, Leah's double and shadow. Beginning a dynasty of temporary sanctuaries[20] and of a removed kingdom[21] the covenant in the personage of Rachel is one of patience. Deprived of all presence, she is consecrated to the future; her talent and strength lie in being confident, and her confidence is the occult sign of the undertaking. Queen Esther keeps silent as well, exemplifying in the palace of Shushan the sequestered mode of the Revelation.

The Talmud attests[22] that in these uncertain, troubled times the Jewish people authentically shouldered the Law of the covenant that they had accepted in Sinai, the Law which marked the climax of all previous accords with the Fathers. Ahasuerus's indecisiveness and the intrigues of the harem appear distant from the formidable quaking of the Revelation in Sinai. Even so, it is in this fall, this secularization of the Word in favor of a more secret miracle, that the Talmud perceives the completed stage of the human response to the offer of a covenant. At the foot of Mt. Sinai, driven into a corner by overwhelming evidence, Israel recognized the God and the Law which compel its conscience. Subjugated before it could understand, Israel had acquiesced in the absolute violation of its will which dazzled it. That covenant is solemn, manifest, and traumatic. But within the tempests of palace revolutions, in the ever-diminished crescent of the moon, Israel well and truly enters into the covenant, in the obscure freedom of hidden signs. In Shushan the Jews claim their acceptance and responsibility for the law which had been forced upon them by the miracles in Egypt.

Thus, if history is the working out of the Promise and its temporal substratum; if the Word must necessarily be "detoured" through multiple truths, through the disparate paths of its realization, this hesitation has to be understood as natural: a wisp of shadow fallen on Rachel's face which enjoins her to give signs, to reinvent them out of her own silence in their most subtle, because most indistinct, form.

Finally, it should be no surprise to find that ambiguity coiled up within the word-sign which enunciates it. The primal mediation between promise and reality, which creates the problematics of the covenant, is ensured in the formulation of the promise itself, caught in the snares of language. In a double deciphering which puts faithfulness to the covenant on trial, the verse from Jeremiah finds its semantic resolution at the same time that the promise is given its elucidation in event.[23] The nature of the sign is to be both single and dispersed.

Reflecting upon the surprises of the word may thus inure us to the incomprehension of History. The interpretation of the text is also a practice of patience which develops in us an aptitude for conceiving multiplicity as we contemplate truth. There is always a distance, created by the word, between promise and reality. The Jew feels this distance to be reducible by means of exegetical labor, as confusion and as consolation.

The Oral Law, which itself embraces human modes of sign-making via observance of the commandments, may thus appear as the privileged place where the covenant is born,[24] in the double perplexity of meaning as read and meaning as lived. Thus the Oral Law is the rational form of revelation: divine law in a permanent state of dialogue with the earth.[25] A symbol of history, because it has been transmitted, and at the same time a symbol of difference, because it is forever distinct from the primal Word, the Oral Law appears like the covenant. Being itself a covenant, and thus an attempt to inscribe the Law in the world, it is perpetually in a state of readjustment to reality via the jurisprudence of interpretation.

This interpretation is based on the sage's authority, distinct from that of the prophet in its absence of absoluteness; it is linked to the source of knowledge through the more intimate means of *ruach ha'*kodesh, or "spirit of holiness." The sole sign of the Oral Law is that it appeals to be recognized as truth; it offers an utterly subjective and indefensible evidence—the taste of truth before any proof can be offered, like that which Delilah sensed upon Samson's lips.[26] Nonetheless, the Talmud teaches that the sage with his less glaring truth, is preferable to the prophet[27]. The sage is before his time;[28] he is devoted to the exactness of what will be, discovering it in the maze of history's illegible signs. The Oral Law is Rachel within us, secretly handing over the signs she has received.

This perspective brings a new light to prophecy itself and to the greeting of Revelation, which is perhaps nothing more than a sharper perception of a still obscured sign. Hence, the Jewish prophet is in opposition to the Gentile prophet because of the ignorance which fills his faithfulness. The shining of the visible always bespeaks a diminished light. This Moses knows, who does not know. Only Balaam could read the intentions of the Most High in the stars and accurately calculate the instant of His rage.[29] It is this which excluded him from the Promise. Apart from this calculation he can do nothing, annihilated by the surprise of a reversal. Moses, on the other hand, is perpetually ready for dialogue, and thus uncertain of the place and time of meeting. His closeness to God makes him ignorant; forever being called, he is like a bird blinded by the sun.[30] The extreme presence blurs the signs at the same time that this occlusion indicates presence. Even in Revelation, the divine sign is a sign of effacement, and effacement is a sign of proximity.[31]

While the sign, demanded by God, fills a lack, it also indicates human entry into the covenant as a partner. The divine sign occupies a space of disquiet which is little by little absorbed by the reading of truth at the heart of uncertainty, by uncertainty itself as a new sign. The accomplishment is delayed and expectation weakened to that point of risk where the necessity of the sign seems to disappear, is projected in its entirety into the consciousness as an internal image. The accomplishment is delayed until that point of engagement where the alliance is subsumed in the name of the human sign which ratifies it and disentangles it, like a brotherhood that no longer needs to proclaim itself.

NOTES

1. On the dual formula for taking a spouse, see Rambam, *Hilchot Zechiya U'matana*. Sefer Kinyan, 3:7–8.

2. Thus are all God's promises to Israel redoubled by an order: You shall enter the land, You shall return to your God. Cf. Ramban on Deut. 30.

3. See Rashi on Gen. 9:9.

4. See Rashi on Gen. 9:12.

5. At first the promise seems independent of its reformulation in the covenant.

6. See Rashi on Gen. 15:1 and Ramban on Gen. 15:7.

7. See Ramban on Gen. 15:2.

8. See Rashi on Gen. 17:1.

9. Ramban comprehends this integrity as an integrity of faith. The text itself underscores time and again this problematic of belief concerning Abraham.

10. Exod. 12:21–23. See also *Mehilta,* ch. 11, 76 on these verses.

11. See Rashi on Exod. 24:3 and Tractate Shabbat 88a and b.

12. "There is not before and after [i.e, no chronological order] in the Torah."

13. This is grounded in a parallel with a passage located before the Decalogue and assimilated to our episode. (Exod. 19:7–8).

14. See Exod. 12:40 and Rashi's commentary on it.

15. The precipitate deliverance from Egypt had been made necessary by cruel oppression and by the despair of the oppressed.

16. The covenant is not directly evoked here. Nevertheless, the parallelism of the situations and the reappearance in the commentary of the idea of a covenant seemed to me enough to authorize the assimilation of the notions—founded in any case upon the immutability of the promise.

17. See Tractate Megilla 11b.

18. See Deut. 13:18 and Tractate Hullin 139b.

19. See Tractate Megilla 13b.

20. Ibid., 16b.

21. King Saul is alluded to here.

22. See Tractate Shabbat 88a.

23. According to tradition, it was eventually Darius who, seventy years after the destruction of the Temple, ordered its rebuilding.

24. "The covenant with Israel was concluded only for the sake of the Oral Law." Tractate Gittin 60b.

25. See Tractate Baba Mezia 59b.

26. See Tractate Sota 9b.

27. See Tractate Baba Batra 12a.

28. "He sees what is to be born." Tractate Tamid 32a.

29. See Tractate Berachot 7a.

30. *Sifri, Ve'zot Ha'beracha,* 39.

31. Only the feast of Purim, which marked the entry into the covenant of the unsaid, will remain as a "sign" at the end of time. *Shocher* Tov, *Mishlei* 9.

Covenants and Texts

CHAPTER 7

Redesigning Redemption: *Covenant in the* Testament of Moses

Betsy Halpern-Amaru

Although it is not regarded as a midrash, the *Testament of Moses,* a pseudepigraphic work redacted, if not composed, in the early decades of the first century C.E.,[1] is a prime example of a work fruitfully interpreted as midrash, that is, as a text with a close thematic and linguistic relation to specific biblical texts with which the reader is assumed to be well acquainted.

A clearer understanding of the intertextuality of this pseudepigraphic work and its scriptural subtexts allows us to identify the specific theological concerns of the author or redactor of the work. It will allow us to appreciate the attempt of a first century Judean to treat creatively the vexing issue of the apparent contradiction between his historical period and the deuteronomic posture which would have brought Jewish history to an end with the return from Exile. By means of a subtle and creative strategy the author of the *Testament of Moses* redevelops the covenantal theology of specific passages of Deuteronomy such that his own historical time becomes encompassed within the biblical perspective.

In their concern for dating this work, modern scholars have so focussed their textual analyses on evidence of historical milieu that they have passed over the issue of the relationship between the pseudepigraphic and the scriptural texts. As a result, the biblical allusions and clues that provide substance and cohesion to a text which otherwise appears most disunited have not been sufficiently appreciated.

Using the account of Moses's imminent death, the appointment of Joshua as successor, and the prediction of Israel's future history in Deuteronomy 31–32 as his base structure,[2] the author (or redactor) constructs a dialogistic frame. Within this frame he places a revelation composed of an historical preview of Israel's history from the conquest of Canaan to the reigns of Herod's sons (2:2–10:10) and an apocalyptic poem describing the immanent end-time. The major sections of the work are connected by virtue of their mutual relationship to Deuteronomy 31–32. Focussed on the transfer of leadership from Moses to Joshua, the opening frame is developed along the general lines of Deuteronomy 31:1–8, 14–15, 23–26. The closing frame (chaps. 11–12) presents Joshua's reaction to the revelation and Moses's response. Although these last chapters are not as closely tied to Deuteronomy 31–32 as the introductory one, the author does use the transfer of leadership as his point of departure for a concluding dialogue which makes the theological perspective of the work explicit. The historical revelation and apocalyptic poem which comprise the central part of the *Testament* replace, respectively, God's prediction of Israel's future in the prose of Deuteronomy 31:16–21 and the poem of Deuteronomy 32.

Whereas in Deuteronomy God is the source of the prediction of Israel's violation of the covenant and the subsequent divine wrath (31:15ff.), in the *Testament,* Moses (speaking to Joshua) conveys the prediction. The revelation attributed directly to God is the more positive one of reaffirming the promise of the Land. This reaffirmation includes the first of several explicit recollections of the covenant expressed either in terms of a promise to the "fathers" (1:8, 2:1; 4:2–3, 5; 11:11) or in terms of God's "covenant and oath" (1:9; 2:7; 11:17; 12:13).[3] Not surprisingly, the recollections are found only in the frame and first half of the historical revelation, that is, those sections which chronologically parallel the historical period covered within Hebrew Scriptures.

Like comparable recollections in Deuteronomy, the first type, recollection of the fathers, refers either explicitly or contextually to the promise of the Land.[4] However, in contrast to the biblical writer,[5] in none of the recollections of the Land promise "to the fathers" does the author of the *Testament* identify the patriarchs by name.[6] Consequently, it is never quite clear whether the claim to the Land is being made in the name of the first patriarchs or the more immediate fathers of the exodus generation.[7] The vagueness may well be deliberate for in the second recollective pattern (memory of a "covenant and oath"), the two sets of fathers are in fact joined. This intriguing non-deuteronomic phrase appears without clarification five times in the *Testament*. Except for one occasion involving an emended text, it is contextually associated with assurance of the promise of the Land.[8] The covenant and oath assure that Joshua will bring the people to the Land "promised to their fathers" (1:9). It is the basis upon which the tribes beseech God not to forget His promise to the patriarchs that "their seed would never fail from the Land" (3:9). And in the closing frame it is the covenant and oath that assure that the Israelites would not be driven from the Land and completely destroyed (11:17; 12:13). There are only two biblical referents for such a covenant and oath. One is, as might be expected, the covenant and oath entered into by the Israelites before their entrance into the Land (Deut. 29:9–14).[9] Inasmuch as the *Testament of Moses* is constructed around Deuteronomy, it would be natural to assume that the terminology has been drawn from that text. Much more likely, however, is the possibility that insofar as the oath is specifically described in the *Testament* as one "which You (God) swore . . . by Yourself . . ." (3:9), the intent of the phrasing is to recall the scene of the *Akedah*.[10]

> By Myself I swear, the Lord declares: because you have done this and have not withheld your son, your favored one, I will bestow My blessing upon you and make your descendants as numerous as the stars of the heaven and the sands on the seashore; and your descendants shall seize the gates of their foes. And all the nations of the earth shall bless themselves by your descendants, because you have obeyed My command. (Gen. 22:16–18).

In order to explore further the possibility that the author of the *Testament* deliberately exploited a connection between the covenantal promises and the merits of Abraham as demonstrated by the scene of the *Akedah*, one may examine some of the verbal echoes connecting various biblical texts and the appearance of those same echoes in the *Testament*. There are many subsequent references in the Pentateuch to God having sworn to maintain the covenantal promises with the seed of Abraham, Isaac, and Jacob;[11] but only in Moses's intercession at the time of the Golden Calf (Exod. 32:13) is reference made to God having sworn an oath "by Himself" to the patriarchs as set forth at the *Akedah* scene.[12] In the *Akedah* context the oath stresses the promise of progeny, mentioning the Land aspect of the covenant only indirectly. ("Thy seed shall possess the gates of its enemies" [Gen. 22:17]). However when Moses at Sinai reminds God of the oath, the promise of the Land is clearly stated.

> Remember Your servants, Abraham, Isaac, and Israel, how You swore to them by Your Self and said to them: I will make your offspring as numerous as the stars of heaven, and I will give to your offspring this whole land of which I spoke, to possess forever. (Exod. 32:13)

The implicit connection between the *Akedah* and Moses's intercession at Sinai in the biblical narratives is the key to understanding the *Testament of Moses* and its otherwise puzzling structure. The single occasion on which the content of the oath is stated in the *Testament* is in the context of an intercession created by the author. Narrowing the focus of the appeal solely to the Land promise and expanding the historical scope of the *Akedah* as a source of merit to a later period, this intercession, occasioned by the exile to Babylonia, structurally as well as substantively recalls the Exodus passage cited above:

> God of Abraham, God of Isaac, and God of Jacob, remember your covenant which you made with them, and the oath which you swore to them by yourself, that their seed would never fail from the land which you have given them (3:9).[13]

The *Testament* thus presents an early form of the aggadic tradition which treats the *Akedah* as a source of intercessory merit for future generations. But whereas the association between the *Akedah* and intercession is explicit in later legend and lore,[14] in the *Testament,* as in the biblical narratives, it is only implied by the use of certain crucial terminology. Abraham's willingness to sacrifice his son at God's command is nowhere directly mentioned in the *Testament.* Indeed, although much is made in the work of Moses's intercessory powers, there is also no direct reference to the intercession at Sinai. Instead, by employing the phrase covenant and oath, that is, by associating the covenant with an oath involving the Land promise which God "swore by Himself" (3:9), the author of the *Testament* triggers memory of the relevant biblical passages. Thus the writer calls attention to a causal connection between martyrdom and promise in the life of the first patriarch and between intercessory appeal and recollection of that promise in the life of the nation. Moreover, by using that connection in the context of the Babylonian exile, he transforms it from a single historical event into an ongoing force, reflecting a relationship that persists long after the exodus and Sinai.[15]

The phrase covenant and oath ultimately provides a unity otherwise missing in the *Testament*. It links together the outer frames, the revelations and the eschatology. As noted above, the phrase is used by way of historical introduction in the opening frame and reappears in the intercessory prayer of the ten tribes at the beginning of the Babylonian exile, in Joshua's description of Moses's intercessory role, and again in Moses's own assurance that the nation would never be driven from the Land and completely destroyed. It does not appear in the second half of the revelation which covers the period from the time of the return from Babylonia to the eschaton. Instead, we find a counterpart to the *Akedah,* the story of Taxo and his sons, which connects the end of Israel's history to its beginnings. It is a comparable narrative to the *Akedah,* enacted *l'shem shamayim* (for the sake of heaven),[16] and serves as the final intercessory deed which activates the end-time of Israel's history. The recollected patriarchal deed which occasions the covenant and the oath regarding the Land promise thus foreshadows the post exilic act of intercessory martyrdom which will precipitate the divine eschaton.

Before turning to the final act, however, let us look at some other accounts of intercession in the *Testament*. From them we may reasonably conclude that the connection between obedience to the law and the endurance of the covenant is not of major concern in the *Testament of Moses*. One finds numerous references to the covenant, but no mention of specific *halachot* and relatively little stress on the law per se. In fact, the only section of Deuteronomy 31 which is not in some fashion incorporated into the frame chapters or into the survey of biblical history in the *Testament* is the description of Moses's command to have the Torah Law read every seven years when the Israelites would come to the Temple to commemorate Succot (Deut. 31:9–13). The emphasis in the *Testament* is on the Torah Book as eschatological revelation, not as Law. Thus, instead of instructing the Levites to preserve the Torah in the ark (Deut. 31:26), here (1:16–18) Moses instructs Joshua on how to preserve the revelation ("this writing") until the end-time.

Nonetheless, in the presentation of his own theological perspective, the author of the *Testament* does set forth the general position that those who adhere to the commandments are rewarded and those who violate them are punished (12:10–11).[17] Following the pattern of Deuteronomy, the sin—violation "of the covenant of the Lord" (2:7)—is idolatry, specifically described as offering "their sons to foreign gods" and setting up "idols in the Temple that they may worship them" (2:8).[18] The punishment which immediately follows is invasion of the Land by a king "from the east" who will burn "their city (colony) with the holy Temple of the Lord," and exile the people to his own country (3:1–3).[19]

Although the *Testament* is not as rich in descriptive detail as the Deuteronomy text, the cycle it describes begins in the traditional way. Were the author using the chastisement (*tochacha*) of Leviticus 26, Deuteronomy 4, or of Deuteronomy 28–30 as his base, then a description of repentance in exile ultimately climaxing in a return to the Land could be expected to follow. Instead, apparently using the incomplete cycle of Deuteronomy 31–32,[20] the *Testament of Moses* moves in a significantly different direction. The two tribes, it is predicted, will reproach their previously exiled brethren (the ten tribes) for their fate.[21] In response all the tribes will turn to God with the intercessory plea which parallels Moses's petition on behalf of Israel in Exodus 32:13.[22] Their prayer is the first of a pair which effects turning points in the cycle.[23] Here the exiled remember Moses's prophecies,[24] acknowledge that their exile is a consequence of their violation of the commandments, and appeal to God to remember his covenant and the oath to preserve eternally the seed of the patriarchs in the covenanted Land. While the substance of the petition is drawn from Exodus, the sequence of events which follow are structured like Deuteronomy 31. The witnessing ceremony the tribes recollect is that of Deuteronomy 31:28; and the change brought about by the prayer is no more than that described in Deuteronomy 31:21, that is, the Israelite's recognition of a causal relationship between their disobedience and their situation of exile.[25] Affirmation of that relationship is as close as the *Testament* comes to a description of repentance. It is followed neither by a confession of sins nor by any indication of a "return" to fidelity.[26] As a preface to redemption, therefore, the scene remains incomplete. The author immediately moves on to describe a second intercession scene seventy-seven years later.

In that scene, the second prayer is offered in exile by an unnamed figure usually identified with Daniel.[27] Functioning as an intercessor, the offerer of this prayer recalls the covenantal relationship that originated with the fathers and appeals to God's compassion to end the exile.

> Lord of all, king on the lofty throne,
> you who rules the world, who has willed
> that this people be for you a chosen
> people, yea, who has willed to be called
> their God according to the covenant which
> you made with their fathers, yet they,
> with their wives and children, have gone
> into a foreign land, surrounded by the gates
> of strangers where there is great majesty.
> Have regard for them and have compassion
> for them, O heavenly Lord. (4:2–4)

It is this plea, according to the *Testament* narrative, that effects the return to the Land (4:5–6). The prayer may well be modelled after the intercessory prayer of Daniel 9:4–19;[28] both open with a statement of the covenantal relationship and both appeal to God's compassion. But those similarities aside, there are major differences in structure and content between the two prayers. The deuteronomic pattern of the Daniel prayer is that displayed in Deuteronomy 4 and 28–30—punishment (i.e., exile) follows sin and restoration, be it implicit as in Deuteronomy 4 or explicitly stated as in 28–30, is clearly preceded by repentance. Presenting neither repentance nor return, the prayer in the *Testament of Moses* again evidences the more limited pattern of Deuteronomy 31–32.[29] Neither this second prayer nor the earlier one by the tribes contains a confession of sins or a repentant statement. The plea for compassion is based on God's relationship to the world and to Israel, not on Israel's repentant condition. It opens by addressing God as the "Lord of all," "who rules the world;" and goes on to state that the "chosen people," with whose forefathers this God has covenanted, is now in the dejected state of being held captive in a foreign land. This statement implies, though does not state, that Israel's lowly condition reflects poorly upon the ruler of the world who "has willed to be called their God."

One might hypothesize that Deuteronomy 32 was chosen by the author of the *Testament* specifically because of the unusual closing in its description of the cycle. In Deuteronomy 4 and 28–30 Israel's repentance effects divine forgiveness and return to the Land. In Deuteronomy 31–32, however, not only are these aspects of the process omitted, but as well, God's vindication of Israel is attributed to the provocation of the arrogant Gentiles who defame God's omnipotence by believing that their victories stem from their own hand (32:27–33). Here, as in the *Testament,* divine intervention is related to concern with the perceptions of the nations. The absence of engagement between God and a repentant people in the cycle offers the author of the *Testament* the chance to rewrite it so that it demonstrates the power of intercession used as a replacement for repentance.[30]

Much as the first intercessory plea by the ten tribes parallels Moses's intercession at Sinai as described in Exodus 32:13, the second intercessory plea in the *Testament,* the one that activates the return to the Land, has a close parallel in that same Sinai intercession as it is recollected in Deuteronomy 9:26–29.[31] Appeal is made there to God's promises to the forefathers (9:27), to His election of Israel (9:29) and, albeit in an historical as opposed to cosmic context, to His great power (9:29). Moreover, the crux of the argument implied in the *Testament,* that is, the dejected state of God's chosen in exile reflects poorly on the Chooser, is explicitly stated in Deuteronomy 9: the failure of the Israelites to obtain the Land promised to their forefathers will be attributed (by the Egyptians) to lack of power or ability on the part of their God.[32]

That the author of the *Testament* might specifically have Deuteronomy 9 in mind as an example of intercession replacing repentance might be argued as well from the doubling of the intercessions in both texts. In the Deuteronomy recollection of Moses's intercession at Sinai the exchange between God and Moses is interrupted so that Moses's response to God's anger comes after the description of his descent to the camp of the Israelites and after a general rehearsal of various examples of their rebelliousness.[33] The break in the dialogue on the mountain results in a doubling of the accounts of Moses's fasting and praying, the first presented in reaction to the sight of the molten calf (9:18–19) and the second coming after the destruction of the calf and a rehearsal of subsequent apostasies (9:21–29). It is in the second exchange that we find Moses's belated response to the dialogue begun before his descent. The two accounts are in fact one, broken up only by reason of the recollective nature of the biblical narrative. Nonetheless, the consequent doubling provides a precedent and a structural model for a pair of intercessory prayers such as we find in the *Testament of Moses*.[34]

Repentance on the part of the apostates is not a factor in either the intercessory prayer of Deuteronomy 9 or in the *Testament*. In both cases the intercessor presumes the unworthiness of those on behalf of whom prayer is offered. In the biblical narrative, however, intercession is used solely to assuage divine anger—to inhibit, not to invite divine action. If the author of the *Testament* had limited intercessory prayer to an attempt on the part of the united tribes to stay an immanent exile he would have stayed within this tradition.[35] But such is not the case. Instead, in an attempt to rewrite deuteronomic eschatology such that it will encompass post exilic history, the *Testament* places both the tribal prayer and the one that follows it into a structure that does not so much supplement Deuteronomy 9 and Deuteronomy 32 as offer an alternative to them. Using a *doppelschema* to create a chronological framework, he combines an intercession (modelled on Deuteronomy 9) with a cyclical paradigm (modelled on Deuteronomy 32) to design an historical cycle which produces a significant interpretive resolution. It accounts for the fact that the return to the Land was not accompanied by the kind of spiritual renewal prophesied in the more traditional paradigms of Deuteronomy 4; 28–30.[36] In this new cycle repentance is no longer a factor; it does not even follow, let alone precede,[37] the return of the exiles to the promised Land.

The absence of the notion of a repentant nation may reflect historical realism on the part of the author, a sense that the repentant nature of the generation immediately preceding the Return was no greater than that of the generations which succeeded it. But I would argue that it also reflects the author's effort to maintain in his own fashion a tension between divine and human control over Israel's destiny. In the dialogues which open and close the work, the author makes a point of stressing the extent of God's total foreknowledge and control of all history "from the beginning of the creation of the world even to the end of the age" (1:13; 12:4–5). The election of Israel, her future punishment at the hand of the gentile nations, as well as the appointment of Moses as intercessor were all foreknown and predetermined from the beginning of the world (1:13–14; 12:6). Thus, God's omnipotence over history and his predestination of Israel's future within history are paradoxically combined with the reward/punishment motif so dominant in Deuteronomy.[38] The author of the *Testament* handles this paradox by creating a distinction (in the most non-deuteronomic way) between "historical" and "eschatological" time. Repentance is a factor only within the latter. At the end of days there will be a *diem paenitentiae,*[39] but it is a metaphysical rather than an historical phenomenon. Instead of preceding and initiating the eschaton, it will be an antecedent, a consequence, of the move out of historical time.

The exclusion of repentance from the historical cycle, that is, from the predetermined "before time" acknowledges Israel's incapacity to self reform through the historical experience of exile and creates a place within the theological system for the extended pre-eschatological period in the Land after the Return. By substituting intercessory prayer for repentance as the initiating force for the Return stage in this historical cycle, the author essentially deprives the troublesome postexilic period of eschatological significance. This is not to say that the claim to possession of the Land is negated. To the contrary, on a number of occasions the author pointedly refers to the land as "home," as "their" (the Israelites') Land (2:3; 3:1–3; 4:3; 5:6; 6:3, 5, 8). Rather, the Return is so theologically underplayed that one suspects that the review of biblical history primarily serves as the background for the eschatological cycle which immediately follows.

That second cycle begins with the Maccabees and the Antiochan persecution and historically ends with the reign of Herod's sons.[40] Theologically this cycle completes the unfinished business of its predecessor and brings Jewish history to the eschaton which the author believes is immanent in his own day. In structure, but not in substance, it duplicates the pattern of the first cycle in the *Testament:* sin, punishment, an intercessory act, and redemption, this time 'Return' in the form of an eschaton.[41] There is no repentance, not even a statement comparable to the earlier acknowledgement of the fulfillment of Moses's prophetic warnings. Instead, required by unnamed oppressors to violate the commandments, an historically unidentified character named Taxo,[42] proposes to his seven sons that they join him in fasting and withdrawing to a cave where they will die with the assurance that their deaths will be avenged by God (9:6–7). Immediately following the narrative of Taxo comes an apocalyptic poem describing the eschaton in which the guardian angel of Israel[43] and God Himself wreck vengeance on the oppressor nations. The poem and the revelation close with the exaltation of Israel and the destruction of her enemies.

There is no overt biblical covenant theology in this second cycle. The setting does not involve exile, and no recollection of the patriarchal or Sinai promises is included; settlement in and possession of the Land is simply assumed.[44] In the description of Israel's various sins, one finds a stress on pollution of the cult and of the Sanctuary, but nothing of pollution of the Land. Moreover, although the sins described include transgressions which directly threaten the covenant in biblical literature,[45] no connection is made between these violations and the conditional nature of that covenant.

The Taxo narrative not only is devoid of any affirmation of the connection between obedience and covenant, it denies the basic deuteronomic assumption of an inherent connection between violation of the covenant and the misfortunes which befall Israel in the unfolding of her history. In direct opposition to that assumption, Taxo tells his sons that their fathers and "ancestors" had never violated the covenant;[46] and that the oppression Israel suffers in his own generation is ill deserved in relationship to the sins of other peoples and nations.[47] Indeed, the suffering goes beyond "all bounds of mercy" and is worse than the destruction and exile that befell the First Jewish Commonwealth (9:2).[48]

In the context of traditional intercessions in biblical and post biblical literature, such a claim to purity and sinlessness is strange and unfitting.[49] However, if one views Taxo's martyrdom and the argument that the suffering of Israel is undeserved in the general context of the *Akedah* recalled by the references to God's covenant and oath in the frame and the first part of the revelation, the entire martyr story takes on a new perspective. The father urging his sons to martyrdom, the assertions of purity, and the confidence of divine response all suggest an intercessory typology based on the *Akedah*. Taxo's willingness to martyr his sons has its parallel in Abraham's comparable willingness. The purity of Taxo and his sons reflected in the sinlessness of Israel is paralleled by the purity of Abraham and Isaac.

The narrative of Taxo is framed as intention, rather than as accomplished fact, thus making the parallel with the *Akedah* even stronger. Moreover, in both cases martyrdom activates divine intervention in the destiny of Israel. In the prehistory of the patriarchal period the intervention is a promissorial consequence of, rather than a motivation for, the martyrdom. In the end-time of Israel's history the impact is foreknown and forecast by Taxo: "For if we do this, and do die, our blood will be avenged before the Lord" (9:7). An important transformation has taken place. In the *Testament of Moses* the *Akedah* has been turned back to its original Genesis form. It is no longer the basis upon which appeal to the merits of the forefathers is made on behalf of sinful patriarchal progeny as it was when the Israelite nation first appeared on the historical stage at Sinai. Rather, at the end of Israel's history martyrdom becomes what it was in the patriarchal beginning—an activating force for the divine promise.

Insofar as the eschatological poem which follows focuses almost entirely on God's vindication of Israel against her enemies, it would appear in the broadest sense to be an elaboration on Deuteronomy 32:36–43.[50] This eschaton contains no reference to Israel's life in the Land. Israel will be raised to the "heaven of the stars" from whence she will view God's avenging destruction of her enemies on earth (10:9–10). The scholarly debate over the extent to which the extramundane abode should be understood literally or metaphorically[51] does not clarify the relationship between covenant and eschatology in the *Testament*. If Israel's place in the end-time is literally "in the heaven of the stars," has the covenantal promise of Land repeatedly referred to in the *Testament* been abrogated? And if the description is a metaphorical one, what specifically is the temporal future of Israel within such a metaphor?

The answers to such questions require refocussing them on the very aspect of the work which contemporary scholars have neglected, in the relationship between the *Testament* and the sacred text which it is recasting. It is no accident that the author has chosen Deuteronomy 31–32 as the base structure for his eschaton. In that particular paradigm for Israel's future there is no exile in the punishment stage and hence no return in the restoration—a perfect model for an eschaton that is to take place within the historical circumstances of the post Herodian era when Israel is, and in fact, for some period of time has been, settled in the Land. The single reference to the Land in the cycle of Deuteronomy 31–32 appears at the very end of the poem when God assures that He "will cleanse (atone for) the land of His people" (Deut. 32:43). Modelling the structure, but not the substance of that ending, the author of the *Testament* places his eschatological reference to the Land promise not in the poem, but in Moses's response to Joshua's anxiety over Israel's future at the end of the *Testament*—"It is not possible for the nations to drive them out or extinguish them completely. For God who has foreseen all things in the world will go forth, and his covenant which was established, and by the oath which . . ." [MS ends] (12:12–13). The closure is a crucial one which, like the chapters it is rewriting, ends as the biblical story of Israel begins—with God's commitment to the covenant.

In conclusion, then, although Deuteronomy serves as the structural frame of reference for the *Testament*, the controlling metaphor is not Deuteronomy, but rather the covenant and oath as set forth at the scene of the *Akedah*. In the biblical description of the "oath" in that scene (Gen. 22:13), the Land aspect of the covenant is notably limited. The content of the oath expands to a full statement of the covenantal promises only later when the *Akedah* serves an intercessory function within Israelite history (Exod. 32:13).[52] By shifting the context of the covenant out of an historical context back to the metaphysical stage of the patriarchs, namely to the scene of the *Akedah*, the martyrdom of Taxo and his sons reverses the process. Again the covenant is primarily understood in terms of the promise of a future to the progeny of the martyrs; and again God's action on behalf of Israel is direct rather than mediated by the merits of the fathers.

The dialogue between Moses and Joshua immediately following the eschatological poem in the closing chapters of the *Testament* confirms the shift in perspective. In that dialogue Joshua expresses his anxiety about a future without Moses the intercessor who is capable of "reminding the Lord of the ancestral covenant and the resolute oath" (11:17–19). Moses's response is to assure Joshua that neither his intercessions nor "the piety of this people" ultimately govern the destiny of Israel (12:8). That control rests only with God who has foreseen everything from the beginning of Creation to the end of time and has assured Israel's future through His covenant.

The perspective at the end of the *Testament* is, thus, firmly extra-historical—the surety of the covenant and oath is set outside of an historical frame of reference. The immediate context for Moses's response is conquest of the Land under the leadership of Joshua. However, his perspective is not governed by that context, but rather by the author's own theology and eschatology. "The end of the age" (12:4) returns to the beginning from which it was foreknown. The covenantal promises will be kept in spite of what experience seems to indicate, be it from the perspective of Abraham and Isaac ascending Mount Moriah or of Israel in the post exilic period with fulfillment of the promises so little in evidence.

Within the parameters of historical time Israel will be rewarded and/or punished for its sins; the innocent and pure will be martyred and their martyrdom will have meritorious value. But ultimately God's covenant and oath stand outside the parameters of experienced time. In the end, it is that divine covenant and oath, not covenantal nomism and not intercessory appeal to patriarchal merit, which make it "not possible for the nations to drive (the Israelites) out or extinguish them completely" (12:12). The structure of the *Testament of Moses* evidences a purposeful design. Calling forth the intertextual relationship between intercession and martyrdom through the phrase covenant and oath, the author uses that relationship as a thematic base to present his story of the post exilic period as an eschatological prophecy within the framework of Deuteronomy 31–32. Playing on the relationships between biblical texts and developing parallel ones in a rewritten narrative thus becomes an effective technique for creating a unified, if complex, covenant theology that incorporates the writer's own historical and eschatological perspectives.

NOTES

1. Robert H. Charles (*The Assumption of Moses Translated From the Sixth Century Manuscript* [London, 1897]) attributed the work to a single author and on the basis of references to Herod and his sons and an attack on the Jews by Varus in 4 B.C.E. (ch. 6) placed the date of composition around the turn of the era (7–30 C.E.). This view was challenged by Jacob Licht ("Taxo, or the Apocalyptic Doctrine of Vengeance," *Journal of Jewish Studies* 12 (1961), 95–103) and George W. E. Nickelsburg ("An Antiochan Date for the Testament of Moses," in *Studies on the*

Testament of Moses: Seminar Papers, George W. E. Nickelsburg, ed., Septuagint-Cognate Studies 4 (Cambridge, 1973), 33–7). (Hereafter referred to as *Studies.*) Nickelsburg argued on the basis of form criticism that the work was originally composed in the time of Antiochus IV Epiphanes and that post Maccabean material (chaps. 6–7) was added by a post Herodian redactor. John J. Collins ("The Date and Provenance of the *Testament of Moses,*" in *Studies,* 15–32) originally held to composition by a single hand after the death of Herod, but subsequently came to accept the argument for a Maccabean base with significant reworking by a later redactor. D. M. Rhoads ("The *Assumption of Moses* and Jewish History: 4 B.C.–A.D. 48," in *Studies,* 53–58), J. Priest ("Some Reflections on the *Assumption of Moses,*" in *Perspectives on Religious Studies* 4 [1977], 92–111 and "*Testament of Moses,*" in Charlesworth, ed., *The Old Testament Pseudepigrapha,* I, 919–34) and E. Brandenburger (*Himmelfahrt Moses,* JSHRZ 5.2 [Gutersloh, Mohn, 1976]) continue to reject the two stage view of composition. They do however acknowledge that "some of the materials" used in the text "may have had a considerable prior history in either oral or written form." (Priest, "*Testament of Moses,*" in *Studies,* 921).

2. Although the *Testament* is often described by scholars as a "rewriting" of Deut. 31–34, in the text as it currently stands there is sparse evidence of attention to chapters 33 and 34.

3. The use of "oath" in 2:7 (". . . [Four], however, will violate the covenant of the Lord and defile the oath which the Lord made with them") involves understanding the Latin *finem* ("end," "purpose") as a corruption from the Greek (*aron* in place of *arkon*). On the emended text, see R. H. Charles, *The Assumption of Moses* (London, 1897); J. Priest's translation and notes in *The Old Testament Pseudepigrapha,* James Charlesworth, ed., vol. 1 (New York, 1985), 928; and A. S. Hartom's comments on the verse in the Hebrew edition (*Tzavat Moshe,* in *Sefarim Hachizoniim* [Tel Aviv, 1981]).

4. *Testament of Moses* 1:8 and 2:1 specifically recall the promise of the Land to the fathers; 4:2–3, and 5 refer to the covenant with the fathers, but the Land aspect of that covenant is clearly implied in the contexts. 11:11, emended from *araborum* to *atavorum,* simply describes the Land as "land of their forefathers."

5. In the recollections of Deut. 1:8; 6:10; and 30:20 the patriarchs are referred to by relationship and by name; in 34:4 they are named without reference to their status as forefathers.

6. The single reference to the patriarchs by name in the *Testament* appears in the tribal prayer addressed in direct voice to the "God of Abraham, God of Isaac, and God of Jacob" (3:9).

7. The attitude toward the wilderness generation in the *Testament* is intriguingly contradictory. In the last scene Moses describes his role as intercessor and mediator "for their sins" (12:6). But in chapter 9, Taxo, the martyr who brings on the eschaton, says to his sons, "never did (our) fathers nor their ancestors tempt God by transgressing his commandments" (9:4).

8. On the exception, the emended text of 2:7, see note 3 above.

9. In the Latin "covenant and oath" is "*testamentum et jusjurandum*." In the *Akedah* context, "oath" is expressed in the language of "נשבע." In *Deuteronomy*, however, the "oath" is expressed as "אלה" a reference to the negative stipulations if the covenant is not kept.

The concept of a divine oath to the patriarchs also appears in *Pseudo-Philo* in the context of a promise never to abandon Israel (30:7). In the *Testament of the Twelve Patriarchs* (T. Judah 22:3) and in the *Psalms of Solomon* (17:5) the divine oath refers to the eternality of the House of David.

10. Used throughout this study, *Akedah* refers to the biblical narrative of the binding of Isaac. In Ps. 105:9–11 and I Chronicles 16:15–18 reference is made to God's covenant with Abraham and oath to Isaac regarding promise of the Land. But the only oath mentioned in the promissorial scene with Isaac (Gen. 26:3) is in fact the oath to Abraham at the time of the Akedah (Gen. 22:16) now being transferred to his son. The association between "covenant and oath" and the *Akedah* appears in the *Zichronot* Liturgy of Rosh Ha-Shanah, dated no later than the third century C.E. and also in medieval penitential poetry. In the latter see particularly Rabbi Eliezar Bar Natan's "Et haBrit v'et haShvuah" in A. M. Habermann, *Sefer Gezerot Ashkenaz we-Sarefat* (Jerusalem, 1945), 107–108.

11. For example, Ex. 6:8; 13:5, 11; 33:1; Deut. 1:8; 6:10; 30:20 among many.

12. The concept of God swearing by Himself appears in Jeremiah (22:5; 49:13; 32:13) and in Isaiah (45:23); but in these contexts the oath involves destruction rather than promises of progeny and land and hence does not fit the contexts in which it appears in the *Testament*.

13. The intercession is made by the tribes on behalf of the new exiles.

14. See Shalom Spiegel, *The Last Trial* (New York, 1967). Spiegel repeatedly notes the antiquity of the aggadic tradition, but does not discuss the *Testament of Moses*.

15. For a similar transformation of an historical event in the biblical narrative into an ongoing condition in *Chronicles*, see Sarah Japhet, *The Ideology of the Book of Chronicles and its Place in Biblical Thought* (Hebrew) (Jerusalem, 1977) 327ff.

16. In early rabbinic aggadic literature the *Akedah* is treated as though Isaac had in fact been martyred and therefore as having atoning value whenever Israel sins. For examples, see *Targum Yonatan* on Gen. 22, *Sifra,* Behukkotai 112c, *Lev. R.* 36.5; *Gen. R.* 94.5; *b. Taanit* 16a, *b. Yoma* 5a, and *Mekilta d'R. Shimon* 4. The tradition is also reflected in *Pseudo-Philo* (18:5; 32:2–4; 40:2). For full development of the theme, see Spiegel, *op. cit.*

17. ". . . those who truly fulfill the commandments of God will flourish and will finish the good way, but those who sin by disregarding the commandments will deprive themselves of the good things which were declared before. They indeed, will be punished by the nations with many tortures" (12:10–11). John J. Collins has described this theology as "thorough-going 'covenantal nomism'" ("Testaments" in *Jewish Writings of the Second Temple Period* [Assen-Philadelphia, 1984], ed., Michael Stone, 347.)

18. For biblical sources see 2 Kings 16:3; 21:6; and Ezek. 8:8–16; 16:20. The description of idolatry includes the presence of carved images of all sorts of animals in the Temple (2:9).

19. The emphasis on Jerusalem and the Temple here is typical of the literature of the Second Temple period when socially and economically Jerusalem became so central. See M. Weinfeld, "Inheritance of the Land—Privilege versus Obligation: The Concept of the Promise of the Land in the Sources of the First and Second Temple Periods," *Zion,* 49 (1984), 115–37 (Hebrew). The transition of focus from 'land' to 'city and sanctuary' in the Second Temple period was a gradual one. The writer of the *Testament* reflects that transition by shifting his interest from the land to the Temple in the second half of the historical revelation, i.e. the period after the return from Babylonian exile.

20. In neither its prose (ch. 31) nor its poetic (ch. 32) form does Deuteronomy 31–32 include the stages of exile, repentance and return in the cycle. Divine withdrawal is the punishment; and acknowledgement of this withdrawal as the source of Israel's troubles (vv. 17–18) is substituted for repentance without reference to return. In the poem Israel's repentance is replaced by the arrogance of the punishing Gentiles (Deut. 32:27–33); and return to the land is limited to the promise to atone "for the land of His people" (33:43).

In his analysis of the adoption of the deuteronomic scheme in various works of post exilic Jewish literature, George Nickelsburg uses Deuteronomy 28–32 as a single block and adopts the terms "turning point" and "salvation" in place of "repentance" and "return." See Nickelsburg, "An Antiochan Date for the Testament of Moses," in *Studies* 33–37 and *Jewish Literature Between the Bible and the Mishnah* (Philadelphia, 1981), 80–1; 118–21. The adoption of such terminology overgeneralizes and neutralizes the significant differences between eschatological patterns in Deuteronomy.

21. The notion that the Judean tribes suffer for the sins of their northern brethren also appears in 2 *Bar.* 77:10.

22. "Then all the tribes will lament, crying out to heaven and saying, 'God of Abraham, God of Isaac, and God of Jacob, remember your covenant which you made with them, and the oath which you swore to them by yourself, that their seed would never fail from the land which you have given them'" (3:8–9).

"Remember Your servants, Abraham, Isaac, and Jacob, how You swore to them by Your Self and said to them: I will make your offspring as numerous as the stars of heaven, and I will give to your offspring this whole land of which I spoke, to possess forever" (Exod. 32:13)

23. None of the various analyses of the structural pattern of the *Testament of Moses* attributes significance to the prayer of the tribes. Nickelsburg includes the passage in the stage he labels "turning point," but like Collins and Harrington, he has little to say regarding the purpose or significance of this first prayer. See Nickelsburg "An Antiochan Date for the *Testament of Moses,*" in *Studies,* 33–37; Collins, "The Date and Provenance of the *Testament of Moses,*" in *Studies,* 15–32; and Harrington, "Interpreting Israel's History: *The Testament of Moses* as a Rewriting of Deuteronomy 31–34," in *Studies,* 59–71.

24. "Then, in that day, they will remember me, saying from tribe to tribe, even each man to his neighbor, 'Is this not that which was made known to us in prophecies by Moses, who suffered many things in Egypt and at the Red Sea and in the wilderness for forty years (when) he solemnly called heaven and earth as witnesses against us that we should not transgress God's commandments of which he had become the mediator for us? These things which have come upon us since that time are according to his admonition declared to us at that time. And (those words) have been confirmed even to our being led as captives in the land of the East" (3:10–13).

25. "Gather to me all the elders of your tribes and your officials, that I may speak all these words to them and that I may call heaven and earth to witness against them." (Deut. 31:28)

"And when the many evils and troubles befall them—then this poem shall confront them as a witness, since it will never be lost from the mouth of their offspring" (Deut. 31:21).

26. Experience occasions comparable confirmations of Moses' prophecies in II *Bar.* 84:2–5, in *Dan.* 9:12–13, and perhaps in II *Macc.* 7:18. In each of these contexts, however, the confirmation is accompanied or followed as in Deut. 4:28–30 and 30:1–2 by repentance expressed in terms of a confession of sins and/or a call to return to the command-

ments. See II *Bar.* 84:6–85:4; *Dan.* 9:7–11, 15–16; II *Macc.* 7:18, 32. The reference to "when all these things happen to them" in *Jub.* (1:5–6) is in response to the question raised in Deut. 31:17 and is not part of the cycle. It is presented as an explanation for the Sinai revelation that *Jubilees* itself portends to be, that is, the evidence that God had not abandoned them in spite of their sins (1:5–6).

27. This prayer is offered by "one who is over them" (4:1). Ezra or an angel such as in Zech. 1:12 have also been suggested.

28. While J. Licht and G. Nickelsburg stress the relationship between the *Testament of Moses* and *Daniel* (*op. cit.*, in *Studies*), J. Priest argues that the "identification of the prayer with Daniel" is "probable," but this does not necessarily indicate "that the author of the *Testament* was familiar with the book of Daniel, but rather with certain Danielic traditions" ("*Testament of Moses,*" in *Old Testament Pseudepigrapha,* 924).

29. This point is stressed by Daniel Harrington against Nickelsburg who, as noted above, does not distinguish between the historical patterns of Deut. 28–30 and 31–32 (Daniel J. Harrington, "Interpreting Israel's History: *The Testament of Moses* as a Rewriting of Deuteronomy 31–34," in *Studies,* 66ff.).

30. In their essays on the *Testament,* J. J. Collins and D. J. Harrington both note that intercession functions as an analogue or counterpart to repentance (Nickelsburg, *op. cit.,* 15–32; 59–71.

31. "I prayed to the Lord and said, "O Lord God, do not annihilate Your very own people, whom You redeemed in Your majesty and whom You freed from Egypt with a mighty hand. Give thought to your servants, Abraham, Isaac, and Jacob, and pay no heed to the stubbornness of this people, its wickedness, and its sinfulness. Else the country from which You freed us will say, 'It was because the Lord was powerless to bring them into the land that He had promised them, and because He hated them, that He brought them out to have them die in the wilderness.' Yet they are Your very own people, whom You freed with Your great might and Your outstretched arm."

The substance of the intercession in the *Testament* is cited in the text, p. 8. Note that the sequence is reversed—the statement of God's power is made first in the *Testament;* in Deuteronomy 9 it follows the justification for forgiving the sin.

32. This is one of the two perceptions attributed to the nations in the Deuteronomy version of the intercession. The related second perception—that God hated the Israelites and brought them to the wilderness to kill them (9:28)—is the one presented in the Exodus narrative of the Golden Calf (32:11–13). The two are compressed in Deut. 9 where Moses's recollection of his intercessory role encompasses both occasions.

33. In Exodus a full intercessory scene (the dialogue between God and Moses and acknowledgment of divine acceptance of Moses's appeal) comes after Moses has been told of the worship of the calf but before he has himself witnessed the deed (Exod. 32:7–14). Yet here too there is a doubling. When Moses returns to the mountain after he has destroyed the image, he acknowledges the great sin of the people, and urges God to erase him also if He has not forgiven the sin (32:31–32). God responds by urging him to continue leading the people even as He assures him that those who participated in the great sin of the calf will in fact be punished (32:33–4).

34. *Pseudo-Philo* (12:4–9) also uses the Deuteronomy version of the intercession on Sinai where Moses's response to God comes only after his destruction of the calf.

35. Interestingly, the author of II *Bar.* (85:1–4) makes a point of the effectiveness of intercession by "helpers," "prophets," and "holy men" being limited to only so long as "we were . . . in our country." Once exiled, the Judeans have no recourse but to "direct and dispose" their hearts toward the commandments in order to effect the eschatological return.

36. He notes that the returned exiles were not able "to offer sacrifices to the Lord of their fathers" (4:9). J. Priest ("*Testament of Moses,*" notes to 4:9 in *Old Testament Pseudepigrapha*), argues that the author is asserting no more than the inferiority of the Second Temple to the First. However, such a comparison does not fit the description of the post exilic period which follows the comment about sacrifices.

37. The author of *Jubilees* also tries to place post exilic history within the deuteronomic schema, but he deals with it by creating a failed intercession and emphasizes the necessity of full repentance before the onset of the final end-time.

38. On the dominance of the deterministic theme in the *Testament,* see J. Priest, "*Testament of Moses,*" in Charlesworth, ed., 922ff. On the apocalyptic determinism generally see J. J. Collins, "Jewish Apocalyptic Against Its Hellenistic Near Eastern Environment," in *Bulletin of the American School of Oriental Research,* no. 220, (December, 1975), 27–36.

39. "Ut invocetur nomen illius usque in diem paenitentiae in respecta quo respiciet illos Dominos in consummatione exitus dierum" (1:18).

40. Neither events nor major characters are specified by name. But the descriptions in chapters 5 and 6 are sufficiently clear that scholars generally agree that chapter 5 describes the Hasmonean period and 6, the reign of Herod, his sons, and the invasion of Varus. Chapter 8 has been identified with the Antiochan persecution; but that identification, like the historical nature of chapter 7, continues to be the subject of some debate.

On the chronological sequence of these chapters, see George W. E. Nickelsburg, *Resurrection, Immortality and Eternal Life in Intertestament Judaism* (Cambridge, 1972), 43ff., and the studies by Collins, Licht, Priest, and Rhoads cited above in note 1.

41. Like several of those described in Deuteronomy, the cycle contains a doubling of the sequential stages of sin and punishment: Sin 5:3–6:1; Punishment 6:2–9; Sin 7:3–10; Punishment 8:1–5. If one treats chapters 7 and 8 as an interpolation as argued by Licht and Nickelsburg (see above, note 1), and places the chapters chronologically, the double sequence of sin/punishment would no longer be in order. Hence, on the basis of the interpolation theory, the pattern found in the work as it stands is the work of the final redactor.

For examples of the doubling of the sin/punishment pattern in Deuteronomy, note 28:15–68 (15; 16–57; 58; 59–68) and 31:16–21 (16; 17–18; 20; 21).

42. On the identity of an historical Taxo, see H. H. Rowley, *The Relevance of the Apocalyptic* (New York, 1963), 149–56 and S. Zeitlin, "The Assumption of Moses and the Bar Kochba Revolt," *Jewish Quarterly Review* 38 (1947/48), 4–5. On Taxo as a messianic figure, see C. J. Lattey, "The Messianic Expectation in 'The Assumption of Moses,'" *Catholic Biblical Quarterly* 4 (1942), 9–21. On the function of the Taxo story, see J. Priest, "Some Reflection on the Assumption of Moses," in *op. cit.*;" J. Licht, "Taxo, or the Apocalyptic Doctrine of Vengeance," in *op. cit.*; A. B. Kolenkow, "The Assumption of Moses as a Testament," and D. M. Rhoads, "The Assumption of Moses and Jewish History: 4 B.C.–A.D. 48," in *Studies*.

43. "The messenger who is in the highest place appointed" (10:2) is usually identified as the angel Michael. See Priest's note on 10:2.

44. In the descriptions of the reign of Herod and the invasion of the "powerful king of the West" (6:5, 8), the Land is referred to as "their" land.

45. The specified sins include idolatry ("they will play the harlot after foreign gods" directly cited from Deut. 31:16); pollution of the sanctuary and cult (5:3–61); injustice and oppression of the poor (7:3–10). In the Pentateuch and prophetic literature, idolatry (which frequently is described as harlotry) and injustice are sins which result in loss of the land.

46. "Never did (our) fathers nor their ancestors tempt God by transgressing his commandments" (9:4).

47. In sharp contrast, the author of II *Macc.* prefaces his tales of martyrs with the assurance that the "misfortunes . . . were meant not for the destruction of our people, but for their correction" and that Israel's suffering was in fact a mark of God's love (8:12ff.).

48. The reference to the end of the First Commonwealth in 586 is only implicit. Taxo refers to what is happening in his own day as "a second punishment." If one accepts the Nickelsburg thesis that the Taxo narrative is from the Maccabean period, the "second punishment" is understood as a reference to the persecution by Antiochus and the first punishment is the Babylonian Exile of 586. If one does not accept that thesis, the "second punishment" could refer to some later oppression perhaps under Herod; and the first could be 586, the Antiochan persecution, or some later event. See Priest's note on 8:1.

49. With the exception of J. Priest, generally scholars have not commented upon Taxo's unusual perspective. Priest notes that it "may support the view that the chapter had an independent origin." See Priest, "*Testament of Moses,*" in *Old Testament Pseudepigrapha,* note "d" on 9:4.

50. If the mounting upon the wings of an eagle (v. 8) is understood as a return to God's protective custody, the parallel with Deuteronomy 32:11 is clear. However, if the eagle is identified with Rome and the verse understood as victory over enemies, the parallel no longer functions, for in Deuteronomy 32 it is God, not Israel, who destroys the subjugators of Israel. On the eagle as Rome, see Adela Yarbro Collins, "Composition and Redaction of the *Testament of Moses 10, Harvard Theological Review* 69 (1976), 184–86.

51. On the literal interpretation of the verse see the work of George W. E. Nickelsburg, particularly, *Resurrection, Immortality, and Eternal Life in Intertestamental Judaism* (Cambridge, 1962), 28–31; 43–45. Nickelsburg's argument rests heavily on the parallels he sees between the passage here, *Dan.* 12:3 and I *En.* 104:2–7 as well as later descriptions of the endtime in II *Bar.* 51:5–12.

52. In Exod. 6:8 the oath is transferred through the merit of the fathers to the Israelites whom Moses is to lead. In Exod. 32:13, it becomes the basis upon which Moses bases his plea on behalf of the Israelites who have constructed the Golden Calf.

CHAPTER 8

Placing Reading: Ancient Israel and Medieval Europe

Daniel Boyarin

> Reading for pleasure is an extraordinary activity. The black squiggles on the white page are still as the grave, colorless as the moonlit desert; but they give the skilled reader a pleasure as acute as the touch of a loved body.
>
> Victor Nell

INTRODUCTION

Robert Alter's book, *The Pleasures of Reading in an Ideological Age* is a vigorous description of (and defense of) the European practice of reading literature for pleasure. I hasten to add that this "pleasure" does *not* mean a hedonistic experience, but rather one of affective identification with the characters, an experience understood in our culture to be gratifying, but nonetheless edifying and

---

This paper was originally delivered in earlier versions at a conference at Bar-Ilan University on the occasion of the retirement of Professor Harold Fisch in November, 1989 and at the MLA session on the "Ethnography of Reading" in Washington, D.C. in December of that year and is being published in the volumes generated by both conferences. I wish to thank all of the respondents at those meetings as well as Robert Alter, Piero Boitani, Jonathan Boyarin, Joan Branham, Ken Frieden, Steven Fraade, Dell Hymes, Chana Kronfeld, Ellen Spolsky, Brian Stock, and an anonymous (and very nasty) reader for the University of California Press for their helpful comments. The section on European reading and the erotic was presented at a colloquium entitled "Is Reading a Universal?" at the Townshend Center for the Humanities at Berkeley on November 13, 1990, and some important final revisions incorporated in response to the discussion thereafter.

improving of the reader. Alter identifies several of the distinctive features of this practice: "Very few people will take the trouble to read a novel or story unless they can somehow 'identify' with the characters, live with them inwardly as though they were real at least for the duration of the reading" (Alter 1989:49). If we pay close attention to this statement, we will see that it conjures up several features of our reading-practice. It assumes that reading is a voluntary act; people can choose to do it or not (Nell 1988:2). Accordingly it must cause some kind of pleasure to the reader or he or she will abandon the activity (Nell 1988:8–9). Second, the pleasure is produced by an affective identification between the reader and the characters in the story, a sympathy between the real reader and imaginary people and their imaginary adventures (Nell 1988:39). Third, at least ideally, the pleasure of this identification is produced when the reader is in private and can "forget" reality in the illusion of the reality of the characters and their story.[1]

"Reading" as spoken of and described in the Bible has none of these features. The Torah names the function of its reading as a speech act. It declares of itself that its intention is, "it shall be with him, and he shall read in it every day of his life in order that he will learn to fear the Lord his God, to keep the words of this Torah and to perform the commandments" (Deut. 17:19). Reading is not a voluntary act, nor one that is supposed to produce pleasure. It is not an excitation of the emotions or sentiments but simply a demand that the reader fulfill the obligations which the read document contains. This is not a claim of lack of literary value and beauty in the biblical text. To our ears and eyes, the poetry of Jeremiah is full of such poetic value; nevertheless, it can hardly be said to have attempted to persuade or seduce its hearers with its poetry. There is nothing *dulce* in the *utile* of Jeremiah. It should be made absolutely clear that I am not invoking a positivistic content-form distinction; indeed, I am asserting that the very notion of form is a historicizable practice and not a given of language.[2]

In an extraordinarily suggestive recent interview, the French Jewish poet and theoretician, Henri Meschonnic spoke about the biblical term "Miqra," the word that best translates the English word reading. Meschonnic's central claim is that reading means something entirely different in biblical Hebrew because the written text is always read orally:

> Keeping the tie between writing and reading is in the biblical name of *Mikra* itself. In a manner very characteristic of our European languages, the biblical corpus is called *Writing*. . . . I think that to say *Writing*—holy Writing, Writings, from *Scriptura* onward—makes the texts thus named enter culturally into a field radically different from the Hebraic, Jewish field, in the sense that to say *Writing* or *Scriptura* is to conceive fully an opposition, finally, of the subject and the social, of writing and reading, of the act and the word. . . . In the Hebraic field it is completely otherwise: the very term *Mikra,* which designates the biblical corpus, etymologically and functionally at the same time, signifies *reading*—not reading as we speak of reading by contrast to writing. *Mikra* assumes the gathering during which one reads or has read the texts in question, and since this reading is done out loud, the notion conjoins, indissolubly to my understanding, orality and collectivity in reading. (Meschonnic 1988:454)

There is great insight in Meschonnic's remarks. However, since Meschonnic's claim that *Scriptura* is unknown in Hebrew is exaggerated—we do find, after all "kithvei haqqodesh" (Holy Scripture) as a title for the Bible—the relevant distinction seems to be not the designation of the Bible as the Writing or the Reading, but the fact that the word reading means, as well, the Bible. In other words, the point is not to situate the text in Jewish culture in the metaphysics of the reading—writing opposition, but to situate reading in that culture in its sociocultural semantic field. Reading, in ancient Jewish culture signifies an act which is oral, social, and collective, while in modern (and early-modern) Europe it signifies an act which belongs to a private or semi-private social space.

By studying the structure of the semantic affinities and fields of the Hebrew words for reading, I hope to show that they do not belong to the same lexical categorization of practices that reading does in modern European culture. However, that alone would leave my investigation open to the sort of theoretical questions posed by Keesing:

> To what extent are conventional metaphors, and the schemas they express, constitutive of our experience? Do varying schemas, whether of emotion, time, causality, social relationships, and so on, reflect contrasting modes of subjective experience, of thought and perception—or of simply different conventions for talking about the world, as creatures with our human brains and sensory

equipment and bodies experience it? There is no simple answer. (Keesing 1987:386)

In order, therefore, to corroborate the findings from this semantic inquiry, I will analyze biblical narrative texts that describe scenes of reading; the descriptions of practice coincide with the semantics of the words involved. Then, I will interpret some European scenes of reading which through contrast will point up how different reading is in the two cultural formations. In the last section of the paper, I will attempt to shed some light on an important critical debate vis-à-vis biblical narrative from the perspective developed in my paper's main argument.

THE BIBLE: "READING" AS A SPEECH-ACT

A semantic analysis of the distribution of the root *qr'* in biblical Hebrew reveals the following points. The root encompasses a range of meanings including "to call," "to proclaim," "to summon or invite" and "to read." It will be immediately observed that the whole semantic field to which these glosses belong is that of speech acts and not of passive reception. And indeed, as I shall argue, reading in Biblical Hebrew is a speech act. It nearly always means "to read aloud to someone," as confirmed by the complements "in the ears of PN"[3] or "before PN." In all of these cases the activity described is the reading of some kind of a message and its communication or proclamation to an audience. The following verses will point up the force of *qr'* in the Bible:

1. "And the Lord *called out* to the Adam and said to him 'Where are you?'" (Gen. 3:9)
2. "And the angel of the Lord *called out* to him from the heaven and said, 'Abraham, Abraham.' And he said, 'Here I am.'" (Gen. 22:11)
3. "And now, *call out* in the ears of the People, and say, 'Whoever is afraid and terrified, let him sit and watch from the Mountain of Gilead!'" (Judg. 7:3)
4. "And he took the Book of the Covenant, and he *read* it in the ears of the People, and they said, 'All that the Lord has spoken, we will do and we will obey'. And Moses took the blood and sprinkled it on the People and said, 'This is the blood of the

Covenant, which God has enacted with you with regard to all of these words." (Exod. 24:7)

5. "When all of Israel come to appear before the Lord, your God at the place which he shall choose, *read* this Torah in the presence of all of Israel, in their ears. Gather together the People, the men, the women and the children and the stranger within your gates, in order that they hear and in order that they learn and they fear the Lord your God and watch to perform all of the words of this Torah." (Deut. 31:11)
6. "And you shall come and *read* out the Scroll which you have written in accord with my dictation." (Jer. 36:3)

We learn several things from this very partial list of verses with *qr*'. First of all, in every case, the usage indicates an oral act, an act of the speaking of language. Second, the usage of *qr*' when there is a written text present is virtually identical to that when there is no written text present. From the point of view of the semantic structure of Hebrew, this is not even polysemy, but simply the same meaning. Thus, comparing example 3 with 4 and 5, we are hard-pressed to find any reason from the Hebrew to translate the verb differently in the latter cases than in the former one. I think it might not be going too far, indeed, were we to translate "call out [or proclaim] this Torah"![4] The Rabbis seem, at any rate, to have understood this point well, for they commented on example 6, "Was Barukh used to speaking out in the presence of Jeremiah?"[5] Finally, all of these acts of speaking in which the verb *qr*' is used are immediately followed by the desired or actual result of the performance of the speech act in the performance of the listener. Looking into the semantic affinities of the root *qr*', then, certainly seems to suggest that for the biblical culture, reading occupies a different place in the social world than it does for us, so different that it is nearly an entirely different practice.

When we begin to look at narrative scenes of reading—both prescriptive and descriptive—in the Bible, we will find the semantic analysis strengthened by the accounts of our informants, as it were.[6] In all of the Hebrew Bible, there is no unequivocal usage of *qr*' in the sense of "to read to oneself," no place where someone is described as silently (or even orally) consuming a text alone and/or without immediate public consequences.[7] Although in Deuteronomy 17:19, we are told that the king must write for himself a copy of Deuteronomy, and "it shall be with him, and he shall read in it every day of his life in order that he will learn to fear the Lord his God, to keep the words of this Torah and to perform the commandments," we can learn what this "reading" would have been like from the description of the first occasion in which a king "read" this scroll:

> [8] And Hilqiahu the Priest High Priest said to Shafan the Scribe: I have found a Scroll of the Torah in the House of the Lord, and Hilqiahu gave the scroll to Shafan and he read it. . . . [10] And Shafan the scribe told the king, saying: Hilqiahu the Priest has given me a Scroll and Shafan read it before the king. [11] And it happened that *when the king heard* the words of the Scroll of the Torah, he rent his garments. [12] And the king commanded Hilqiah the Priest and 'Ahiqam the son of Shafan and ʿAkbur the son of Mikiah and Shafan the scribe and ʿAsaya the king's servant, saying: [13] Go seek the Lord for me and for the people and for all of Judea with regard to the words of the Scroll which has been found, for the wrath of the Lord which has been kindled against us is great, because our ancestors did not obey [lit. hear!] the words of this Scroll to do all that is written for us. [14] And Hilqiah the Priest . . . went to Huldah the Prophetess . . . and she was sitting in Jerusalem in Mishneh and they said to her. [15] And she said to them: Thus has the Lord the God of Israel said, Go tell the man who sent you to me: [16] Thus has the Lord said: I hereby bring evil to this place and upon its inhabitants—all of the words of the Scroll *which the King of Judea has read.* (2 Kings 22:8ff.)

We can learn several things about the ethnography of reading in ancient Israel from this scene of reading. This event is portrayed by the Bible as the founding moment for the practice which Deuteronomy—the very Scroll which was discovered in the Temple—prescribed, so we can take it as a model for that practice. The scribe reads the Torah before the king and his attendant councillors of various types, and then the king is declared to have "read" the Scroll. According to Deuteronomy he is expected to respond to its import immediately, and according to the Kings text, that is exactly what happens. "Reading" is a proclamation, a declaration and a summons. Even though the original reading, that of the scribe itself, here described in verse [8] seems to have been a silent reading, it is quite clear that it is preparatory for the real reading, that is, the public, oral proclamation and receipt of the message which the Scroll contains.[8] Each of the readers has to act, and the act of each is contingent on his social function: the scribe, having read, must read to the King. The King, having read, must send men to seek the Lord. As claimed by Meschonnic's text,[9] the noun form, "miqra" means both the "reading" and the "Holy Assembly" at which the reading takes place. Moreover, even this last sense of miqra has a double meaning, because it refers to the summons to come to the convocation as well as the calling out or reading that will take place there. The text, Miqra is the place one is summoned to and the place which summons. To dramatize the difference in structure between that culture and ours, I would claim that the field of our social practice which most nearly fits that of *qr'* in the biblical culture would be "preaching" or even "adjuring" and not reading.[10] It is certainly significant that in English there is a synchronic semantic opposition between reading and "lection"—the reading of the Bible in church or synagogue—while in biblical usage, of course, no such opposition exists. Reading in that culture is a public, oral and illocutionary speech-act, an act, moreover, which when successful always has perlocutionary effect. And this is the only type of reading of which the Bible knows. There simply is no other word in Biblical Hebrew which conveys the sense of processing and receiving written language, and there are no scenes described in the text which indicate private reading.

The above scene of reading is doubled in the famous incident described in Jeremiah 36. Exactly one generation after the discovery and reading of Deuteronomy described in Kings, the king and the people have been backsliding. God commands Jeremiah to "take a scroll and write on it all of the words that I have spoken to you about Israel and Judea and all of the nations, since the day when I first spoke to you in the days of Josiah and until now . . . Perhaps the House of Judea will hear of all of the evil which I intend to do unto them, and will repent each one from his evil ways, and I will forgive their sin and their transgression." [1–2]. The prophet, of course, performs as commanded. He has his scribe Barukh write down all of the words in a book, which is then read before all of the people, before the king, the son of Josiah and all of his councillors, the sons of the very same officials described in the Kings story. The emphasis on citing the genealogies of the persons—note that in the Kings story the officials' genealogies are not given—seems intended to establish that this scene is a (reversed) antitype of the former one.[11] The reading of prophetic text, as that of the Torah, is expected to function as the speech-act of command, and its intended perlocutionary effect is obedience—as opposed, for example, to an illocutionary act of exhortation whose intended effect would be persuasion. In this case, however, the speech act does not have the desired perlocutionary effect. The king defies the warning in the scroll which has been read to him. The experience is, however, so threatening that he has the scroll burnt bit by bit as it is read to somehow neutralize its power. Once again, we see, that even when disregarded, the act of reading is public, social and illocutionary, not private and subjective in nature:

> And it was in the fifth year of Yehoyakim, the son of Josiah, the king of Judea in the ninth month, they called [*qar'u:* Note that this is the same verb as the one used for the reading! The root is *qr'*.] a fast before the Lord, all of the people of Jerusalem and all of the people who come from the cities of Judea in Jerusalem. And Barukh read [*qara'*] in the book the words of Jeremiah in the temple in the office of Gemaryahu, the son of Shafan the scribe, in the upper court, near the entrance to the gate of the new House of the Lord, *in the hearing of all of the People.* (9–11)

After this reading, the text is brought before the king and all of the rest of his councillors, once more identified as the sons of the very ones who heard the first reading of Deuteronomy as above. When the scroll is read before them, "When they heard these words, each man was very afraid, and they said, *we will tell the king, all of these words.* And they asked Barukh, saying, 'tell us, how did you write all of these words from his mouth?' and Barukh said to them, 'He called-out [*qara'!*] all of the words, and I write them on this scroll'." (16–18) The same root is used to signify the calling of the fast which is the setting for the reading, Jeremiah's oral declamation of his prophecy, and the scribe's reading out of that prophecy to its destinators.

> And the king sent Yehudi to take the scroll and he took it from the office of Elishama the scribe and Yehudi *read it in the ears of the king and in the ears of all of the princes who serve the king.* And the king was sitting in his winter house in the ninth month and the fire-place was burning before him. And it was, that as Yehudi read three or four columns he ripped them with a razor and threw them into the fire that was in the fireplace until the

> entire scroll was consumed in the fire on the fireplace. And the king and all of his servants who heard these words were not frightened and did not rend their garments. (21–25)

In its very description of the *failure* of the speech-act and in its explicit contrast between this event and its type in the previous generation, we have further evidence for how "reading" was conceived as a practice in the biblical culture. We see clearly that it was a social and public practice, more akin to a court's sentence than to anything like the practice of private, recreative self-improvement and ethical growth that we conceive it to be. The concept of a silent and private reading and that of the aesthetic pleasure of being taken up in an imaginative world (Alter 1989:49), even only for a moment, is simply excluded from possibility both by the semantic structure of the language and by the actually described practices of reading in the text.

"READING" WITH THE RABBIS

When we turn to rabbinic literature, the texts of the Talmud and midrash, we find that the situation is somewhat more complicated, but still much the same picture will emerge. There are more relevant terms in this linguistic field. In addition to *qr'*, also *drsh, grs,* and *ʿyn* belong to the semantic field which can be generally characterized as the processing of written language. The last two can be dealt with very briefly, for neither of them have anything to do with interpreting the marks on the page as text or discourse, *grs* meaning to repeat over and over again and thereby memorize, while *ʿyn* denotes merely the physical process of training one's eyes on the writing. Thus, one who translates the Torah in the synagogue is required not to *ʿyn* in the Torah, because the onlookers might err and think that his translation is actually written there.

Beginning once again with *qr'*, we find that in addition to the biblical usages of "to call, to invite, to summons," it has several senses relating to the processing of texts in the Hebrew of the rabbinic period. The first is, as in biblical Hebrew, to read Scriptures aloud in a communal, ritual setting. The sememe of "aloud" is attested in the contrast between what is written and what is read, as in the type of interpretation called "al tiqre," that is, do not read what is written but read (pronounce) it differently, or in the Masoretic distinction between the "k^{e}thiv" and the "q^{e}re," that is the "written and the read." Although certain words are written in the text, one is commanded to "read" them differently. Thus, for example, everywhere that the Holy Name of God [the Tetragrammaton] is written, we read "The Lord." Since this is not an injunction to emend the text, "q^{e}re" here cannot mean that which is read in our sense of to read, for to read something other than what is written is an oxymoron in our culture. It is only because reading means oral recitation of the text that this distinction between the written and the read can mean anything at all. *Qr'*, in this sense, is typically used for the public, ritual reading of a portion of the Torah at every synagogue service.

The second sense of *qr'* in rabbinic Hebrew is to perform certain biblically ordained rituals which involve the recitation of passages from the Torah, once again out loud. Thus the daily recitation of "Hear O Israel, the Lord our God, the Lord is one," is designated "reading the Hear O Israel." The third sense attested for this root in rabbinic Hebrew is to study Scripture. Even in this last sense, the verb does not cover the ground of our to read, because a different root is used for the study of Mishna, as we clearly see in the following text: "And Rabbi Shefatia said that Rabbi Yohanan said, 'Anyone who *reads* Bible [qore'] without a melody or repeats Mishna [shone] without a song, of him Scripture says, *And also I have given them bitter laws*' (Ezek. 20:25) [TB *Megillah* 32a]." The semantic dominant of *qore'* here is not reception of a text, but participation in the religious act of studying Scripture. Indeed, to this day, the study of religious texts in traditional Jewish societies is typically carried out in pairs called "*hevrutot*" or in small study conventicles[12] and the term "reading the Talmud" simply does not exist in any Jewish language, while "reading the Bible" still exclusively means reading it out loud in the ritual setting. One could fairly say that reading in the European sense just does not exist in that traditional culture.

If we attempt a sememic analysis of all of these usages of *qr'* in this state of the language then, we notice that:

1. They all belong to the field of religious practice.
2. Most of them, indeed, belong to the semantic field and the social sphere of prayer.
3. They are all activities carried out in public places.

4. They are all speech acts, not only performed out loud, but having some illocutionary or perlocutionary force.[13]

The second important root for us to consider in the context of rabbinic Hebrew is *drsh,* the verbal root from which "midrash" is derived. However we characterize that special style of interpretation, it is interpretation of narrative texts, and is therefore close to what we call reading. In this context what is important for us is, however, not what kind of reading it is in the sense of how it interprets texts, but rather what kind of social practice it is in the sense of what social settings it takes place in. Again we will find that the social setting of *drsh* is public and religious exclusively.

The two situations in which we find the practice of *drsh* are the study house, called the House of Midrash and the synagogue. In the first situation, we truly have an activity which seems closest to what we mean by "reading a text," that is perusing it carefully and trying to make sense of its various linguistic levels. However, the project is undertaken always as part of a dialogical encounter. Thus, a typical situation involves a claim made by a given Rabbi, which is challenged by his fellows, and to which he answers, "I am reading [doresh] a verse from the Torah."[14]

The second setting of *drsh* simply involves what we would call lecturing or, once again, preaching. The rabbi stands in front of a congregation and interprets for them the lection of the day with a view, of course, that they assimilate the messages intended and act on them. Thus there are subjects about which one is enjoined not to *drsh* at all. Again the contrast between *drsh* and reading can be sharpened by pointing out that while reading is typically understood as consumption (except in very special institutional settings like MLA meetings), *drsh* is *always* production of text. Clearly, *drsh* also, while covering some of the ground of to read does not provide a semantic fit.

Summing up the results of this brief semantic analysis, we can conclude that the structure of the semantic field which includes the practices analogous to what we call reading was entirely different in the Hebrew of the biblical and talmudic periods. In this light, there was simply no word in that language at all which meant what we mean by "reading a book," that is the essentially private, individual consumption of narrative with the effect of and for the purpose of "pleasure."

EUROPE: READING IN THE SOCIAL SPACE OF THE EROTIC

Reading in the Bible and Talmud occupied the public social spaces of the forum, the synagogue, the House of Study and the court. In contrast, there are two privileged social sites for the practice of reading in Europe in Late Antiquity, the Middle Ages and the Early Modern period: the study and the bedroom. Horace, in a famous and much discussed passage, refers already to "reading and writing which I like to do in silence" *Sat.* 1.6.122–23. The silent and private study of a sophisticated Christian like Ambrose also belongs to the tradition of studious, private reading.[15] Monastic reading of saints' lives grows out of this tradition as well.[16] This sort of private reading, whose architectural trajectory takes it from the monk's cell to the scholar's study has a powerful ascetic element.

More revealing for our purposes here is the pervasive association of reading in the West with the private social spaces and meanings of the erotic. In order to evoke this moment of Western culture, I will take now a lightning tour of several of the most privileged scenes of reading in our European tradition. First, of course, is Augustine for any inquiry into European reading. Augustine is describing his early education and remarks, "Better indeed, because more certain, were those first studies by which there was formed and is formed in me what I still possess, the ability to read what I find written down and to write what I want to, than the later studies wherein *I was required to learn by heart I know not how many of Aeneas's wanderings, although forgetful of my own, and to weep over Dido's death,* because she killed herself for love, when all the while amid such things, dying to you, O God my life, I most wretchedly bore myself about with dry eyes"[17] (Augustine 1960:56 [emphasis added]). Now, on the one hand, it is quite clear that this text does not record an experience of the practice of reading for pleasure which our culture knows. Augustine is *required* to do these things, including weeping (apparently in the classroom) for Dido. One suspects, as have earlier readings of Augustine, that it was at least as much Dido's representation of Africa as her dying for love that produced this school requirement to weep over her fate (Brown 1969:23). Be that as it may, there can be very little doubt that Augustine's story is one of the major sources of the practice of affective identification, and particularly affective identification with a female character, which is so emblematic of our reading practice. It is important to note as well that Augustine is drawing an implied contrast between the perverted ludic reading of his youthful education and the converted reading of his later life, between the weeping for Dido and the response to *tolle, lege.*[18]

It seems to me that it is not over-interpretation to see this affective identification as a development out of the cathartic identification with the characters which was earlier the mark of the tragic theater, and indeed Augustine's description of theater-going is not altogether different from his description of reading the *Aeneid* in school (Augustine 1960:78).[19] This interpretation is supported as well by explicit notations in Aristotle himself:

> In the next place, [tragedy is in fact the better form] because it has everything that epic poetry has, and has in addition an element of no small importance in its music, which intensifies our pleasure in the highest degree, then also it has the advantage of vividness *both when read and when acted. Poetics* 26 (Aristotle 1982:78 [emphasis mine])

It is, moreover, Aristotle as well who is among the first to speak explicitly of pleasure as the telos of literature *Poetics* 4 (Aristotle 1982:47). We can locate, then, one historical source of reading in the pleasurable catharsis of ancient theater as theorized by Aristotle in the *Poetics*. However, we have not yet located the source of the strong association of reading pleasure and erotic experience in our culture.

A vital necessity for this move to take place is the transferral of reading from public to private spaces. Thus with regard to one of the poetic genres of the Middle Ages a recent scholar remarks:

> Despite its high degree of self-reflectiveness, the *canso* remained public in that it was performed. Hermeticism for the troubadors was not possible in the same way as it was for, say, Mallarmé. A modern poet can occasion a private, silent confrontation between himself and his reader through letters on a printed page. But the troubadors worked within a tradition that was largely oral. The *cansos* which they composed were destined to be sung by a *jongleur* before a number of people. There was, then, an unavoidable tension between the private realm created by the song and the public setting in which it had to be verbalized. One

> way in which the troubadors reduced this tension was to use *senhals,* or pseudonyms. In giving secret names to the *personae* of the *canso,* the poet discouraged connections between the men and women mentioned in his song and those assembled in the audience. (Poe 1984:15)

It follows that in order for such connections to be promoted by a reading practice and not discouraged by it, a private setting (not necessarily individual—"alone together" works fine) had to be invented for reading. One very important viaduct of this transition would seem to be the *Vidas* of the Provençal troubadours. These were prose biographies of the troubadors who composed the *cansos.* They seem to have developed when the *cansos* became collected into volumes called *chansonniers,* which from the thirteenth century were produced for private reading (Schutz 1939). They thus serve as a double transitional moment in the "erotic" formation of European reading, as a transition from oral, public to written, private and as a transition from poetry to prose as well. We have here a specific site of origin for an erotic connection between the book, its author, its protagonist and the reader, an eroticized connection which is central to our notion of ludic reading. As a modern commentator on reading for pleasure evokes it, "Reading for pleasure is an extraordinary activity. The black squiggles on the white page are still as the grave, colorless as the moonlit desert; but they give the skilled reader a pleasure as acute as the touch of a loved body" (Nell 1988:1). This is, in itself, an extraordinary comment, if only for the way that it testifies to how naturalized the sense of reading as erotic experience has become in our culture.[20]

Another crucial moment in the history of European reading is the story of Héloïse and Abelard, which marks the site of a cross or a juncture between the two traditions of reading that Augustine represents. On the one hand the reading of this couple belonged to the tradition of reading as monastic study, but on the other hand it quite obviously activates the Augustinian *Aeneid* topos of reading as erotic experience as well. Indeed Abelard in his autobiographical *Historia calamitum,* admits almost to a willful manipulation of these common-places (Abelard 1974:66–67). This hybridization (or contamination) will find its fullest flowering, however, in Dante.

Perhaps the most famous "scene of reading" in European literature, and a crucial one for the association of reading with erotic experience, is the narrative of Paolo and Francesca in *Inferno*, Canto 5 (127ff.) The text both alludes to earlier eroticized scenes of reading, Augustine and Dido,[21] and Héloïse and Abelard (Dronke 1975), and forms a distillation of the history of European reading. Encountering the pair, Dante (the pilgrim narrator) is told:

> "One day, for pastime, we read of Lancelot, how love constrained him; we were alone, suspecting nothing.[22] Several times that reading urged our eyes to meet and took the color from our faces, but one moment alone it was that overcame us. When we read how the longed-for smile was kissed by so great a lover, this one, who never shall be parted from me, kissed my mouth all trembling. A Gallehault was the book and he who wrote it; that day we read no farther in it."
>
> While the one spirit said this, the other wept, so that for pity I swooned, as if in death, and fell as a dead body falls. (Dante Alighieri 1970:55–56)

This is a text which explicitly thematizes a scene of reading for private ("we were alone") pleasure ("to pass the time away"), but as we can easily see, it renders precisely that practice thoroughly problematic as well.

The crux of the problem, and indeed of the text, is Francesca's charge "Galeotto fu 'l libro e chi lo scrisse." How can the author and his book be accused of having caused the downfall of Paolo and Francesca? One possibility would be to understand Dante as indicting a certain type of literature as socially dangerous, much as Flaubert would do centuries later. However, this reading seems excluded by the fact that Dante in other places indicates approval of the Romances, precisely the texts that the couple were reading here.[23] How can its author, then, be referred to as a Galehot? Put somewhat differently, although the situation of these illicit lovers is comparable (and has intertextual connections) with the narrative of Héloïse and Abelard in the *Roman de la Rose* (Dronke 1975:131–35), no one to my knowledge has accused the book that they were *studying* or its author of leading to the downfall of *that* couple. This innovation is Dante's, and it is a crux. The question, of course, is to what extent is Francesca's claim that she was seduced by a book to be relied upon. Some critics (Dronke refers to them as the "hawks") have understood that Dante is merely indicating here Francesca's Eve-like dissembling, an attempt to mislead the pilgrim and justify herself, reading his text as referring to a topos of feminine misreading (Musa 1984:119 and see Hatcher and Musa [1968:107–08]). However, the swoon of pity on the part of the Pilgrim militates against this reading. Although the pilgrim pities other sinners (and indeed expresses pity for Paolo and Francesca's fate even before hearing their story), in all the *Inferno* there is no such extravagant expression of identification with the plight of the condemned as here. His pity can only have been so aroused, I would argue, if he accepted (at least in part) Francesca's argument that the book and its pious author were in fact Panders and she and Paolo thus innocents.[24]

How then can the book and its author be accused of pandering? The question is even stronger according to the view of some Dantean commentators that the book that Paolo and Francesca were reading was the Cistercian[25] prose *Lancelot,* an anti-Romance, one in which the love of Lancelot and Guinivere is presented grotesquely (Hatcher and Musa 1968:108) and with an awful end. On that interpretation, the trouble that Paolo and Francesca got themselves into was not at all because they were reading the wrong texts. Susan Noakes is one of the adherents of this interpretation. She concludes, "In short, the prose *Lancelot* cited by Dante had transformed the Lancelot story (already condemned by the Papacy a hundred years before the *Commedia* was written) into a religious attack on chivalrous values, showing that adulterous love brings only unhappiness. Paolo and Francesca are thus depicted as reading a text designed expressly to keep potential adulterers out of Hell" (Noakes 1988:44). Noakes, in contrast to Musa, doesn't read this as dissembling on Francesca's part so much as denial and lack of insight, "'Galeotto fu 'l libro e chi lo scrisse,' expresses an appalling blindness that she has carried with her into Hell, for it is she and Paolo (rather than a textual or authorial panderer) who have undone themselves by misreading a work written to edify them" (Noakes, 1988:46). The pilgrim faints, on this account, in terror at the "evidence of readerly blindness." Both of these exegeses have in common that the author is *wrongly* accused of pandering.

I would like to suggest a different interpretation, namely that even if the text that Paolo and Francesca were reading was the pious prose Lancelot, (and all the more so if they were reading Chrétien), the text and its author can be *justly* accused by Dante of causing the evil that befell Paolo and Francesca, because of the very scene of reading which it presupposes—even against its overt intentions. Francesca emphasizes that the reading was private and "to pass the time away."[26] I speculate, therefore, that notwithstanding the pious contents of a text, Dante is suggesting that the very practice of reading for pleasure can be morally dangerous.[27] This interpretation is supported by the swoon of the pilgrim as a sign of moral identification between him, Paolo and Francesca. How so? The privacy and intimacy of the very act of reading of the anti-Romance covertly supports the practices of Romance, even as it overtly attacks them. Put another way, the way that the text wishes to achieve its effects is by stimulating and exciting the reader, and that is indeed what it did. Because the text is intended to seduce the reader to the moral life, it necessarily excites him or her, and the effect that it has willy-nilly is a seduction.[28] The similarity between the pragmatics of reading the Romance and that of the anti-Romance is stronger than the oppositions of their semantics and sufficient, indeed, for the text and its author to be condemned as panderers.

As Noakes argues, Dante's narrative can be understood on the background of the *newly emerged practice of private reading for pleasure* (Noakes 1988:42). This historical shift has been best documented by Paul Saenger (1982), who concludes most relevantly for us, "the habit of private silent reading among laymen seems to have begun at least a half century earlier in Italy than in northern Europe. Dante's *Inferno* and *Paradiso* were intended to be held under the eyes of the lay reader"* (Saenger 1982:410). Thus if one of the intertexts of Canto 5 is assuredly the tale of Héloïse, another is such texts as Guillaume de Saint Thierry's exhortation against silent (and thus, private) reading even of Scripture (Saenger 1982:390). On this view, then, Dante announces here precisely the

*Erich Auerbach, *Literary Language and its Public in Late Latin Antiquity and in the Middle Ages*, trans. R. Manheim (London, 1965) 299–302 [note in Saenger's text].

blurring of the two moments of private reading, the ascetic and the erotic, because of the social practice and space which they share. The moment of this blurring is most clearly marked, I suggest, by "that day we read no farther in it," almost surely an echo of Augustine's "I had no wish to read further" at the climax of his conversion by the book (Confessions viii.12). The cell can be a bedroom, and holy literature read in a *boudoir* can be erotic. Indeed, I would argue that the very ambiguity of the nature of the text that the lovers are reading is a thematization of the perceived moral ambiguity of "reading for pleasure."[29] Dante is aware that this practice is not necessarily conducive to uplifting and moral behavior on the part of its practitioners no matter what they read. It is, after all, Francesca's identification of herself with the heroine that got her into all that trouble, as pointed out by Mazzotta (1979:169). "The new privacy afforded by silent reading had dramatic and not entirely positive effects on lay spirituality. Private reading stimulated a revival of the ancient genre of erotic art" (Saenger 1982:412). Note that this will be the case whatever Paolo and Francesca were reading, for even while the prose *Lancelot* thematically exhorts against the values and practices of Romance, *a fortiori* of erotic literature, as act of communication it works by indirection—seduction. The theory of *dulce et utile* is explicit in medieval poetics, including, of course, Dante's. The pilgrim, Dante, is panicked by the thought that given the reading practices of his time and place the same accusation might be leveled against him, and indeed, he was right, for the bitter, almost Sartrean irony of "as you see, he never leaves my side" has actually often been read by Romantic readers, themselves half in love with Francesca, as love conquering hell! (Dronke 1975:127 and see Hatcher and Musa [1968:107]).[30] This mistake too was, of course, only possible because of the reading practices of our Romantic culture, and indeed of Dante's. Well might the pilgrim faint: If even so pious an author as the Cistercian who composed the prose *Lancelot* can be rightfully accused of being a Galleoto, what will be said of his intentions and his text which will also be read in such a culture?[31] Dante's text, then, can be said to be a historical sign of the rise of reading as a practice in the modern sense in the centuries just before his writing.

A final step in the distancing of reading from public, ritualistic and controlled space to private, ludic, eroticized space is the development of the practice of reading in bed. Two of Chaucer's scenes of reading are very much to the point here. The first is his *The Book of the Duchess,* which both opens and closes with the insomniac protagonist reading in bed and proceeds to a romantic dream (Chaucer 1986) and see Boitani (1982:140–49). The other is, of course, *The Parliament of Fowls,* once again the dream of a reader who after reading in bed falls asleep and proceeds to a dream whose thematics are explicitly concerned with the erotic (Boitani 1982:169–83). Nell documents convincingly how preeminent the bed is as a privileged site for ludic reading even now (Nell 1988:250).[32] Carrying out the sort of ethnographic characterization that I did for the Bible and Talmud suggests that here reading occupies a sociocultural space entirely different from the one that it did in the biblical and rabbinic culture. Rather than being speech-act, public and liturgical in nature, reading is passive, private or semi-private, and belonging to the sphere of leisure and pleasure.

"READING," "HISTORIOGRAPHY," AND "THE BIBLE AS LITERATURE"

This analysis of the pragmatics of reading in Ancient Hebrew may help us get a clearer take on a recent debate in biblical hermeneutics. An important new development in the interpretation of the Bible is the application of literary canons of reading to its prose narrative. Two of the most subtle and skillful of practitioners of this criticism are surely Robert Alter (1981) and Meir Sternberg (1985). Both of them treat the art of biblical prose, showing through myriad examples how we can derive great aesthetic pleasure from an appreciation of such devices of linguistic art as repetition, variation, echoing, irony and the like. The question at hand is, what historically justifies such a practice? Or indeed, is the practice justified? Some have argued, after all, that in truth it is not, because it is in the very nature of the biblical discourse to battle against such "trivialities" as aesthetics and literary art. To be sure, both Alter and Sternberg are sensitive to the theoretical problems which their critical/hermeneutic practice raise. I, for one, am convinced that their reading practice is justified by the profound effect that it has on the richness of our perception of the biblical text.[33] While I find their *practice* telling, however, I find its theoretical grounding in both of their works much less so for reasons that

I will now adduce. That is to say, using a talmudic apothegm: I am in accord with their practice but not their theory. I wish, nonetheless, to suggest that the practice of reading the Bible *as literature* (I use this disdained terminology advisedly—see below.) can be reestablished on another theoretical footing, provided in part by the ethnography of reading approach here adumbrated.

I will begin by setting out the terms of the issue as Alter and Sternberg themselves laid it out. In his comprehensive work on biblical narrative, Alter has defended the thesis that, "prose fiction is the best general rubric for describing biblical narrative" (1981:24). Among the criteria that Alter applied are the signs of intervention on the part of the narrator in the presentation of the story, that is, the conventionality of narrated events and other signs of verbal artistry. In a recent paper Alter (n.d.), has further elaborated and exemplified his thesis. He argues from three "test-cases" (n.d.:5) that, "If virtually every utterance of biblical narrative points toward the imperative concerns of covenant faith, it is also demonstrably evident that virtually every utterance of biblical narrative reveals the presence of writers who relished the words and the materials of storytelling with which they worked, who delighted, because after all they were writers, in pleasing cadences and surprising deflections of syntax, in complex echoing effects among words, in the kind of speech they could fashion for the characters and how the self-same words could be ingeniously transformed as they were passed from narrator to character or from one character to another" (Alter n.d.:9–10). I find Alter's identifications of "pleasing cadences" and all the rest persuasive, but here's also the rub.

Sternberg disagrees strongly with Alter's description of biblical narrative, claiming that it must be understood as historiography. What is relevant in the distinction between historiography and fiction is the truth claims which the text makes as a function of its discourse—certainly not our judgment of those truth claims, nor our judgment of the plausibility of the evaluation of the events which the text presents (Sternberg 1985:33–34). Sternberg argues that the fact that the "narrative . . . illegitimates all thought of fictionality on pain of excommunication," makes it impossible for us to understand it as anything but historiography. It seems to me doubtless as well that Sternberg has also put his finger on something important here. Our understanding of biblical narrative *must* at some level take into account the evidence that many people, including very likely its authors and first audiences did believe in its literal truth. I believe that the "ethnography of reading" approach adumbrated in this paper will give us a way out of the dilemma thus created by showing that the terms of the debate should be recast. Rather than talking about what biblical narrative is or is not, we should be talking about strategies and pragmatics of reading in different cultural moments.

In a recent essay, I have argued against Sternberg's position that biblical narrative is historiography, to the effect that *since biblical narrative does not generally verify its factual claims by referring to evidence, but in fact at nearly every moment presents its data as that of an omniscient narrator,* from the point of view of our own time and our conventions of writing-reading, it belongs to the genre of fiction and not historiography (Boyarin 1990). Indeed Sternberg reads the Bible in essentially the same way that Alter does, providing also illuminating readings of verbal artistry. His critical practice thus shows that the Bible's narrative reads like fiction. (The fact that much historiography is written like fiction does not obscure this argument; when historiography tells what goes on in the mind of a character, we read it as more or less plausible historical fiction.) All of his comparisons to various discursive strategies in texts closer to us in time and place are to fictional texts, and this is not accidental. Sternberg complains against the terminology of reading "the Bible as literature" (or of "literary approach to the Bible"), unless they are taken as shorthand for "reading the Bible as the literary text that it is" (Sternberg 1985:3), but historiography is not the typical case of literary text for our culture. Indeed, when we read Gibbon in a literary way, precisely what we are doing is reading historiography as literature. He suggests that when we read the Bible we must suspend disbelief, but that also is an argument for its fictional status—not historiographical! When we read ancient historiography, we may enjoy its style and wit and be fascinated to learn what people thought about the world once, but we do not ask ourselves to suspend disbelief. Such suspension of disbelief is a practice which belongs in our culture to the reading of fiction, not of historiography. Indeed, the "suspension of disbelief" is one of the prime mechanisms of reading for pleasure. Since the major discursive gesture which Sternberg finds, the omniscient narrator, and its concomitant requirement of the reader that she or he "believe" this narrator, belongs in our literary system exclusively to fiction, I think that Alter is right when he asserts "prose fiction is the best general rubric for describing biblical narrative."

Here I would like to propose that there is a real contradiction or tension in the very practice of literary criticism of the Bible which Sternberg senses and which produces his problematic. As convincing as Alter's readings are, they seem also to be missing something by referring to the texts as fiction. Sternberg is surely right about something here; after all we *don't* excommunicate people for not believing in the literal truth of fiction. Sternberg, in fact provides one argument which I take to be very similar to the one I am promulgating here when he says that the Bible, "internalizes its own rules of communication, whereby the remembrance of the past devolves on the present and determines the future" (Sternberg 1985:31). However, this suggests exactly that my own discourse is prone to very much the same contradictions as his, for I seemingly assert at one and the same time with Alter that the Bible is prose fiction and with Sternberg that fiction (and indeed "literature") is an irrelevant concept for the language *cum* reconstructed culture of the Bible. If reading, as we know it, did not exist in the biblical culture, then certainly neither did literature, *a fortiori* fiction! We seem, then, to be caught in an adamant aporia.

It seems to me that cognitive anthropology will offer us possible avenues of rescue from the horns of this dilemma. In recent years a great deal of very important theoretical and descriptive work has been done in cognitive anthropology. One important area of research in this branch of ethnography has been based traditionally on the study of semantic fields in various languages, with the understanding that they are informative of ways of worldmaking of the respective cultures.[34] Before getting into the substantive argument, I think it is necessary to spend a little time assessing the current status of this method. Holland and Quinn have put the question in the following way:

> It has been colleagues from the more materialist traditions in anthropology, and indeed from some of the ideationalist traditions within the discipline as well, who have been at pains to point out the limitation of a research program for validating cultural models solely on the basis of linguistic behavior. These anthropologists observe that people do not always do what

> would seem to be entailed by the cultural beliefs they enunciate. . . . Do cultural models, they want to know, influence more than talk, and if so how? (Holland and Quinn 1987:5)

For the type of research engaged in here the question is even sharper, since we have virtually no access to the culture other than what people said. Can linguistic behavior teach us anything significant concerning behavior in cultures about which we know very little other than their written and material remains?[35] Do linguistic cultural models reveal anything more than the "talk" of the ancient culture?[36] Recent work suggests that they do, but we must seriously nuance and qualify what precisely it is that they reveal. As Holland and Quinn put it, "culturally shared knowledge is organized into prototypical event sequences enacted in simplified worlds. That much of such cultural knowledge is presumed by language use is as significant a realization to anthropologists as to linguists. For the latter, these cultural models promise the key to linguistic usage; *for the former, linguistic usage provides the best available data for reconstruction of cultural models*" (Holland and Quinn 1987:24 [emphasis added]).

One way out of our aporia of biblical narrative which claims to be historiography but looks like fiction would be to regard this as a particular instance of a familiar ethnographic problem, one that could be defined as the gap between what a culture says about its practice and its observed practice. A classic instance of this in the literature is the "long-standing debate in social anthropology over the reported disparities between Nuer descriptions of their kinship system and Nuer kinship behavior 'on the ground'" (Holland and Quinn 1987:5–6). Now one way of resolving this debate in the literature is that of Holy which Holland and Quinn discuss. He argues for a solution based on Caws's two types of native or folk models, "representational" and "operational." "The former are indigenous models of their world that people can more or less articulate; the latter are indigenous models that guide behavior in given situations and that tend to be out of awareness. Representational models, from this view, are not necessarily operational nor are the latter necessarily representational; thus inconsistencies between what people say and what they do need not be cause for puzzlement" (Holland and Quinn 1987:5–6). Following this reasoning, what we have in the case of biblical narrative is a similar situation where the Bible's representational models (what they say) deny both at levels of semantic organization and of explicit representation the existence of a category like fiction or indeed literary art while their operational models (what they do) certainly presuppose such categories. This is a formalizable way of talking about the distinction between explicit and implicit poetics in literary theory.

I would like to take this distinction a step farther and suggest that we need to historicize the very opposition of fiction and historiography. My claim in brief is that it is from the point of view of *our own* practices of reading that biblical narrative reads as fiction. That does not imply, in any way, that for the biblical culture itself, fiction is a relevant category, nor, for that matter, need we assume that historiography is a relevant category for the biblical narrator. Indeed, I would argue that the whole theoretical debate between Alter and Sternberg is non-essential, precisely because we cannot assume an a-historical organization of cultural productions into the genres familiar from our own. In this way I hope to account for the evident fact that the practices of both critics are virtually identical in principle. Both read the Bible *as* didactic fiction. There are other genres and possible organizations of textual cultures than history ~ fiction. Just to take an obvious example, in many cultures myth makes truth-claims every bit as serious as those of historiography in ours, and indeed, disbeliefs in myths might well lead to excommunication or worse in some cultures, but that certainly does not define them as historiography.[37] On the other hand, while myths are emphatically not fictions, certainly not made-up narratives for the production of pleasure, for us, the practices of reading fiction may be the only ones available for the reading of myths. We must accordingly make a sharp distinction between reading strategies and practices which we adopt vis-à-vis given texts from other cultures and the assumption that the rules and practices of those cultures were the same as ours. The evidence cited above suggests, therefore, that whatever pleasure biblical narrative may produce for us, when we read it for the aesthetic values that we find in it, producing pleasure was the farthest thing from the "minds" of the authors of that narrative.

This point can be honed by examining another claim of Alter's:

> One should add that the very act of writing in one respect makes the writer more craftsman than communicator, for he is directed in the first instance not to his—necessarily, eventual—audience

> but to the medium of words, which has its own intricate allure, and which he works and reworks as a sculptor models his clay, to produce the pleasing curve, the intriguing texture, the satisfying symmetry. (Alter 1989:79)

I dare suspect that Jeremiah would have been horrified at such a description of his practice, however much *we* may find "intriguing texture and satisfying symmetry," in his rhetoric. Communication and not craft was his primary (if not only) aim, and any craft involved was only to serve that aim. An analogy may be helpful here. We in Metropolis read the statuary of Others in accord with the practices of our culture as art. We find genuine aesthetic value in precisely "the pleasing curve, the intriguing texture, the satisfying symmetry" of what was for that Other perhaps a god—sometimes an icon and producer of terror—directed certainly in the first instance to its audience or its function and not at all to the medium or to the beauty that we legitimately, nevertheless, find there. Indeed, it is not uncommon that the very statues that we place in museums were in their original cultural contexts normally hidden entirely from sight! Thus, reading the Bible as fictional art may indeed be the only way appropriate or available for many of us to read it, without requiring us, however, to assign that meaning to it in its original cultural context or contexts.

As Sweetser (1987:49) has shown "fiction" in our culture is part of an intricately structured cultural model, in which such entities as jokes and white lies also have a place. What possible reason is there to assume that the model of this general area of culture in ancient Israel was anything like in ours? To be sure, cognitive anthropologists no longer assume radical discontinuity between human cultures in basics such as emotions, but in the details there certainly are significant differences (Keesing 1987:374, 386). Thus the Rabbis *do* have a category that means something like fiction, that is, they have a term for narratives which are not referentially "true." The term is "parable," that is *mashal.* The concept of true versus false stories was, therefore, part of their socio-mental world. But let us just imagine how different fiction would feel if the only fiction we knew of were *romans à thèse,* "authoritarian fictions," in Susan Rubin Suleiman's phraseology!

Both Alter and Sternberg read biblical narrative appropriately for our cultural context *as if* it were fiction. That is the only way we can read texts (I can hear somebody saying, "What do you mean 'we', white man?") which tell us what went on in the hearts of men, women, and angels and report private conversations with all their psychological nuances. For the Talmud, however, it was precisely these features that "proved" Divine intervention in the authorship. I cannot, therefore, accept Sternberg's claim that the Bible is ". . . not just an artful work; not a work marked by some aesthetic property; not a work resorting to so-called literary devices; not a work that the interpreter may choose (or refuse) to consider from a literary viewpoint or, in that unlovely piece of jargon, as literature; but a literary work" (Sternberg 1985:2). I believe that the semantic/ethnographic analysis performed here supports the view that reading and indeed literature are the historically generated practices of a particular culture, and not the one in which the Bible was produced. Indeed, Alter's "prose fiction is the best general rubric for describing biblical narrative" is valid, if when he says, "for describing" he means, "for us in our culture, given our practice of 'reading', to describe." I suggest then that by engaging in literary reading, that constructed (but not less valuable for that) practice of European culture, that precisely what we are doing is *reading the Bible as literature*.

NOTES

1. Alter emphasizes, of course, that a reader who is psychologically normal never really forgets that he or she is reading a fictional story. To imagine that anyone claims otherwise is to set up a straw man (Alter 1989:50).

2. Thus, for example, while modern critics discover exceedingly "artful" word-play in Jeremiah 36 (a text that I will be analyzing below), there is very little reason to suppose that the author/s of Jeremiah had any aesthetic (that is, ludic) intentions. The paronomasia serves not to delight and thus win over the hearer/reader but only to increase the effectivity of the speech-act, or, at any rate, this is a strong possibility. On the word-play of Jeremiah 36, see now the paper of J. Andrew Dearman (1990). His paper was published too late to be fully integrated into my text, so the reader will find some overlap in the discussion of Jeremiah 36 below.

3. For non-Semitists let me explain that PN is a convention referring to unnamed persons; it stands for "personal name."

4. Dearman also translates Jeremiah 36 "proclaim the words of the scroll" (1990:405).

5. *Sifre Bamidbar* 52.

6. Robert Alter has argued (personal communication) that my "informants" are not clearly a random sample of the culture, as they are all centered around the Deuteronomistic school with its very heavily didactic tendency. He questions whether such documents as J and E would share D's concept of reading. However, since J and E do not seem to ever mention reading at all, it is hard to argue from silence. Moreover, I believe that there is other corroborating evidence for my analysis of reading in the Bible which is not from the Deuteronomists per se. See, for instance the description of a scene of reading in Nehemiah 8, although it could be argued that this late text reflects the devolutionary influence of Deuteronomy, and that argument would have some merit. On the importance of the Deuteronomistic connections of Jeremiah 36, see now Dearman (1990:403–4) and passim and especially (420); and on the Nehemiah passage (409, n. 16). Moreover, we have not only evidence from "informants" but also the report of an ancient "ethnographer," Hecateaus:

> At all of the gatherings of the people, the High Priest explains the commandments of the Torah, and the people listen with such willingness that they immediately fall on their faces and bow to the High Priest who reads and expounds to them.

The caution remains, nevertheless, important. We have, at best, only partial data for any culture that we know only through literary remains, and allowance must be made, as sophisticated, recent critiques of ethnoscience teach us for variation, diachronic development (expressed as synchronic variation), ideological interests and cultural conflict (Keesing 1987:371 and especially 388: "Models are created for the folk as well as by them").

7. There are, to be sure, cases in which the orality of the reading is not explicit. However, even in those cases we find that the act of reading is accompanied by perlocutionary force—that is, it demands an action in response. The following example will make this clear:

> And the King of Aram said, 'Go and I will send a scroll [*sefer,* the same word that refers to a scroll of the Torah, or the Book of the Covenant!] to the King of Israel', and he went and he took with him ten talents of silver and six thousand golden coins and ten suits of clothes. And he brought the scroll to the King of Israel which said, 'And now, with the coming of this scroll to you, I have sent to you Naʿaman my servant. Cure him of his leprosy!' And when the King of Israel *read* the scroll, he rent his clothes, and said 'Am I God that I can kill and revive? For this one has sent to me to cure a man of leprosy, but indeed, he is seeking a cause against me.' (2 Kings 19:5–7).

Since there is no more reason to believe that this king was himself literate any more than the king-protagonists of the texts that I will presently discuss, it is very probable that "when the king had read" means here "when the king had heard the reading of," just as it does explicitly in the next text cited in the body of the paper.

8. That is, *a perlocutionary effect!*

9. In that text, it is Alex Derczansky (Meschonnic 1988:454) who makes this point explicitly, but it is already contained within Meschonnic's remarks. I think it best to read that "round table" as a single dialogical text, a fiction with several voices.

10. Dell Hymes remarks: "Perhaps, in other words, qr' indicates a type of communicative event (a mode of communication, a way of 'speaking,' using 'speaking' figuratively, in the sense of my chapter in R. Bauman and J. Scherzer, *Explorations in the Ethnography of Speaking* (Cambridge, 1974, 1989). A certain configuration, or set of relations, among participants and text and channels" (letter to the author, Spring 1991).

Prof. Hymes's remarks seem right on the mark.

11. For a general literary comparison of the two chapters see Isbell 1978 and see now Dearman (1990:409).

12. See Jonathan Boyarin 1989 for an ethnographic description of such a contemporary conventicle—not, to be sure, an entirely typical one, but then none is.

13. For an illuminating analysis of liturgy as a speech-act, whose perlocutionary force is to convince of the "truth" of the unprovable, see Rappaport 1976.

14. Gerald Bruns is one of the few theorists who has connected the social situation of midrash, that is its dialogical setting, with its hermeneutic practice. He has also clearly talked about how midrashic, "understanding always shows itself as action in the world" (Bruns 1987:629–31). See also David Stern 1988, who has addressed the social setting of midrash importantly.

15. See discussion in Knox (1968:423), however the Horatian text cited in Hendrickson (1929:187) seems to contradict the interpretation that Horace enjoyed silent reading. In any case, he does refer here to reading as a pleasure. Notice that I am decidedly not claiming that "silent reading" was unknown or impossible in the Ancient World. In spite of the celebrated astonishment of Augustine at finding Ambrose reading silently, this might very well reflect just his backwater origins. Moreover, the practice of "reading for pleasure" can be an oral one in which the reader murmurs to himself or herself, and it is possible for readers to read certain kinds of documents silently even when the general practice is for narrative to be read publicly and orally. Knox makes it abundantly clear that reading silently was certainly possible for the Ancients.

16. Private reading was developed especially among the Cistercians. See n. 25 below.

17. *Confessions,* Book 1, chapter 13. I am using the translation of

John K. Ryan (Augustine 1960). There is another moment in this text which Jonathan Boyarin has called to my attention, namely the contrast between reading/writing and memorization with Augustine's valorization of the former over the latter.

18. This is one, then, of a series of binary oppositions which structure the *Confessions,* which are, of course, in that work set out temporally. See now the reading of Jill Robbins (1991) chapter 2. What Augustine figures as perversion and conversion remains a synchronic structure in European culture, just as do Virgil and the Bible.

19. Book 3, chapter 2.

20. There is a serious problem with Nell's book. From this formulation, it would seem that the reading practice that leads to this kind of erotic pleasure is a trained one, that is not a given of being human. This "skill" would seem to be supremely cultural, like the erotic arts of ancient Indian culture for example. However, it is clear from other places in the book that the skill involved is the purely technical one to "rapidly and effortlessly assimilate information from the printed page" (Nell 1988:7). This skill is more analogous to the ability to remove a partner's clothing than anything else. Now, I can testify from personal experience that while I believe that I can rapidly and effortlessly assimilate information from a printed page, I do not share the pleasure of ludic reading, so something else is clearly required. Not being able to partake of that erotic experience in reading fiction, I have a feeling sometimes of inadequacy that would lead me to seek a reading-therapist, who would presumably provide me with a surrogate book. More seriously, the very cultural precariousness of ludic reading as a practice is attested to by many teachers, including, most eloquently Robert Alter:

> Perfectly earnest, reasonably intelligent undergraduates, exposed for the first time to the fantastic proliferation of metaphor in Melville, the exquisite syntactic convolutions of the late Henry James, the sonorously extravagant paradoxes and the arcane terms in Faulkner, are often simply baffled as to why anyone should want to do such strange things with words, and to make life so difficult for a reader. (Alter 1989:78)

Complaints such as this, and they are legion, testify eloquently, sometimes against the manifest intention of their authors, with how much cultural effort is the practice of ludic reading constructed even today.

21. "Further, in both scenes [Augustine and Dido, Paolo and Francesca] the act of reading is disclosed as an erotic experience" (Mazzotta 1979:168).

22. Or "innocent of suspicion" (Musa).

23. For Dante's positive remarks on the Romances, see *Purgatorio* 26:118–19 and *De Vulgari Eloquentia* 1, 10:2. Professor Boitani supplied these references.

24. Against the argument that the pilgrim's reaction here is occasioned by his "falling in love" with Francesca is the fact that his pity is explicitly engendered by both of the figures and in particular by Paolo's weeping.

25. This is a particularly interesting datum in light of the fact that the Cistercians particularly emphasized pious reading as a monastic practice, as pointed out in a recent lecture by Brian Stock.

26. Or "for our delight" (Dronke 1975:127); the Italian has *per diletto*.

27. Since writing this, I have become aware that my reading is anticipated in large part by Mazzotta (1979:166ff.).

28. Much has been written on the narrative text as seducer. Most recently, several articles in Hunter 1989 deal with this theme.

29. Note that this reading also disempowers an easy division of reading by genre, for example, into fiction and nonfiction.

30. Indeed, Dronke himself, while he does not share, of course, the ideology of the Romantic readers, proposes, nevertheless, a version of this reading (127, n. 29). Ironically, my reading implicitly answers Dronke's question that, "Did it ever occur to Dante, I wonder, that for some later readers Francesca's words might become as inflammatory as the tale of Lancelot and Guinivere had been for her and Paolo" (Dronke 1975:116–7)? My reading suggests that Dante thematizes an answer to this very question. Dronke does suggest that Dante saw an analogy between the prose *Lancelot* and his *Vita Nuova* (127).

31. This is a culture, after all, which has finally produced a text like the recent film, *La Lectrice,* in which a young and attractive woman hires herself out to read *belles lettres* to people in intimate surroundings with predictable results.

32. See also his comment on a nineteenth century homology between the "degenerative physiological" effects of habitual masturbation and those of prolonged reading (Nell 1988:29–30).

33. This is not to claim, of course, that I agree with all they say, either on the theoretical level or on the level of "practical criticism." See Boyarin 1990.

34. Immediately below I will discuss recent thinking on this subject. We no longer think that we have access to the true world picture of other cultures through semantics, however something remains valid nevertheless. At any rate, the semantic division of the world *is itself practice and worthy of analysis and "thick description."* For a definitive statement of an early and positivistic stage of this type of research, see the collection of Stephen Tyler (1969).

35. The alerts of Keesing (1987:387) against relying on inadequate field knowledge of languages are even more to the point here, but what else can we do?

36. "Early efforts sought to describe the semantic structure of lexical domains. If analysts could recover or reconstruct what one needed to know in order to label pieces and portions of the world correctly in the native's own language, it was reasoned, then the resulting model would capture an important part of those people's culturally constructed reality" (Holland and Quinn 1987:14). But "The semantic structures recovered in these earliest analyses did provide insight into the organization of some domains of the lexicon. However, the organization of lexicon was soon recognized to offer only limited insight into the organization of cultural knowledge." (Holland and Quinn 1987:14).

37. Dell Hymes remarks in a letter of October 5, 1990:

> I think it would be true to say that many American Indians heard performances of myths, and thought about them in between performances as both enacting a message and as pleasurable. In some groups some kinds of stories would be framed as not true, not necessarily true. Among the Nootka of British Columbia for example, what we typically call 'myths' can be referred to in English as 'fairy stories.' They express truths about the world but whether they happened or not is not essential. What *are* true, and history, are the accounts (equally mythological in important part to us) of how the privileges of a lineage were acquired by an ancestor. Those are known to be true because they have been recited, exactly, from one generation to another.

The very fact that Professor Hymes refers to different practices of reception of "myths" among different groups only proves my main point that genre is a set of culturally specific practices; however, I would continue to dissent from his characterization of the lineage accounts as history. Just as in the biblical case, the belief in the referentiality of the narrative does not constitute it as historiography, given my argument that historiography is a particular discursive practice developed in European culture for particular sociocultural functions. Even the very appeal to memory or oral tradition as authority and not documents is a fundamentally different practice, as is also the pointing out of a pillar of salt to validate the story of Lot's wife.

Because I fear that I may still be misunderstood here, I want to make it absolutely clear that my purpose is not to privilege "Western" culture and its signifying practices over those of "others." Quite the opposite, my point is to disrupt that privilege, making it clear that what others do with stories of their pasts is not failed (or even successful) historiography but a different practice of story-telling of the past. An example may make my point clearer. I recently attended the lectures of a colleague on Ancient History. In a review session, he asked the students what the beginning date of the course's purview was and the correct answer was 2500 B.C., because that is when the first *contemporaneous document attesting to a state occurs*. We have buildings and other material remains from people much earlier, of course, than 2500 B.C., but what we say about them is not historiography. We can easily see how culture-bound the practice of historiography is, and we do others no favor by seeing their practices as something like ours—but not quite. Once more, none of this has anything to do with the referential truth or falsity (historicity!) of events represented in any practice of telling the past. Non-historiographical practices of communal memory may often be more "true" than the reconstructions of historians.

REFERENCES

Abelard, Peter. 1974. Historia calamitum. In *The Letters of Abelard and Heloise*. Ed. and trans. Betty Radice. Pp. 57–108. The Penguin Classics. Harmondsworth: Penguin.

Alter, Robert. 1981. *The Art of Biblical Narrative*. New York: Basic.

———. 1989. *The Pleasures of Reading in an Ideological Age*. New York: Simon and Schuster, Touchstone.

———. n.d. Biblical Imperatives and Literary Play.

Aristotle. 1982. *Poetics*. Trans. James Hutton. New York: W. W. Norton.

Augustine. 1960. *The Confessions of St. Augustine*. Trans. and ed. John K. Ryan. New York: Doubleday, Image.

Boitani, Piero. 1982. *English Medieval Narrative in the 13th and 14th Centuries*. Trans. Joan Krakover Hall. Cambridge, England: Cambridge University Press.

Boyarin, Daniel. 1990. The Politics of Biblical Narratology: Reading the Bible Like/as a Woman. *diacritics* 20 (Winter):31–42.

Boyarin, Jonathan. 1989. "Voices Around the Text," *Cultural Anthropology* 4, 399–421.

Brown, Peter. 1969. *Augustine of Hippo: A Biography*. Berkeley: University of California Press.

Bruns, Gerald. 1987. Midrash and Allegory. In *The Literary Guide to the Bible*. Robert Alter and Frank Kermode, eds. Pp. 625–46. Cambridge, MA: Harvard University Press.

Chaucer, Geoffrey. 1986. *The Book of the Duchess*. Helen Phillips ed. Durham: Durham and St. Andrews Medieval Texts.

Dante Alighieri. 1984. *The Divine Comedy*. Vol. 1: *The Inferno*. Trans. Mark Musa. Harmondsworth: Penguin.

Dearman, J. Andrew. 1990. My Servants the Scribes: Composition and Context in Jeremiah 36. *Journal of Biblical Literature* 109 (Fall):403–21.

Dronke, Peter. 1975. Francesca and Héloïse. *Comparative Literature* 27 (Spring):113–35.

Fisch, Harold. 1988. *Poetry with a Purpose.* Indiana Studies in Biblical Literature. Bloomington: Indiana University Press.

Hatcher, Anna, and Mark Musa. 1968. The Kiss: *Inferno* V and the Old French Prose *Lancelot. Comparative Literature* 20:97–109.

Hendrickson, G. L. 1929. Ancient Reading. *The Classical Journal* 25:182–96.

Holland, Dorothy, and Naomi Quinn. 1987. Culture and Cognition; Introduction. In *Cultural Models in Language and Thought.* Dorothy Holland and Naomi Quinn, eds. Pp. 3–43. Cambridge, England: Cambridge University Press.

Hunter, Dianne. 1989. *Seduction and Theory: Readings of Gender, Representation, and Rhetoric.* Urbana, IL : University of Illinois Press.

Isbell, Charles D. 1978. II Kings 22:3–23:4 and Jer. 36: A Stylistic Comparison. *Journal for the Study of the Old Testament* 8:33–45.

Keesing, Roger M. 1987. Models, 'folk' and Cultural: Paradigms Regained. In *Cultural Models in Language and Thought.* Dorothy Holland and Naomi Quinn, eds. Pp. 369–93. Cambridge, England: Cambridge University Press.

Knox, Bernard M. W. 1968. Silent Reading in Antiquity. *Greek, Roman and Byzantine Studies* 9:421–35.

Mazzotta, Giuseppe. 1979. *Dante: Poet of the Desert: History and Allegory in the Divine Comedy.* Princeton: Princeton University Press.

Meschonnic, Henri. 1988. Poetics and Politics: A Round Table. With Alex Derczansky, Olivier Mongin, and Paul Thibaud. *New Literary History* 19 (Spring):453–67.

Nell, Victor. 1988. *Lost in a Book: The Psychology of Reading for Pleasure.* New Haven: Yale University Press.

Noakes, Susan. 1988. *Timely Reading: Between Exegesis and Interpretation.* Ithaca, NY: Cornell University Press.

Poe, Elizabeth Wilson. 1984. *From Poetry to Prose in Old Provençal: The Emergence of the Vidas, the Razos, and the Razos de Trobar.* Birmingham, AL: Summa Publications.

Rappaport, Roy A. 1976. Liturgies and Lies. *International Yearbook for Sociology of Knowledge and Religion* 10:75–104.

Robbins, Jill. 1991. *Prodigal Son/Elder Brother: Interpretation and Alterity in Augustine, Petrarch, Kafka and Levinas.* Chicago: Chicago University Press.

Saenger, Paul. 1982. Silent Reading: Its Impact on Late Medieval Script and Society. *Viator* 13:367–414.

Schutz, Alexander. 1939. Were the *Vidas and Razos* Recited? *Studies in Philology* 36:565–70.

Stern, David. 1988. "Midrash and Indeterminacy," *Critical Inquiry* 15, 1:132–162.

Sternberg, Meir. 1985. *The Poetics of Biblical Narrative: Ideological Literature and the Drama of Reading*. Indiana Studies in Biblical Literature. Bloomington: Indiana University Press.

Sweetser, Eve. 1987. "The Definition of *lie*: an Examination of Folk-Models Underlying a Semantic Prototype." In Holland and Quinn, eds.

Tyler, Stephen A. 1969. *Cognitive Anthropology*. New York: Holt Rinehart & Winston.

CHAPTER 9

Binding and Unbinding: The Summons to Interpretation in The Merchant of Venice

Elizabeth Freund

The postulate that *The Merchant of Venice* both dramatizes and thematizes a sequence of interpretive predicaments hardly requires urging. Starting with the enigma of Antonio's sadness (a question which generates a good deal of interesting surmise but no conclusive answer), the economy of the play's fable—that which the classical rhetoricians called *dispositio*—hinges throughout on the staging of a series of scenes of interpretation whose enactment drives the play to its teleological conclusion. Three such central scenes organize the main action: in Belmont, in order to win the lady richly-left, Bassanio must choose by interpreting the riddle of the strange lottery bequeathed by Portia's father; in Venice, with Antonio's life at stake, the court must interpret the terms of the

All quotations from *The Merchant of Venice* are taken from the Signet Edition, ed. Kenneth Myrick, New York: New American Library, 1965.

An earlier and shorter version of this paper was presented at a conference on "The Covenant in Law and Literature," held at Bar-Ilan University, Israel, in November 1989; in February 1991 a longer and revised version was presented to audiences at the University of California, Berkeley, and Irvine; and at Yale University in October 1991. I am grateful to these audiences for their hospitable receptions and for useful discussion. I would also like to express my special gratitude to Geoffrey Hartman and Alexander Gelley for their stimulating suggestions and responses.

contract between the Christian merchant and the Jewish moneylender. Two binding contracts, "the will of a dead father" and a "merry" bond, on whose interpretations human bodies and destinies depend, generate yet further contracts and bonds, and more summons to interpretation. The play's concluding scene, set in a Belmont significantly marked by repeated intrusions of Venice, constitutes the canonical comic scene of recognition and resolution, enacted in the losing and finding of the rings. In accordance with the normative generic and thematic economy I have sketched here, this traditional comedic resolution takes the form of a reinterpretation or clarification of the binding force of conjugal vows.

My present concern, however, is not with the economy of plot but with an economy of interpretation and response, at once thematized and solicited by the plot of *The Merchant of Venice*. In foregrounding the word "economy" my purpose is to relocate the attenuated formalism of a rhetorical term within a field of *affect*—a circulation of responses and feelings within the text and between the text and its readers—without losing the word's root meanings (from the Greek oikos = house; nomos = law) pertaining to household arrangements, modes of production, distribution, and consumption. Such modes explicitly inform the broader social institutions of human exchange represented in this play (the Home: both Belmont and the Jew's household in Venice; the Law: the dramatization of distributive and retributive justice in one of drama's most compelling court scenes; Wedlock: the exchange of rings, property, sexuality) and have received extensive attention from critics of all persuasions.[1] Less notice, however, has been given to another central human institution also copiously represented in this play: the mode of conversation or dialogue we call interpretation. It is to the exchange and circulation of words or texts and their frequently slippery or unruly behaviour that I shall address myself in this essay. But before I do so, I should like to reflect a little further on the questions of economy, exchange, and circulation.

These terms are associated today with the critical agenda that goes by the name of neo-historicism, or cultural poetics.[2] The impulse to revise our perceptions of the past seeks to perform a "restitutive criticism" (Hartman)[3] which painstakingly recites (also sites/sights—the multiple pun is a propos) the previously overlooked or suppressed events, voices, objects of history. This task of retrieving, reconstructing, and rehabilitating a previously silenced or marginalized experience provides the reader/critic at once with a respectable social agenda, a greatly increased inventory to contemplate, and a set of new ways to contemplate it. The project also effectively (if not always intentionally) stages what Alexander Gelley, in a commentary on Walter Benjamin's "Arcades Project," has called the "dynamic intervention into the temporal process that activates a past in the present: citing as an *in*citing. The citation, strategically chosen and implanted, has the effect of an iconic intrusion within a discursive fabric."[4] The text is still there but it is now telling a different story.

Benjamin described his fantasy of exhibiting a compilation of citations thus:

> Method of this work: literary montage. I have nothing to say. Only to show. I will steal nothing of value and appropriate no witty formulation. But the rags, the rubbish: these I want, not to inventory, but to let them come into their own in the only possible manner: by putting them to use.

The theatricality of "only to show" accords well with the shrewd usage of anecdote or marginalia (the startling fragments of "rags," or the revealing remnants of "rubbish" which are the traces of everyday life) in much neo-historicist writing on the Renaissance. Not so the strange reticence of "I have nothing to say." The act of exhibiting these graffiti of the past, letting them "come into their own," in itself constitutes a "putting to use," a "usance" (to borrow a central trope from *The Merchant*) which, by disrupting our received narratives of the past, is bound to generate something else—different and other. Regardless of whether we interpret this difference, or allow it to interpret us, reading and interpretation are still at stake.

We all know that formalism in literary theory has been discarded, and there are few mourners at the demise. But in practice the work of literary interpretation always remains to be done and redone, often, though not exclusively, by formal methods. For all its interesting by-products, we are still anxious lest close reading continue to be literary criticism's starting point and sole destination. That is why so many of us would like to know what, if anything, is to be learned, or what mastered, "what interest made good," in the pursuit of close critical readings of the literary text.

One answer which continues to appeal to me, but often threatens to leave me too close to formalism, is the ever-renewed privileging of the question itself; the vigilant and thoughtful putting into question of essentialist propositions about "aboutness" or meaning. Thus, having pronounced in my primmest pedagogical voice that *The Merchant of Venice* is *about* interpretation and its consequences, I feel compelled to scrutinize and theorize my pronouncement metacritically. One direction in which I might proceed would be to assume apodictically that any such proposition of aboutness can and should be questioned, since it will no doubt run the familiar risks of an interpretive impasse, leading perhaps all too tediously to a derridean gesture of suspended judgement: "on the one hand . . . but then on the other . . ."[5] It is neither a gesture I wish to forego, nor one which I care to linger on indefinitely, but rather to incorporate into the nexus of my reflections.

Add to that the further twist that, for obvious historical, cultural and political as well as personal reasons, reading against the grain of the text and/or of history (and these are not cognate readings) a play as ambivalent, as haunted by nemesis as the text of *The Merchant of Venice* has become, will highlight not only the grain of the reader's biases, but lead her into strange loops and contortions of reading against reading against the grain . . . Simply put: no amount of either old or new historicizing, or deconstructing, will liberate us from the text's (no longer entertainable) invitation to hate Shylock and love Portia; or from our post-holocaust sensibilities; or from the imperative of attentive reading. Under these circumstances—and to raise the question of the reader's response even more bluntly—what critical poise or stance, what economy of response, what gesture of "showing" can the literary critic (and *a fortiori* the Jewish literary critic) summon in order to cite once again the anti-semitic, jew-baiting and yet compelling Shakespearean representation?

I should like to focus on the dominant rhetorical gesture informing the enactments of interpretation in *The Merchant of Venice,* namely, the citation of text. Citation occurs in a remarkable variety of forms in this play. With no pretensions to the rigor of a taxonomy, I shall list three heuristic categories mainly for the convenience of indicating the diversity and scope of this intra- and intertextual language game.

The first category consists of the embedded quotation which repeats verbatim the precise words of an antecedent text: for instance, Portia's wooers repeating the inscriptions upon which they proceed to exercise their interpretive skills—"Who chooseth me must give and hazard all he hath" (2.7.9)—or, in another instance, Shylock quoting from the text of the bond: "So says the bond, doth it not, noble judge? / 'nearest his heart'; those are the very words" (4.1.252–53); or the obverse of this strategy, when Portia quotes in order to identify a precise blank or omission in the text: "This bond doth give thee here no jot of blood; / The words expressly are 'a pound of flesh'" (305–06)—the precise omission upon which she constructs her legal triumph.

The second category consists of an approximation or paraphrase of a specific antecedent text, related either intertextually, as in Shylock's retelling of the story in the book of *Genesis* ("Mark what Jacob did . . ." [1.3.74]), or intra-textually as when Nerissa reminds Gratiano without necessarily quoting the exact words of his oath that "You swore to me when I did give it you / That you would wear it till your hour of death" (5.1.152–53).

The third category goes beyond the intra-textual and runs the risk of collapsing the notion of citation into the totality of linguistic or rhetorical behavior. It would include the text's sources or analogues (for instance, Giovanni Fiorentino's *Il Pecorone* or Marlowe's *Jew of Malta,* or the book of *Genesis*), and even Shakespeare's reliance on a certain generic convention (romantic comedy, five-act structure), as well as any reference to an imaginary "encyclopedia" of proverbial wisdom—the anonymous cultural text made up of allusions, adages, gnomic sayings, maxims and apothegms which circulate as communal cliches, topoi, commonplaces. The *Merchant of Venice* seems to be particularly rich in this mode of citation. Wisdom literature seems to be at the fingertips of all in Venice, and the dialogue is studded with proverbs[6] (what the rhetoricians called *paroemia*): "Fast bind, fast find, / A proverb never stale in thrifty mind" (2.6.53–54), or "All that glisters is not gold; Often have you heard that told" (2.7.65–66). Thus, the scroll—presumably composed by Portia's father—which poor Morocco pulls out of the golden casket and has to suffer the indignity of reading aloud, is an example both of the category of proverbs as well as an instance of word-for-word citation or repetition of the text of Portia's father, itself a citation. (This is not the place to comment on the sagacity, poetical gifts and rhetorical originality, or perhaps tongue-in-cheekiness, of that ghostly patriarch. Note, however, that even Launcelot can do better with the hoary proverb, itself a citation from Corinthians: "He that hath the grace of God hath enough." By "parting" it he wittily comes up with something new: "The old proverb is very well parted between my master Shylock and you sir" he says to Bassanio; "You have the grace of God, sir, and he hath enough" [2.2.148–50].)

What interests me about the rhetoric of citation is the way in which two prominent and seemingly essential features of this rhetorical gesture stand in an antithetical and even agonistic relation to each other. On the one hand, citation invokes a Logos, the authority of a prior text or, more precisely, the authority of an (absent) but binding original voice or intention underwriting the text cited. This is the case whether Shylock cites Scripture, or the words of his bond (or Portia its blanks), or the wooers cite the proverbial "truths" (which then become legally binding) cited by Portia's father. On the other hand, even though citation constitutes an act of deference to the authority of the original text, it is inescapably transformed into a speech act—which is to say, a performance—of parting or unbinding from the origin, an act of dislocation and appropriation and, as such, an act of interpretive intervention whose effect is to recycle and defer the antecedent, and to produce a fresh redistribution within the existing economy of interpretations. The dual or (very possibly) duplicitous character of the act of citation[7] stems from the obvious condition that repetition can never be itself; in its most precise reflection or reproduction of the original, there is always an increment of difference and self-difference. Another way of putting this is to say, as Stanley Fish says, following Derrida, following Austin, that words are always unbound, but that unbound words are never not bound by a frame or context. There is always a context.[8] It is no accident that my own rhetoric also reproduces the point I am trying to make: citation, in this case of Fish or Derrida or Austin, is at once an appeal to their authority and an appropriation, a dislocation of the original (con)text, which is also an intervention or a rebinding with new contexts.

This particular language game of citation also raises the question of interpretive reflection, in both senses of the word: the sense in which interpreters meditate upon and unfold or explicate the textual meaning, as well as the self-reflexive sense spotlighted by the specularity of deconstructive readings, or the sense in which interpreters ponder the enigma of textuality or rhetoricity and trace the intricacy with which texts resist unfolding, folding back into themselves in structures of infinite regress. Interpretive reflection thus seems to have the same duplicitous or antithetical structure as citation. The root meaning of citation, as I have argued elsewhere, is a summons or an arousal to respond. "Interpretation has traditionally responded to the summons by reflecting upon the strangeness of texts or citations in order to reproduce as faithful an image as possible of the object of reflection. But the implication of disinterested thoughtfulness is already disqualified if an act of reflection is always *en abîme*. The French locution has become a loose name for the production of an effect of infinite regress spiralling towards a vanishing point—call it logos or stable meaning—which is always beyond reach or stabilization.

But if that is the case, why bother with a task—the task of interpreting—which seems able to achieve little more than a "show" of ascetic reflection of/upon the conditions of its impossibility? What *more* does/can the deconstructing interpreter desire? To rephrase the question in terms of the trope of usury: Is there a hermeneutic thrift at play, a parsimony of response (cf. Benjamin: "I have nothing to say"), whose obverse side is a hermeneutic hunger or greed for the "excess," or "advantage" or "usance," a desire to "make interest good?" I shall leave this question (which has metamorphosed into a hypothesis) about the desires of interpreters hanging unanswered over the remainder of this text, while I return to Shakespeare's.

Act 1 scene 3 of *The Merchant of Venice* dramatizes a formidable conflict of words and interpretations between Shylock and Antonio over the issue of usury. This is the keystone scene of exposition in which Antonio, Bassanio, and Shylock negotiate the loan of three thousand ducats to finance Bassanio's courtship. I propose to read closely the section in which Shylock cites the Biblical story of Jacob's covenant with Laban (a recital which turns into a discussion of the moral and legal status of certain business transactions), in order to explore the unfolding representation of a relationship between rhetorical and ideological interpretations performed by the dialogue.

> SHYLOCK: Ay, ay, three thousand ducats.
> ANTONIO: And for three months.
> SHYLOCK: I had forgot—three months, you told me so.
> Well then, your bond. And let me see—but hear you:
> Methoughts you said you neither lend nor borrow
> Upon advantage.
> ANTONIO: I do never use it.
> SHYLOCK: When Jacob grazed his uncle Laban's sheep—
> This Jacob from our holy Abram was,
> As his wise mother wrought in his behalf,
> The third possessor; ay, he was the third—
> ANTONIO: And what of him? Did he take interest?
> SHYLOCK: No, not take interest—not as you would say
> Directly int'rest. Mark what Jacob did:
> When Laban and himself were compremised
> That all the eanlings which were streaked and pied
> Should fall as Jacob's hire, the ewes being rank
> In end of autumn turned to the rams;
> And when the work of generation was
> Between these woolly breeders in the act,
> The skilful shepherd pilled me certain wands,
> And in the doing of the deed of kind
> He stuck them up before the fulsome ewes,
> Who then conceiving, did in eaning time
> Fall parti-coloured lambs, and those were Jacob's.
> This was a way to thrive, and he was blest;
> And thrift is blessing if men steal it not.
> ANTONIO: This was a venture, sir, that Jacob served for,
> A thing not in his power to bring to pass,
> But swayed and fashioned by the hand of heaven.
> Was this inserted to make interest good?
> Or is your gold and silver ewes and rams?
> SHYLOCK: I cannot tell, I make it breed as fast.
> But note me, signor—
> ANTONIO: Mark you this, Bassanio,
> The devil can cite Scripture for his purpose.
> An evil soul producing holy witness
> Is like a villain with a smiling cheek,
> A goodly apple rotten at the heart.

O what a goodly outside falsehood hath!
SHYLOCK: Three thousand ducats—'tis a good round sum.
Three months from twelve—then let me see, the rate—(1.3.63–101)

I begin my reading of the passage from the end mainly because Antonio's position represents the normative Venetian interpretation (cf. 3.2.73ff.) against which Shylock's counter-interpretation articulates itself.

Mark you this, Bassanio,
The devil can cite Scripture for his purpose.
An evil soul producing holy witness
Is like a villain with a smiling cheek,
A goodly apple rotten at the heart.
O what a goodly outside falsehood hath!

What can we learn about interpretation from Antonio? His response to Shylock's citation of a puzzling Biblical narrative takes a good deal of exegetical authority for granted: not only does he assume the equation of Jew and Devil shared by other Christians in the play, but also, and by extension, he assumes a direct knowledge of "his [Shylock's] purpose." Antonio's presupposition is that the use of citation in the act of interpreting is extremely powerful—"holy witness" assumes both sacred and legal authority—but it is also extremely treacherous because everything depends on the moral probity of the interpreter. Indeed, the horror of Shylock's citational distortions, as Antonio sees it, lies in the fact that the diabolical character of the citer is in reverse ratio to the holiness of his citation.[10]

But on what grounds does Antonio reach this conclusion? How does he *know* the Jew is a devil? At least rhetorically speaking (but of course never just) he knows in the way in which all of us possess certain kinds of so-called "knowledge": on grounds of the authority of common knowledge, wisdom of the it-goes-without-saying variety. Every fool in Venice knows Jews are devils, the word made flesh. "Certainly the Jew is the very devil incarnation" (2.2.26–27), Launcelot points out. These self-evident grounds are then rhetorically embellished by Antonio with a simile or analogy ("an evil soul is like a villain . . .") which is no more than a simple tautology. The villain's duplicity is reaffirmed by a metaphorical commonplace ("a goodly apple rotten at the heart"—Shakespeare's texts abound in similar tropes), both figures leading to the conclusive and confident assertion of a universal and indisputable truism about the deceitful relationship of manifest to latent, outside to inside, appearance to reality ("O what a goodly outside falsehood hath!"). Antonio's commentary upon Shylock's citation of a biblical text cites the topoi or axioms circulating as sound moral sense in the sociolect of his interpretive community. His interpretive procedures are as bound and constrained by a cultural codex and its written and unwritten rhetorical sententiae as he will later be himself bound by the words of the aberrant "merry" bond.[11]

Let me tentatively characterize this rhetoric of assent to cultural dominance as a conservative economy of interpretation, conserving, by repeated affirmation, an existing and powerful consensus regarding a mode of discourse, or a set of values and beliefs, a cultural identity. What is remarkable is that this economy is curiously at odds with the venturesome and prodigal spirit of gentile Venetian merchants.

Shylock's citation of Scripture suggests a rather different rhetorical economy or system of interpretation. Observe first how the biblical citation is staged and framed so as to deliberately obscure Shylock's "purpose." His attention seems to wander (but perhaps he is faking) from the immediate business of negotiating the terms of the loan as he muses his way into a digression.

> S: Ay, ay, three thousand ducats.
> A: And for three months.
> S: I had forgot—three months, you told me so.
> Well then, your bond. And let me see—but hear you,
> Methoughts you said you neither lend nor borrow
> Upon advantage.
> A: I do never use it.

Framed thus, the recital of the Jacob story seems to come as a commentary on Shylock's hidden thought. And although this hidden thought remains concealed to the end, it is evidently related to the question of "use" and the alternative modes of making a profit which divide Christian from Jew in the world of Venice.

Observe also how Shylock strangely interrupts the beginning of his tale in order to "overname" the dynasty of Patriarchs (just as Portia, in the preceding scene [1.2.35], asks Nerissa to overname the suitors so that she can mock them). Shylock's intention appears to be a desire to emphasize the exalted historical and cultural status of "the third possessor."

> S: When Jacob grazed his uncle Laban's sheep—
> This Jacob from our holy Abram was,
> As his wise mother wrought in his behalf,
> The third possessor; ay, he was the third—

But this proves to be a puzzling deviation on many grounds. Shylock's elision of Isaac's name, and the displacement of the second possessor in the patriarchal line, by his wife Rebecca (also unnamed by Shylock), the "wise mother" who engineered possession of the blessing on Jacob's behalf, is only one intriguing wrinkle in the citational process. Rebecca enters the representation both forcefully and obliquely, raising a host of questions. Is Shylock's parenthetical reference to the mother an affirmation or obstruction (even a mockery) of the transcendental Logos or the Law of the Fathers? Does it come to privilege the wisdom of female trickery and deception in the distribution of blessings (an issue not irrelevant to the representation of women in this play)? In the allusive and elliptical citation of originary material, how much of the diversity of a past are we supposed to remember and use, or exclude and forget? For that matter, how transparent or singular is the origin itself with which the citation interacts?

In the biblical narrative, Rebecca dresses her favorite son, Jacob, in the skins of animals to conceal his identity lest Jacob "bring a curse upon [himself] and not a blessing" (Gen. 27:12). The second possessor of the blessing, the patriarch Isaac, because he is now old and his eyes dim, is duped into conferring the blessing upon the disguised Jacob, "the smooth man," instead of the "hairy" first-born twin Esau. Yet we must not jump to the conclusion that the dimness of his eyes is a trope for the dimness of his wits. He may well be a conscious accomplice who, like the blind Gloucester in *King Lear,* sees "feelingly" and recognizes perfectly well that "the voice is Jacob's, but the hands are the hands of Esau," choosing, however, not to acknowledge or undo this contradiction. We are not told whether he is guided by some alternative "knowledge" or intuition. The modality of a blessing's itinerary is as moot in the original text as it is in the citation. The narrator shows, but says nothing.

Shakespeare also *shows*, sometimes in the tricky mode of comic subplots and mirrors. In the representation of Launcelot's clownish psychomachia in 2.2., the younger Gobbo determines to "try confusions" (1.37) with his sandblind father to extort a blessing. With the fool's hermeticism he remarks that "it is a wise father that knows his own child" (2.2.76–7), before he kneels with his back to his father (to impersonate a hairy face) and asks for blessing. The unnamed Isaac is a ghostly tragi-comic presence in this text, returning, in another piece of unruly allusion, as an analogue for Antonio in the trial scene, with its undertones of *akedah*—the binding of the innocent victim.

But to return to the instance before us: it is the ambivalent Jacob, wrestling for blessing, who provides a key analogue to Shylock.[12] The biblical Jacob comes into the world on the heels of his twin brother, wrestling for priority, and thrice in the course of his biography is portrayed as wrestling for blessing: with his brother Esau over the birthright, with his uncle Laban for hire, and then with the mysterious man/angel at Penuel, for a name. The ewe/lewe/-ish female gender is central in the confrontation of male opposites, both in the scriptural account of fathers and sons (and sons-in-law) and in Shakespeare's representation of male antagonists. Both Jacob and Shylock wed a Leah, but Shylock's pained reference to *his* Leah, when he discovers the loss of a ring she gave him when he was a bachelor, and which he would not have given for a wilderness of monkeys, adds an asymmetrical twist to the motif of thrift and theft. It was Jacob's first love, Rachel, who—like Jessica—stole the household idols when she and Jacob and the rest of their family fled from her father's home. (In the longer run, of course, Shylock's quest for blessing—birthright, name, and generation—unlike Jacob's, is bitterly frustrated: his "sacred nation" is abominated, his "thrift" stolen, the proper name of "the Jew" rarely spoken, and his heirs will be the Christian children of Lorenzo. But that lies beyond my concern here.)

As for the rhetorical value of "evocalizing"[13] the first Patriarch, Abram, by his earlier name instead of the more usual Abraham, would it be too arcane to speculate upon the embedded "ram" component, and the advantages of sonically anticipating the acts of propagation and generation between "ewes" and "rams" from which thrift and blessing originate? Again, it is not at all clear where such speculations might lead. The excess of allusions and possible meanings resists assimilation into a single and consecutive, or coherent narrative mold.

Not surprisingly, therefore, we find Antonio impatient with these perambulations into the generations of patriarchs, and with the powerful and illicit energies of "verbal usury" (Shell)[14] which they release. He hurries to preempt and foreclose what he takes to be Shylock's meaning in the juxtaposition of shepherd and moneylender: "And what of him, did he take interest?" But Shylock will not be rushed; he denies and doesn't deny this interpretive feint—"No, not take interest—not as you would say / Directly int'rest" (indeed, Shylock generally prefers to avoid the word "interest"). "Mark what Jacob did"—and launches into his story:

> When Laban and himself were compremised
> That all the eanlings which were streaked and pied
> Should fall as Jacob's hire, the ewes being rank
> In the end of autumn turned to the rams;
> And when the work of generation was
> Between these woolly breeders in the act,
> the skillful shepherd pilled me certain wands,
> And in the doing of the deed of kind
> He stuck them up before the fulsome ewes,
> Who then conceiving, did in eaning time
> Fall parti-coloured lambs, and those were Jacob's.
> This was a way to thrive, and he was blest;
> And thrift is blessing if men steal it not.

What triggers the recital of this bizarre narrative of Jacob's bargain with Laban and the occult event of genetic engineering, and what is the recital supposed to illustrate or prove? What is its rhetorical and hermeneutic point? The Biblical narrative, the original itself, is enigmatic enough to invite any number of scholarly, midrashic, or literary interpretations, as well as to resist them.[15] Recycled by Shylock, the narrative becomes even more enigmatic.

What is remarkable, rhetorically speaking, is its deployment as a sort of exemplum—which is, of course, another rhetorical figure of citation—but what is this exemplum an exemplum of? There is no clearly visible or announced text or sermon or proposition to be glossed by it, so that citation here performs the role of commentary on an absent text. All we are left with is surmise about this absence. Is use or "interest" indeed the missing topos, as Antonio conjectures? Is Shylock using biblical authority to defend usury?

He denies this, but then modifies his denial. The matter is complicated by the text's tonality: what does Shylock really think of Jacob? Is his citation a chuckling endorsement of the slyness of this trickster patriarch (Jacob "the heel," as Hartman characterizes him in a fit of midrashic wordplay[16]) or a mockery? Why is Jacob "blest"? "*This* was a way to thrive," says Shylock, but fails to specify an alternative—as opposed to what other way of thriving and achieving "blessing" is *this* way (Jacob's)? Shylock's or the merchant's?

To complicate matters further, the authority of scripture rather disconcertingly gives two rival narratives or constructions of the same event. It is "originally" a twice-told tale, first told in the more familiar J(ahwist) version in chapter 30 of the book of *Genesis* as a third-person narrative, and then repeated, but in a very different narrative mode, in the E(lohist) account in chapter 31, this time as a first-person narration.[17] In this second telling, Jacob has summoned his wives to a family counsel at which he airs his grievances against their father, Laban, and then continues thus (Jacob still speaking, 31:10–13):

> And it came to pass at the time that the cattle conceived, that I lifted up mine eyes, and saw in a dream, and behold, the rams which leaped upon the cattle were ringstraked, speckled and grisled.
>
> And the angel of God spake unto me in a dream, saying, Jacob: and I said, Here am I.
>
> And he said, Lift up now thine eyes, and see, all the rams which leap upon the cattle are ringstraked, speckled, and grisled: for I have seen all that Laban doeth unto thee.
>
> I am the God of Beth-el, where thou anointedst the pillar, and where thou vowedst a vow unto me: now arise, get thee out from this land, and return unto the land of thy kindred.

In the J account (chap. 30) Jacob is the agent of his profiteering, in the E version (chap. 31) it is all revealed in a dream, "swayed and fashioned by the hand of heaven," as Antonio puts it, and providence is the agent. But how far can we credit the account of an unreliable narrator when even the word of God cannot keep the story straight?

Antonio intervenes to appropriate the meaning of the biblical text on behalf of Christian exegesis by calling Jacob's activities "a venture" (the privileged occupation of Venetian gentiles), controlled by providence (as the first-person dream-version of the E narrative suggests), and not by subtle or tricky private enterprise; in other words, not by taking advantage.

> A: This was a venture, sir, that Jacob served for,
> A thing not in his power to bring to pass,
> But swayed and fashioned by the hand of heaven.
> Was this inserted to make interest good?
> Or is your gold and silver ewes and rams?
> S: I cannot tell; I make it breed as fast.

In Antonio's world God is always on the side of merchants, as they are on His. And in Shylock's?

The referent of Antonio's "this" (1.91) is indeterminate—does it point to the Biblical narrative (which one?) or to Shylock's? This question in turn complicates the punning phrase "to make interest good," itself already complicated by the quasi-anagram of "inserted" and interest, causing narrative economy to tangle with social and divine economy. It is as though language will not allow Antonio to ask his plain question which I take to be: does your narrative, Shylock, exemplify the proposition that usury is condoned by scriptural authority, *or* is it used to enforce the unorthodox equation of woolly breeders and barren metal (unorthodox, that is, and even heretical, in Antonio's Christian system of interpretation[18]). We could even construe Antonio's question to be challenging Shylock to declare explicitly the system of interpretation from within which this argument is being conducted, to declare the principles by means of which he expects to earn some hermeneutic hire. "Was this inserted to make interest good? Or is your gold and silver ewes and rams?" And Shylock answers with maddening evasion: "I cannot tell; I make it breed as fast."

"Breed" is of course the operative word; in Shylock's account, woolly breeders *and* breed of barren metal have both been a source of blessing for Jews, and it is easy to detect in his nonresponse the tones of a sardonic triumph. But what does he mean by the pun on "tell"—that he is unable to say, or that he refuses to recount further, or that certain differences cannot be accounted for? But then what *are* the differences to be counted and accounted for? Is it the difference between Jews and Christians, or sheep and coins, or nature and craft, or providence and human resourcefulness, or even God's accountability or unaccountability for the difference in the distribution of his blessings?

"Three thousand ducats—'tis a good round sum." The dialogue returns briefly to the literalist calculation of rates and interest with which it began, but the language is by now infiltrated by some less pragmatic, almost incantatory or folkloristic calculus. In the rhetorical "excess" of insistent repetition (the scene's opening phrase "three thousand ducats" recurs seven times), three thousand ducats for three months chimes oddly with three patriarchs, to say nothing of three caskets, three suitors, three rings (when we include Leah's turquoise). What manner of dark or veiled counting and accounting, what allegorical or verbal expenditure is at work here?

A rhetorical penchant for good round sums is not limited to Shylock. The apparent realism and deliberateness of his accountancy can be compared with Portia's "full sum" multiplications of herself and her fortune to a figure of plenitude beyond computation:

> Though for myself alone
> I would not be ambitious in my wish
> To wish myself much better, yet for you
> I would be trebled twenty times myself,
> A thousand times more fair, ten thousand times more rich,
> That only to stand high in your account,
> I might in virtues, beauties, livings, friends
> Exceed account. But the *full sum* of me
> Is sum of something—(3.2.150–58)

Consider also her characteristically extravagant offer, on behalf of the man who has won the lottery of her fabulous dowry, to pay Shylock six thousand ducats, "double six thousand, and then treble that . . ." (1.300), to redeem the friend of the man she loves. These exorbitant sums can be attributed to the exuberance and generosity of spirit inspired by love, and therefore read as a trope for "fullness"; but rhetorically speaking, they also speak of the "fulsome" (Cordelia would perhaps have done well to emulate both Portia and her sisters); a heaping not only of ready cash but of rhetorical excess to the point where it becomes empty.

My present quarry, however, is not the moral aspect of dramatic character, but a rhetorical approach to the scene of interpretation to which I return. From this point of view, it can fairly be shown that it is at Shylock's witty (rather than, say, sinister) instigation that the complex conflict of interpretations is enacted between the two adversaries of the play; that it is reflexively and symbolically reenacted in the citation of a story dramatizing the conflict between normative and aberrant modes of breeding; and is then repeated in the argument over normative and aberrant modes of making a profit, or acquiring a blessing in Venice.

It is no doubt as perverse to characterize Shylock as witty, as it is to characterize Portia as fulsome. The extraordinary energies of his speech here and throughout the play, lack the grace and elegance we associate with wit. Witness his excruciating habit of spelling out his meanings, as he does with respect to Antonio's solvency ("Antonio is a good man. . . . my meaning in saying he is a good man is to have you understand me that he is sufficient" [2.12–17]), or further on, when he speaks of "land rats and water rats, water thieves and land thieves—I mean pirates—" (2.22–24). But the linkage of "meaning" to the concern with Antonio's "means," and the abrasive return of the clunking pun on "rats/rates," linked to usance, when Shylock airs his grievances first in an aside ("He lends out money gratis, and brings down / The *rate* of usance here with us in Venice" [2.41–42]) and then publicly: "Signior Antonio, many a time and oft / in the Rialto you have *rated* me / About my moneys and my usances . . . and spet upon my Jewish gaberdine, / And all for the use of that which is mine own" [103–10])—are only some of the more trivial instances of a concentration of passion and intellect crowding his graceless witticisms. It has been said of Shylock that he "hoards" his words,[19] that he "uses language as he uses money: carefully, and as a weapon," and, though frugal, he "does occasionally venture a pun, pleased to get two meanings for the price of one."[20] The observation that the exchange of money is commensurate with the exchange of words is a profound one, but it is not at all clear that what such troping reveals is the character's miserliness. I am far more inclined to see in this verbal energy a "deep wit" in which the cheaper pleasures of getting two for the price of one are overshadowed by the more troubling reminders of difference and otherness, within the word as much as within the troubled world of Venice.

Shylock's discourse in the elusive mode of deep wit has the effect of unbinding the ostensible meaning of the text, dislocating it from received contexts, turning it loose, disseminating it. As opposed to Antonio's conservative exegesis, let me tentatively characterize this dissemination as a form of open or subversive interpretation—strangely at odds with the fiercely continent, literalist Jew who locks up (is not shy of locking), binds fast, and clings to the letter of the Law (as traditional Christianity depicts it) yet generates a speculative and venturesome spirit of exegesis.

I began the previous section with the observation that the scene stages a confrontation of opponents, and a conflict of words and interpretations. Normative utopian readings of *The Merchant* all wrestle with, and attempt to demolish, the insurmountable barrier between opposite sets of values in the representation: Belmont and Venice, Christian and Jew, the New Law and the Old Law, Aristocrat and Puritan, feudal merchants and modern capitalists, splendid spendthrifts and thrifty miser, and a host of other conceptualizations, both historical and metaphysical, which have been adumbrated to characterize the antitheses controlling the dynamics of plot and theme. The passage I have been reading is of course also informed by these same antitheses, and most pointedly and painfully by the irreducible difference in ethos between Christian and Jew in the matter of usury. The controlling assumption governing so-called normative readings is a conviction that the reconciliation of these antitheses, or a dialectical assimilation of one into the other, is required by the sense-making process of interpretation, as well as by the strictures of comedic structure and vision. If the drama exhibits a contradiction, a predicament, an agon of wills, it does so in order to work its way towards a resolution into narrative coherence and reconciliation. And when that coherence remains in dispute, as a glance at the body of critical commentary on *The Merchant* will quickly reveal, the debate generated by the confrontation of opposites continues unresolved ad infinitum, duplicating the structure of debate thematized in the play.

One way out of this deadlocked state of affairs is to adopt a different set of critical questions which will require, in the words of Walter Cohen, "not so much interpretation as the discovery of the sources of difficulty in interpreting."[21] Cohen's marxist-historicist strategy is to turn to "the view of the play as a symptom of a problem in the life of late sixteenth-century England."[22] His presentation and rich documentation of the socioeconomic background is fascinating, but there is almost no *literary* criticism to speak of in his discussion of the play. If the production of literary and critical texts is to be seen as contributing to the work of culture, historicist and cultural *poetics* cannot afford to surrender the task of close reading to the currently maligned formalists. The *literary representation* of a complex and evolving attitude to capitalism, and its *affect,* its aesthetic and emotional impact, plays the role of ground as much as of figure in the work of culture. That is why it has seemed to me that a closer scrutiny of the verbal and rhetorical scene, its manipulation of the economy of representation and response is decisive to our understanding of the controversial character of money-lending, or changing banking practices, and their representation by means of apparently symmetrical yet untenable binary oppositions.

My argument has been that a rhetorical scrutiny of the scene of interpretation reveals that Shylock's shrewd citational intervention unsettles the terms of an orthodox economy based on the traditional tension between fixed antitheses: the natural procreation of "woolly breeders" versus the unnatural "breed for barren metal," or the supposedly life-affirming Christian ethos of doing business (informed by Aristotelian doctrine that money cannot breed) on the one hand, and the life-denying Jewish mode of usury on the other. His allegory which is and isn't a defense of usury, is and isn't a defense of "the deed of kind" in commerce, deconstructs (intentionally or not is entirely beside the point) in order to expose the deluded dissociation of spirit and letter, love and profit, luck and lucre, on which the Christian ethic is founded. (In the trial scene Shylock sharply reminds us of the reciprocity or interconnectedness of life and livelihood, of person and purse, of means and their meaning, when he says that "You take my life / When you do take the means whereby I live" [4.1.375–76]). Indeed, it is Antonio's hasty polarisation of these categories (categories which language itself conflates or resists) that so ironically engenders the outrageous bond in which human flesh and economic interest are made interchangeable.[23]

It is worthwhile to recall exactly how the moment of this monstrous birth is represented:

If thou wilt lend this money, lend it not
As to thy friends—for when did friendship take
A breed of barren metal of his friend—

> But lend it rather to thine enemy,
> Who if he break, thou mayst with better face
> Exact the penalty. (1.3.129–34)

Having himself "[broken] a custom" of never taking or giving of "excess" (11.59–61), it is the courtly Antonio's uncompromising animosity which uncannily generates the brief for Shylock's bloodthirsty bond and his uncompromising behaviour in the courtroom. The moneylender's response to Antonio's insolence is hardly innocuous—"Why look you, how you storm! / I would be friends with you, and have your love, / Forget the shames . . ." (134–36)—though it carries its own pathos. Shylock then offers to take, according to the Christian model, "no doit of usance for my moneys" and goes on to say: "This is kind I offer" [137–39]. The pun is familiar to readers of Shakespeare and admirers of Hamlet's wit. It shuttles between light and dark senses of the word: the benign sense of decent and gentle (the sense to which Bassanio seems to be responding naively when he concedes that "This were kindness"), the natural sense (as in Shylock's calling the coupling of animals "the deed of kind" or nature), as well as in the legal and commercial sense of taliation, or commensurability. What Shylock offers now is a legal deed or contract founded on the shifting sands of "kindness" and wordplay. "This kindness will I show: / Go with me to a notary . . ." (140–41). The immediate irony, of course, is that the usurer "breaks" his practice of lending for interest. Indeed, it is his *refusal* of interest in favour of exacting a penalty, as Christians would, on the bond's default, which precipitates the crisis. The ferocity of the irony is not lost on either party.

Bassanio is uncomfortable, but Antonio is greatly amused by the ironies of a "kind" bond, mockingly remarking that "there is much kindness in the Jew" (150), the "gentle Jew" who might even be punned into a gentile. "The Hebrew will turn Christian," he sneers; "he grows kind" (174–75). This courtly and acerbic punster has yet to learn very literally what the graceless but no less acerbic deep wit of Shylock knows about the power of the word to generate curses and blessings both. Despite his generally atrocious puns, Shylock takes the power of language far more seriously than his Christian enemies. His demystified notion of "kind-ness," not accidentally, knows and openly acknowledges the profound kinship which binds propagation, friendship and community with the base barter of the market place. (The shriek of pain underlying "my daughter! my ducats!" caricatured by Salanio and Solerio registers this knowledge movingly.) For Antonio the punning substitutions enacted in language are no more than a casual joke. And so the Christian merchant and exegete, whose practice stands in contradiction to his ideology, who differentiates self-righteously and self-confidently between flesh and ducats, ewes and golden fleeces, blindly signs on the binding dotted line.

As for Shylock, his obsessive insistence on having his bond—after Jessica's flight into the arms of a Christian—enacts the implacable economy of a most terrible retaliation: this daughter, gilded with the stolen ducats, is "my own flesh and blood," the flesh and blood nearest his heart, and he will have her loss repaid in kind, and not in ducats.

Ultimately, these violent inscriptions and voicings of the entanglement of words and wounds, blessings and curses, governing the operations of theological, political, social, and household economies are too potent for the deluded and exclusionary moral vision of romantic comedy, and therefore must, in the inflexible economy of comic genres, be expelled or coercively converted into uniformity.

NOTES

1. I am particularly indebted to Marc Shell's brilliant reading of the play in *Money, Language and Thought: Literary and Philosophical Economies from the Medieval to the Modern Era* (Berkeley: University of California Press, 1982).

2. This project is primarily associated in the American academy with the name of its inaugurator Stephen Greenblatt. See, for example, *Shakespearean Negotiations* (Berkeley: University of California Press, 1988). See also Leonard Tennenhouse, *Power on Display: The Politics of Shakespeare's Genres* (London: Methuen, 1986).

3. Geoffrey Hartman, "Criticism and Restitution," *Tikkun*. Vol. 4, n. 1 (1989) 29–32.

4. Alexander Gelley, "Thematics and Historical Construction in Benjamin's 'Arcades Project'," *Strumenti Critici* n.s., a. 4, n. 2 (1986) 233–51:248. The quotation from Benjamin which follows is cited by Gelley on p. 249.

5. The mass of critical commentary on *The Merchant,* as well as the history of its stage interpretations exhibits this basic gesture repeatedly, without benefit of deconstructionist readings. A useful metacritical

retrospective can be found in Norman Rabkin, *Shakespeare and the Problem of Meaning* (Chicago: The University of Chicago Press, 1981).

6. Keir Elam, *Shakespeare's Universe of Discourse: Language Games in the Comedies* (Cambridge: Cambridge University Press, 1984), is an elaborate investigation of Shakespearean rhetorical practice in relation to semiotics and speech act theory.

7. It is both odd and obvious that writers should be so touchy about being quoted "out of context"—what is a quotation if not a wrenching from context? But the frequency of litigation around this issue will remind us of the deep political, philosophic and social consequences of tampering with the word's truth, credibility, meaning, *and so forth*. See also n. 14.

8. For what these writers actually "say" see J. L. Austin, *How to Do Things with Words* (London: Oxford University Press, 1976); Jacques Derrida, "Signature Event Context" (*Glyph*, 1 (1977) 172–97); Stanley E. Fish, "How to Do Things with Austin and Searle: Speech Act Theory and Literary Criticism" (*MLN*, 91 (1976) 983–1025), and "With the Compliments of the Author: Reflections on Austin and Derrida" (*Critical Inquiry*, 8 (1982) 693–721.

9. Elizabeth Freund, "'Ariachne's broken woof": the rhetoric of citation in *Troilus and Cressida*" in *Shakespeare and the Question of Theory*, ed. Patricia Parker and Geoffrey Hartman (London: Methuen, 1985) p. 27.

10. This neat symmetry has been a literary cliché in the portrayal of villains at least since Chaucer's use of it in his invention of the Pardoner.

11. I cannot resist, athwart professional discipline, imagining Antonio—in some later phase of his life beyond the frame of Shakespeare's play—an elderly bachelor and perennial godfather to the children of his friends, fondly dandling Lorenzo's and Jessica's child on his knee, and reminiscing about the past. In these reminiscences he will claim that he also "knows" the diabolical character of the godchild's grandfather from that indubitably powerful source of knowledge known as "personal experience."

12. For Shakespeare's use of the Bible in *The Merchant*, see M. M. Mahood's useful appendix in her edition of the play for *The New Cambridge Shakespeare* (Cambridge: Cambridge University Press, 1987), pp. 184–88. Barbara K. Lewalski, in "Biblical Allusion and Allegory in *The Merchant of Venice*" (*Shakespeare Quarterly* 13 (1982) 327–43), finds "patently deliberate" (p. 328) allegorical patterns confronting ideological, theological and historical systems in the figures of Antonio (representing love, giving, and forgiveness—the New Law) and Shylock (representing niggardly prudence—the Old Law). Like many other critics, she reads the play as a Christian version of salvation-history.

13. I borrow the term from Garrett Stewart, *Reading Voices: Literature and the Phonotext* (Berkeley: University of California Press, 1990), to designate "the reading that proceeds to give voice, or at least to evoke silently such voicing" (p. 1).

14. "Verbal usury," according to Shell, was a mediaeval category in juriprudence, rhetoric, and philosophy, "an important technical term in the Jewish Talmud, in the Christian church fathers, and in the Islamic traditions. There it refers to the generation of an illegal—the church fathers say unnatural—supplement to verbal meaning by use of such methods as punning and flattering." Shell argues that Shylock "enlarge[s]" and "supplements" the debate about usury by generating a useful pun on use/Iewes/ewes (p. 49).

15. Speiser's scholarly comment (in the Anchor Bible *Genesis*) to the effect that prenatal conditioning of the flock by means of visual aids is in conformance with universal folk beliefs is of little interpretive use here. Midrash can be delightfully unembarrassed by fraud and deception. See Louis Ginzberg, *The Legends of the Jews,* vol. 1 (trans. Henrietta Szold, Philadelphia: The Jewish Publication Society of America, 1909) p. 361. See also n. 16 below. The mainstream literary interpretation (like Antonio's) is that Shylock intends his narrative to represent the practice of taking interest as legitimate "hire." A more lurid reading can be found in Leah Woods Wilkins who believes that "the story of Jacob and Laban indicates Shylock's preoccupation with the problem of how he may feed his grudge against Antonio, how he may match the cunning of his ancestor. . . . Since Jacob took his wages in the form of flesh, Shylock would also take his in terms of flesh. Evilly he decides to practice trickery with human flesh as his ancestor did with animal flesh." (See "Shylock's Pound of Flesh and Laban's Sheep," *MLN* 62 (1947) 28–30; reprinted in *Shylock,* ed. Harold Bloom, New York: Chelsea House Publishers, 1991, pp. 46–47).

16. Geoffrey Hartman, "The Struggle for the Text" in *Midrash and Literature,* ed. Geoffrey Hartman and Sanford Budick (New Haven: Yale University Press, 1986). "Jacob is a ganev" (as *Genesis* 31:20 seems to say); he is "what he is called in the Bible: a heel" (p. 7).

17. I find an interesting analogue to my reading of the struggle for (the meaning of) the text, and for blessing, in Leslie Brisman's extended "midrash" in *The Voice of Jacob: On the Composition of Genesis* (Bloomington: Indiana University Press, 1990). Brisman reads the palimpsest of redactions in the canonized *Genesis* as enacting the struggle between a "Jacobic" and an "Eisaaic" text. In his discussion of the Laban episode, Brisman quotes *The Merchant,* and suggests that the "purehearted" but misguided interpreter, Antonio plays Eisaac to Shylock's Jacob, reacting to Shylock's tale as Brisman's fictional Eisaac would have responded to the fictional Jacobic midrash (p. 79).

18. For the complex and often contradictory contemporary attitudes to usury see Mahood, pp. 19–22, Shell, pp. 47–51, Walter Cohen, *Drama of a Nation: Public Theatre in Renaissance England and Spain* (Ithaca: Cornell University Press, 1985), pp. 197–202.

19. Alexander Leggatt, *Shakespeare's Comedy of Love* (London: Methuen, 1974) p. 137.

20. Lawrence Danson's *The Harmonies of The Merchant of Venice*, (New Haven: Yale University Press, 1978) is the most comprehensive discussion of the play. I can safely be accused of wrenching Danson's words out of their context: Danson does not, in fact, perceive Shylock as a linguistic miser, and makes many useful observations on Shylock's verbal wit. See pp. 126–69. The observation that the exchange of money can be represented by the exchange of words is profound and fruitful but to what conclusions such troping can be read is not in the least perspicuous.

21. Cohen p. 197. But this turn only generates more inconclusive interpretation since the historical evidence is fascinatingly diverse and contradictory. See n. 18.

22. Ibid.

23. Shylock speaks with precision when he says that the villainy Christians teach him he will execute, and it shall go hard but he will better the instruction—by exacting retaliation in "kind."

CHAPTER 10

American Literature's Declaration of In/dependence: Stanley Cavell, Nathaniel Hawthorne, and the Covenant of Consent

Emily Miller Budick

One could say that the following discussion is about the literary criticism of Stanley Cavell or about Hawthorne's short story, "My Kinsman, Major Molineux," or about the relationship between them. But part of what I want to argue is that both Cavell's criticism and Hawthorne's story refute the idea of *about*-ness; that for both Cavell and Hawthorne writing, at least in a democratic society like America, has less to do with a writer's informing or teaching a reader about something than with initiating a negotiation between them. For Cavell and Hawthorne, this negotiation depends upon the uncompromised autonomy of writer and reader. It also depends on the consent each expresses—in language—to enter into relationship with the other. In this way, both Cavell's writings, and Hawthorne's constitute a theory of reading, which is also a theory of politics. These writings also endorse the contract they themselves inaugurate. For both Cavell and Hawthorne, politics and literature in the United States are governed by a commitment to contract or covenant. Far from compromising or mechanizing human relationships, this government by law guarantees such relationships on the highest moral, psychological, and spiritual level.

STANLEY CAVELL'S AVERSIVE CRITICISM AND THE CONTRACT OF READER AND WRITER

It hardly needs saying that one of the central facts of literary studies today is the open competition among different modes of reading texts. In the field of American literature, two chief contenders in this struggle are deconstruction and the new historicism or what Frederick Crews has labeled the new Americanism. A third challenger on the field is Stanley Cavell, whose work has, over the last two decades, become increasingly important for literary criticism (Fischer, Budick 1989). Cavell's criticism has profound implications for reading in general. It is, I believe, even more crucial in interpreting American fiction, specifically the tradition in American writing known as romance fiction. This tradition includes, among other writers, Hawthorne, Poe, Melville, and James in the nineteenth century; and, in the twentieth century, such various and variously different figures as William Faulkner, E. L. Doctorow, Grace Paley, Ralph Ellison, and Toni Morrison. What characterizes this group of texts is its explicit rejection of mimetic modes of representation. In this way, as I have argued in *Fiction and Historical Consciousness,* the tradition evokes the situation known in philosophy as radical skepticism. By radical skepticism I refer, most simply, to the doubt whether we can verify our knowledge of external reality or of other people. Expressing this doubt, romance fiction is less concerned with examining social institutions (though it often does this as well) and more concerned with asking, and then tracing the implications of, the question whether we can know the world. This question the fiction emphatically refuses to answer. Instead, it dramatizes the path from doubt to what Cavell calls acknowledgment. Acknowledgment, according to Cavell, precisely does not settle the question of doubt. Rather it insists on substituting for the desire to know a commitment to responding to the unmistakable attunement between mind and world (and mind and mind) which, despite the question of doubt, most of us experience in the course of our ordinary lives.

Cavell's contract of reading constitutes one form of such acknowledgment, which is also expressed in and summoned by the romance tradition, as, for example, in a story like Hawthorne's "My Kinsman, Major Molineux." This is Cavell in his 1972 *Senses of Walden:*

> The reader's position [is] that of the stranger. To write to him is to acknowledge that he is outside the words, at a bent arm's length, and alone with the book; that his presence to these words is perfectly contingent, and the choice to stay with them continuously his own; that they are his points of departure and origin. The conditions of meeting upon the word are that we—writer and reader—learn how to depart from them, leave them where they are; and then return to them, finding ourselves there again. We have to learn to admit the successiveness of words, their occurrence one after the other; and their permanence in the face of our successions. . . . Words come to us from a distance; they were there before we were; we are born into them. Meaning them is accepting that fact of their condition. To discover what is being said to us, as to discover what we are saying, is to discover the precisely location from which it is said; to understand why it is said from just there, and at that time. The art of fiction is to teach us distance. . . . Speaking together face to face can seem to deny that distance, to deny that facing one another requires acknowledging the presence of the other . . . But to deny such things is to deny our separateness. And that makes us fictions of one another. (SW 61–63)

Informing Cavell's work, here and elsewhere, is his concern to keep "philosophy," hence thinking and writing, "open to the threat or temptation to skepticism" ("Aversive" 4). In the first instance this is exactly what his own writing, as in the above passage, accomplishes. Keeping the reader at arm's length, declaring me, the reader, a stranger who must leave the text's words alone, the text explicitly distances itself from me. This distancing is also a consequence of Cavell's style, which, despite its many moments of personal address, is so densely packed and continuously self-reflective and self-qualifying as sometimes to seem impenetrable. Certainly reading Cavell for the first time (especially in the context of the formalist criticism which characterized much literary reading in the 1970s), one might very well feel strange. But, for Cavell, entertaining doubt motivates the writers he reads. Indeed, it motivates his own writing. It is as if intimacy, for Cavell, is a quality of human relatedness which we must first put aside in order to (re)attain. Hence Cavell's constant breaking of the personal register in his writing, necessitating a continuous process, not of establishing intimacy, but of reestablishing it.

For Cavell, skepticism (which is one way of labeling our sense of distance from the world and from other people) sets the terms for (re)establishing relationships. The "pivot on which skepticism turns," Cavell argues, is that it "is not up for decision." Hence, in Cavell's way of thinking, with no one or nothing in a position to decide the questions skepticism raises, human beings must assume for themselves responsibility for their lives. Such responsibility also pertains to language. "To call [a] matter undecidable," Cavell argues in direct response to deconstruction, "may be just a way of affirming that the words 'can' be taken . . . various ways . . . or a way of denying that you have this responsibility. . . . Nothing in words will distinguish the real [referential?] from the dream [non-referential?] occasion, and this difference is again not up for decision" ("Being Odd" 311). Cavell's basic disagreement with both deconstruction and the new historicism is that each decides the issue of skepticism too soon: deconstruction by opting for the truth of undecidability, the new historicism by brushing indeterminacy aside. Cavell, on the contrary, preserves the pressure of doubt on writing as what necessitates writing, and finally reading, as the writer's and reader's way of acknowledging each other.

The estrangement effected in Cavell's writing is not, therefore, what a particular writer uniquely (or even perversely) foists upon the universe. Rather it is a fact of the universe in which he or she writes. Such a record of cosmic strangeness is no mere minimalism or realism or existentialism on Cavell's part. Estrangement or distance, which is the consequence of doubt, which is itself the result of the limitation of human knowledge, is exactly what forces something to happen, the something we call writing. This writing, which is a form of acknowledgement, does not attempt to state what cannot be stated. It does, however, try to fulfill a responsibility to the world and language. Cavell's enforcement of estrangement, like that of fiction, especially romance fiction, teaches us distance. It reminds us of a strangeness we are likely to forget so that we can remember to acknowledge what we may also forget or take for granted—the existence of other people. In this way, the personal impersonality of Cavell's style establishes relationships of intimacy, or, rather, as I suggested earlier, reestablishes them.

Acknowledgment substitutes for presence in Cavell's vocabulary, as in deconstruction deferral takes its place and in the new historicism, ideology, or consensus. The force of Cavell's acknowledgment is, however, precisely the opposite of both the deconstructive and new historicist substitutions. Deconstruction dismisses presence as nonexistent, a dangerously seductive illusion; ideological criticism exposes it as an undeclared social construct, determining human behavior. Acknowledgment, on the other hand, reconstitutes presence. Such presence is decidedly not metaphysical. Nor is it deterministic. Rather presence as acknowledgment constitutes the effort and consequence of the human will, often expressed in language, but expressed in other ways as well, to establish relationships in the face of language's and the world's alternating undecidabilities and overdeterminations.

This is the kind of acknowledgment enacted in Thoreau, Emerson, Hawthorne, and others. It is the kind of acknowledgment which the above passage from *The Senses of Walden* similarly enacts. It begins with Cavell's opening statement about the reader as stranger. Despite the fact that this statement is cast in the third person, as if constituting a law, and hence a metaphysics, of readership, it functions as no more (and no less) than a personal address to a particular reader (me), who is now reading Cavell's words. (This is so despite the gender inflection of the "he"—Cavell is writing in advance of feminism's correction of that little problem). Cavell will not deny the requirement and responsibility of "acknowledging the presence of the other" which "speaking together face to face can seem to deny." The anonymous, impersonal third-person form of address exhibits Cavell's self-conscious acknowledgment of a reader who is totally separate from himself and whose relationship to him is wholly contingent. Indeed, Cavell's address addresses me only if I agree to become his reader. Thus Cavell's strategy guarantees my rights as a reader. He ensures the totality of my freedom by writing a contract which comes into effect only at the moment I consent to it. Only then do I enter into the relationship Cavell finally specifies as "we—writer and reader." Cavell's statement is a kind of bill of reader's rights, protecting the consent of the governed to their governing, which in turn protects their individualism.

The Senses of Walden simultaneously constitutes a scripture and a constitution of American readership (in much the same way that, in Cavell's view, *Walden* does). It ensures the democratic functioning of the nation's culture. Once the reader consents to enter into contract with the writer, the rights and demands of readership are reciprocal: the writer's vacating his or her words, which guarantees our freedom to enter them or not, must be emulated by the reader, who is obliged to recognize the separateness of these words, their inviolability. "We, writer and reader"—where Cavell is, of course, both—must accept the conditions of our meeting upon the word, where those conditions contain the skeptical and ideological claims of both deconstruction and the new historicism. Accepting those conditions means discovering not what a word (despite its claims to the contrary) *does* mean or *cannot* mean, but "the precise location from which it is said; to understand why it is said from just there, and at that time." Writers must withdraw from their words; readers must listen to them. (We must also withdraw from and listen to ourselves.)

Inviolability and separateness are also what the rhythms of Cavell's style emphasize, stressing the importance of process over statement. The sets of triplet phrases, around which many of Cavell's sentences are built, the triple repetition of phrases like "to deny" and "to discover," convey what Cavell calls successiveness. This idea is also captured in the mutual balancing of words like "permanence" and "succession" or "distance" and "presence" or the internal self-balancing of a word like "fiction," used in two opposing senses. To deny or to discover are neither binary opposites nor limited actions. Rather they are continuing, interdependent, experiences, expressed in the nonending negotiations carried on by language. For this reason I label Cavell's criticism, following his own characterization of Emerson's thinking, as aversive. Writes Cavell, "the relation of Emerson's writing (the expression of his self-reliance) to his society (the realm of what he calls conformity) is one . . . of mutual aversion: 'Self-reliance is the aversion of conformity' . . . figures each side in terms of the other, declares the issue between them as always joined, never settled. But then this is to say that Emerson's writing and his society are in an unending argument with one another—that is to say, he writes in such a way as to *place* his writing in his unending argument . . . an unending turning way from one another, hence endlessly a turning *toward* one another" (HH).

Cavell's idea of culture as a conversation or as aversive thinking summons up certain contemporary ideas in reader response criticism. Specifically it recalls Wolfgang Iser's theories of aesthetic response in which the text does not exist independent of its negotiation with a reader, neither text nor reader existing in any completeness without the supplement of the other. Cavell's aversive criticism differs from Iser's reader response criticism in this way: it does not claim an interdependent relationship between reader and text; rather it insists on what Cavell calls in *The Senses of Walden* the autonomy of writer and reader. The asymmetry of Iser's and Cavell's terms (in Iser's case, text and reader; in Cavell's, writer and reader) is as significant for the difference between them as their disagreement on the issue of autonomy. For Cavell's aversive criticism also expresses his romantic commitment to a self, which Iser's criticism calls into question.

Cavell's idea of autonomy does not, however, return us to formalist notions of organic unity (though it may explain why new criticism evolved as it did, in response to writers such as Hawthorne and James). In Cavell's way of thinking, the autonomous text parallels the autonomous life, not in the perfection of each, outside the socio-political context, but in the requirement under which each labors to establish a relationship with the other, a relationship which nonetheless respects the independence of the other. For this reason Cavell's community of interpreters is also not what Stanley Fish designates an interpretive community. Cavell's interpreters are self-reliant. True, they exist within a community (what the new historicism, to which Fish's ideas are related, would call an ideological consensus). But this community exists solely by will of the governed, the consent of reader and writer (as of citizen and citizen) to enter into this consensus, to voice their consent to it, through their aversive criticism.

HAWTHORNE'S REVOLUTION OF SELF-RELIANT AVERSION

Focusing on various kinds of interpretive communities—the country world in which the major protagonist, Robin, grows up; the world of budding, revolutionary, American nationalism, in which he finds himself during the largest part of the story; the loyalist population within colonial America (represented by Robin's kinsman); and, finally, the new generation of Americans represented by Robin himself—Hawthorne's "My Kinsman, Major Molineux" explicitly exposes the problems inherent in ideological consensus. It proposes in its stead something akin to Cavell's idea of a community of interpreters. These interpreters, in Hawthorne's view, as in

Cavell's, would each be self-reliant. That is, they would bind themselves to each other, not through the consensus (or ideology) which they (like all human beings within a particular social configuration) would inevitably share, but through the contractual consent they would institute (aversively), through the constitutions they would draft and endorse. At the heart of Hawthorne's optimism about America, as at the heart of Cavell's (and Emerson's and Thoreau's), is not the law of nature or of human nature (which are really other names for conformity or consensus). Rather, his faith abides in the laws individuals can draw up and to which they can willingly, explicitly, commit themselves. Such a system of legal documents affirms, for Hawthorne, the idea of interpretation itself. This is so because it places interpretation both inside and outside consensus. Thus it renders interpretation a possible and legitimate human activity, which, though not verifiable by anything outside community, is nonetheless capable of self-conscious self-verification. Romance's contribution to American democracy is a potent defamiliarization of reality, which, like Cavell's strategies of personal impersonality or estranged intimacy, causes reader and writer to establish or reestablish their relationship with one another. To thus actively participate in the constant recreation of consensus is not to submit or conform to consensus. Rather it is to consent to consensus. Voicing consent converts another otherwise dangerously tacit and passive participation into an active one. (Cavell discusses the problem of consent in *The Claim of Reason*, 3–36.)

Hawthorne's story is filled with moments typified by consensual understandings of reality, which the text's explicitly anti-mimetic, symbolic qualities consistently undermine. From the beginning of the story, Robin sees the world, and the world sees him, in terms of types: "This is some country representative," Robin says of his first inexplicable introduction into city life (16); "This low hovel cannot be my kinsman's dwelling," he concludes, on the basis of no more than his assumptions about wealth and position (14); "the next man I meet will do as well" as any one else, Robin determines in choosing his guide (15). Such conclusions might seem no more than further evidence that Robin's famed "shrewdness" suffers from a lack of real experience of and contact with the world (Baym 1976), but the text itself concurs in the inescapability of consensus-making when it tells us that Robin is "evidentally country-bred" (14). Indeed, "dispens[ing] with an account of the train of circumstances that had caused much temporary inflammation of the popular mind" (13), the story depends upon its readership's shared knowledge of early American history in order for its events to be rendered interpretable.

The story's response to the inevitable prominence of consensus in human existence is, simultaneous with its own yielding to consensus, also to create—through the strategies of romance fiction—conditions of estrangement or distance. Estrangement breaks the hold of consensual knowledge. It forces the reader to entertain, and keep unresolved, doubts about what is perceived and what such acts of perception mean. The purpose of raising such doubts is not to destroy consensus and the community consensus creates. Rather it is to compel the reader, as it ought to compel the characters, to recreate the intimacy (the participation in consensus) which has thus been broken. Its purpose is to oblige the citizen commited to the idea of community actively to consent to, rather than simply to accept a place within, the consensual framework. (One is also free *not* to be committed to the idea of community.) For, as the preface to the story already indicates, there exists in Hawthorne's view an "us" (13). This us consists both of reader and writer as of citizen and citizen within the shared text/history Hawthorne's story reports and in some large measure creates. The reader, as the citizen, may or may not choose membership in this us.

The story tempts us to read it as an allegory of the American Revolution and then frustrates us in that attempt. It does this, I believe, in order to promote the value of negotiated relations over inevitable correspondences. This story is not about the American Revolution or the pre-revolutionary period; nor is it about the growth from childhood to adulthood, either for nations or for individuals. It is not about the about-ness of things, which, for Hawthorne, allegory records. In Hawthorne's view, allegory reconstructs as a literary problem the ideological problem of consensus or the philosophical problem of idealism. What refuses allegory and thus mindless consensus (and therefore what his story will insist upon) is an awareness of the way in which events are not about other events but are only themselves (much in the way that people are), necessitating that we own, own up to, and accept them—enter into relationship with them—on their own terms. Two-faced men, hemming and hawing night watchmen, and saucy young women cannot, if they are to be taken seriously, be reduced to figures for something or someone else. For Hawthorne, history, like text, indeed as text, exists independent of the present, independent of its readers, just as people exist independent of our efforts to analyze them. Yet as history affects and is affected by those descendants or readers, at least those who choose to enter into relationship with it, this Hawthornean declaration of independence is simultaneously a declaration of also being in-dependence. For what past and present, text and reader, choose to do to or with one another finally will determine the character of the relationship they establish. In "My Kinsman" the colonists tar-and-feather the past; or, in the form of Robin's gentleman guide, they ignore or disown it, calling it yours and not mine; or, as Robin himself proposes to do, they walk away from it, to go back "home," wherever that might be. All of these are possible—though not equally valid—responses to either past or present. Indeed, each of the possibilities, especially the possibility of walking away from (an option Pearl takes in *The Scarlet Letter*), must exist in order for Hawthorne's other possible response to exist and have meaning. This is the response of acknowledgment, which Hawthorne himself demonstrates when he writes a history of America which he entitles "my."

I have elsewhere discussed the word my in the story's title as explicitly voicing Hawthorne's acknowledgment of his history and as his plea to his reader to do the same (*Fiction and Historical Consciousness*). This "My," which, at the end of the story, Robin's gentleman guide, explicitly refuses, substituting the word "Your" instead ("your kinsman"), seemed to me to indicate a commitment to owning and assuming responsibility for one's past. Hawthorne expresses similar commitments elsewhere, in *The Scarlet Letter*, for example. What I have come to realize, while thinking about Cavell's theory of reading, and (following some recent work by Sacvan Bercovitch) while thinking about reading or interpreting as the specific work of American culture which writers such as Hawthorne propose, is that, playing with the word my, the story constitutes itself a veritable paradigm of aversive relationships; and that, further, it claims this paradigm as the basis for pluralistic democracy in America. Such an aversive stance is precisely lacking in the world of colonial America; and this is why, from Hawthorne's point of view, the colonists' call to democracy is no more than the substitution of one kind of tyranny (call it the rule of the majority) for another kind of tyranny (call it monarchy). The colonists' insistence on ownership is possessive and dictatorial. It will not acknowledge competing claims. To be sure, there is nothing gentle in the word my, and Hawthorne knows this. It establishes a pattern of claim and counterclaim, conflict and competition, which accurately mirrors the dynamics of any society, especially one about to embark upon the path of revolution. Robin's my is not the colonists'; the colonists' is not Hawthorne's; Hawthorne's is not the reader's. Nor can they ever be. Each my is voiced differently, means something else, is spoken in opposition to another my. But Hawthorne also knows that without a my, without a personal sense of commitment to as well as partnership in a society, there can be no community. Therefore, the challenge the story poses, which is the challenge of the emerging nation, is to preserve the autonomy of each my, respecting the separate, aversive claim of each, while forging a collective consciousness, a community joined through its collective ownership of the nation. To put it in other words, Americans must find a way to own America, individually and personally, without usurping the rights of others also to own the nation. They must sign themselves, with a personal my, which is contractual rather than proprietary. To own, for Hawthorne, is to own up to. Ownership is an obligation of reciprocity and not simple possession.

As many critics have noted, "My Kinsman" is suffused with violence, both overt and concealed. One of the story's most striking metaphors for the implicit coerciveness of the new nation is the laying on of hands, which characterizes both Robin's and the colonists' responses to other people. Robin's first response, for example, when he meets his first potential guide, is to lay "hold of the skirt of the old man's coat"; he asks his first question while "still retaining [t]his hold" (15). This gesture is echoed in the old man's threats to lock Robin in the stocks, a threat which is itself repeated, by another character, moments later. (The old man's sepulchral "hem hem" may punningly serve to draw out attention to this holding on to the garment and to its constrictive, imprisoning implications—as in to "hem" in.) This laying on of hands is a figure for control no less terrifying than the actual threats to violence which characterize, for example, Robin's meeting with the two-faced gentlemen (in which Robin flourishes his cudgel and the two-faced gentleman threatens to strike him down) or the colonists' relationship to Major Molineux, which is to say their relationship to England. The kindly gentleman guide who accompanies Robin through the climactic moment of his journey exemplifies this problem of coercion. "'Sit down again, sit down,'" he instructs Robin, "laying his hand on the skirt of the gray coat" (29); and, at the end of the story, "'Well, Robin, are you dreaming,'" he inquires, "laying his hand on the youth's shoulder" (33). The gentleman's refusal to show Robin the way to the ferry suggests that such a laying on of hands is hardly an innocent gesture, though to dismiss the aspects of warmth and affection it also expresses would be equally unfair.

The question, then, becomes, how do we hold on to the past and to each other, without coercion and yet with concern? And how do we hand on with similar generosity and non-graspingness. The gentleman's suggestion that Robin may rise in the world without the help of his kinsman is wrong advice because it ignores the element of relatedness without which society cannot exist. Robin cannot rise without the help of this kinsman, or some other substitute for his kinsman, such as the gentleman himself. He must accept a helping hand, and offer one. But as Jacques Derrida 1987 and Stanley Cavell (AT) have recently argued, in two separate and yet interestingly interrelated essays, hands may serve either to restrain or release, to take or to give. Hawthorne, I believe, would have us hold on to America by simultaneously letting it go. Both such holding on and such letting go are, finally, matters of language. Hence the hands off policy of romance fiction, which refuses mimetic representation. What achieves prominence in Hawthorne's history of America is not the personality of Major Molineux or the political context of his tar and feathering (with which the story explicitly dispenses), but Hawthorne's acknowledgement of him nonetheless. What matters in "My Kinsman" is how we establish kinship; how we speak the word my.

The word my does more than acknowledge a relationship. It also acknowledges a responsibility, which as much entails voicing that responsibility as performing it. Reading *Walden* as raising questions about the power and place of language in what Cavell, in another context (quoting Emerson) calls "this new, yet unapproachable, America" (*This New*) Cavell suggests that

> Writing—heroic writing, the writing of a nation's scripture—must assume the conditions of language as such; re-experience, as it were, the fact that there is such a thing as language at all and assume responsibility for it—find a way to acknowledge it—until the nation is capable of serious speech again. Writing must assume responsibility, in particular, for three of the features of the language it lives upon: (1) that every mark of a language means something in the language, one thing rather than another; that a language is totally, systematically meaningful; (2) that words and their orderings are meant by human beings, that they contain (or conceal) their beliefs, express (or deny) their convictions; and (3) that the saying of something when and as it is said is as significant as the meaning and ordering of the words said. (*Senses* 33)

Throughout "My Kinsman," the fragmentation of language—to its veritible demise—is everywhere in evidence. "I have authority, I have—hem, hem—authority," says the elderly citizen (15), whose speech is continuously interrupted by these "sepulchral hems . . . like a thought of a cold grave obtruding among wrathful passions" (15). "What have we here?" asks the inn keeper, "breaking his speech into little dry fragments" (18). "'Home, vagabond, home!' said the watchman, in accents that seemed to fall asleep as soon as they were uttered" (22). Individuals come hurrying along, "utter[ing] a few words in some language of which Robin knew nothing, and perceiving his inability to answer, bestow[ing] a curse upon him in plain English" (23). The street "murmur . . . was a low, dull, dreamy sound, compounded of many noises, each of which was at too great a distance to be separately heard. Robin marvelled at this snore of a sleeping town" (25). Language, in other words, is, throughout this story, either asleep or dead. It certainly doesn't act to communicate, either knowledge or feelings. The inebriation, the inflammation, of the mind which the story records, seems to have affected the powers of speech along with the powers of thought.

Therefore, Hawthorne's own use of words becomes intensely interesting. How, perhaps, does this story constitute a gesture toward community without either becoming coercively political or, in the opposite direction, dissolving into a sleepy murmur? How is the story's language the key to its political empowerment? indeed, its contribution to the ongoing process of creating and affirming American democracy?

Hawthorne is under no illusions about the political nature of interpretation, whoever is doing the interpreting. But he also believes that the institutionalization of human relations along certain lines—the lines created by the interpretive apparatus of Hawthorne's own story—can foster both human freedom and social commitment. In the prefatory note to the story Hawthorne already raises the specter (confirmed at the end by the more literal "specter" of "Major Molineux") that the American "popular mind," whose "temporary inflammation" the story records, is itself a form of power politics, where the difference between the old definition of power and the new depends only on the fact that "power" now "emanates" from the people (13). The popular mind, in other words, has, as I have already suggested, merely substituted one tyrant (the people) for another (the king). This self-empowerment might well seem a disease peculiar to democracy. But the problem of America is simply one construct, among many, of the problem of ideology or consensus, the problem of our always being inside the situation we would interpret, inside the language we would use to interpret it, and so never free from interpretive prejudice. Indeed, this, I have been arguing, seems to be the problem which the story dramatizes. From the moment Robin steps off the boat, he sees the community, and the community sees him, within highly fixed and easily recognizable stereotypes.

All such attempts to understand of course fail. Hawthorne's story, therefore, exists (to use Cavell's terminology) to teach us distance, to show us that we cannot so easily understand. Hence the non-mimetic form of the story, the dream-like features of both Robin's and our own experience of the story's events. One of Robin's most serious errors in the story is that, at the end of his sojourn, he forgets the defamiliarization (or distance) he has experienced. It is as if he believes that by changing ontological gears he can finally bring into focus a story which at every moment strives to enforce upon him a consciousness of its incomprehensibility. (A major feature of the story has been Robin's constantly siting distant objects and trying to bring them into focus). But Robin's experience is no different from the experience of life itself, revealed through the skeptically-tinted lens of romance fiction.

That we cannot understand turns out not to enslave us to a world of unfathomable and hence uncontrollable mystery, but, quite the contrary, it releases us from the tyranny of consensus.

This tyranny of consensus, making the world seem familiar, would prevent our interpreting it. Even more problematically, it would prohibit our acknowledging it. By this I mean it would prevent our simultaneously granting the unknowability of other people and establishing meaningful relations with them. Robin believes that he will "recognize" his kinsman when he sees him. But in Hawthorne's vocabulary, to *re*cognize is not to know but to know again. Thus knowing, in Hawthorne's lexicon, is neither passive nor automatic. Rather it is a continuous effort of the mind to get beyond what must be a moment of *not* knowing, to reacquire something which has been lost. Recognition is Hawthorne's word for what Cavell calls acknowledgement. It means opting for a sense of knowing which makes space for doubt, which indeed makes doubt integral to knowing. The characters of Hawthorne's story are, if nothing else, smug. They are sure they know about American democracy, as decades later the citizens of America were also sure they knew about their Revolution, and as even decades after that, readers of Hawthorne's story were sure they knew the revised interpretation of the Revolution Hawthorne's story seems to propose. But, according to Hawthorne's story, one cannot "know" in this way. One can only know what one chooses to acknowledge, which means knowing through ways which are not certifiable and which constantly take note of the strangeness of the world. Knowing, thus defined, requires self-imposed commitments external to any category like "truth."

To the credit of the characters in Hawthorne's story (to the credit of America) America would found democracy upon a consensus open to any and all who would share it. Therefore, America does not represent totalitarianism, even in the crudities of the early colonial experience. Robin is finally free to leave, though his gentleman friend will menacingly put off his departure, at least a few days. But neither is the social organization represented in Hawthorne's story the definition of democracy. Democracy, for Hawthorne, depends as much upon the process of consent, let's call it affirmation or acknowledgment, as upon tacit participation within an already established social consensus. What it means, precisely, to consent to a consensus seems to me the issue in "My Kinsman," as it is, as I have argued elsewhere, in *The Scarlet Letter* (1992). Robin's laugh at the end of the story signals his immersion in a consensus to which he cannot voice his consent because he has forfeited the place from which consent is voiced. This is the place of strangeness or defamiliarization which makes us conscious and self-conscious of where we stand, which is always as strangers to the world and to each other. Such consciousness, which philosophers have explored as radical doubt and which a tradition of American writers have investigated through romance fiction, recognizes distance. Thus it makes consent external to consensus, always in the posture of overcoming a resistance we respect as necessary and inviolable, withdrawing from a society which, inevitably a source of contagion, also protects us from this infection by providing us with institutions such as law and literature. This movement away from society, which characterizes Robin's desire at the end of the story to go back home is finally Hawthorne's desire to create a home, in America, on the basis of our collective desire to make it home.

How does one read "My Kinsman?" How does one live in America? resisting, and yet taking seriously, everyone's point of view, including one's own; recognizing that texts and nations are neither natural evolutions nor metaphysical truths but human contracts, which are not (for that reason) less worthy of our assent than either nature or truth. Thus we read Hawthorne's story, as we live in his America, as part of a contractual obligation, respecting autonomy, binding ourselves to community. Indeed, reading Hawthorne's story we may well be living in his America, for taking hold of words (reading them) and letting go our own words (writing them), we sign our own consent to the consent Hawthorne signs in "My Kinsman." Reading and writing, in Hawthorne's view, as in Cavell's, are contractual relationships of aversive acknowledgment. Thus, for Hawthorne, America continues, from generation to generation, to declare its independence as an enterprise of consenting to the condition of being in dependence. This, in the tradition of romance fiction and philosophy, is America's genuine revolution of in|dependence. This revolution turns, not away from but toward community, thus generating the society and history of the democracy.

REFERENCES

Baym, Nina. *The Shape of Hawthorne's Career*. Ithaca: Cornell University Press, 1976.

Bercovitch, Sacvan. *The Office of the Scarlet Letter.* Baltimore: Johns Hopkins University Press, 1991.

———. "The Problem of Ideology in American Literary History." *Critical Inquiry* 12 (1986):631–53.

Budick, Emily Miller. "Sacvan Bercovitch, Stanley Cavell, and the Romance Theory of American Fiction." *PMLA* 107 (1992), 78–91.

———. *Fiction and Historical Consciousness: The American Romance Tradition.* New Haven: Yale University Press, 1989.

Cavell, Stanley. "Aversive Thinking: Emersonian Representations in Heidegger and Nietzsche." *Conditions* 33–63.

———. "Being Odd, Getting Even (*Descartes, Emerson, Poe*)." *Reconstructing Individualism: Autonomy, Individuality, and the Self in Western Thought.* Ed. T. C. Heller, M. Sosna, and D. E. Wellbery. Stanford: Stanford University Press, 1986. 278–312. Rpt. *In Quest of the Ordinary: Lines of Skepticism and Romanticism.* Chicago: University of Chicago Press, 1988. 105–49.

———. *Conditions Handsome and Unhandsome.* Chicago: University of Chicago Press, 1990.

———. *The Claim of Reason: Wittgenstein, Skepticism, Morality, and Tragedy.* Oxford: Oxford University Press, 1979.

———. "Hope Against Hope." *The American Poetry Review.* Jan./Feb. 1986: 9–13; Rpt. *Conditions* 129–38.

———. "The Politics of Interpretation." *Themes Out Of School: Effects and Causes.* San Francisco: North Point Press, 1984.

———. *The Senses of Walden.* NY: Viking Press, 1972.

———. *This New Yet Unapproachable America: Lectures after Emerson after Wittgenstein.* Albuquerque, New Mexico: Living Batch Press, 1989.

Crews, Frederick. "Whose American Renaissance?" *The New York Review of Books.* Oct. 27, 1988:68–81.

Derrida, Jacques. "*Geschlecht* II" Heiddegger's Hand," *Deconstruction and Philosophy: The Texts of Jacques Derrida.* Ed. John Sallis. Chicago, Chicago University Press.

Fischer, Michael. *Stanley Cavell and Literary Skepticism.* Chicago: Chicago University Press, 1989.

Fish, Stanley. *Is There a Text in This Class?* Cambridge, MA: Harvard University Press, 1980.

Hawthorne, Nathaniel. "My Kinsman, Major Molineux." *Hawthorne: Selected Tales and Sketches.* Ed. Hyatt H. Waggoner. New York: Holt, Rinehart. 1950.

Iser, Wolfgang. *The Act of Reading: A Theory of Aesthetic Response.* Baltimore: Johns Hopkins University Press, 1982.

CHAPTER 11

Intertextuality and Reader Responsibility: Living On in Malamud's "The Mourners"

Sharon Deykin Baris

> The purpose of the writer . . . is to keep civilization alive. . . . My premise is that we will live on.
>
> Malamud (1958)

> And to go write-on-living? If that were possible, would the writer have to be dead already, or be living on?
>
> Derrida (1977)

Bernard Malamud's "The Mourners" is a tale of boarders and border crossings. It tells of immigrant boarders in an American house of fiction whose postwar stories must be heard and understood. It also challenges us as readers to define the physical and mental borders that must be both recognized yet somehow crossed over in order to test ourselves as human beings in a postmodern and post-Holocaust period. This brief work seems simply, if hauntingly, to describe dwellers in a decrepit tenement who fail to exchange social amenities or even to acknowledge one another's grief and isolation.[1] Written little more than a decade after World War II and set in that same period, it thoughtfully mirrors a postwar moment when so many people felt they could not bear any

---

This paper is a version of an essay that appeared in *Studies in American Jewish Literature,* Vol. 11 (1992):45–61.

more tales of human suffering and violence. In this context it is not incidental to note that the two main protagonists are Jewish, that the writer is Jewish, and that this story is called "The Mourners." Although the Holocaust is not mentioned, we can surmise that the pervasive mood of numbness in Malamud's story reflects a perplexing inability to share narratives of survival in its aftermath. Yet "The Mourners" drives toward a final scene in which Gruber the landlord is at last moved by "the extent of Kessler's suffering" and tries to imagine some "bad news" as an explanation for what is "wrong here" (25). When Gruber unexpectedly joins Kessler in mourning and winds himself in a sheet (whether wrapping himself in the folds of a prayer shawl or in the pages of another person's story), he responds wholeheartedly to his tenant Kessler's condition. His reaction, however, is too sudden and too ready to be true, and such winding sheets seem only to serve as a cover for his self-enclosed version of someone else's grief. As we in reading the ending of "The Mourners" in turn weigh our own estimation of Gruber's mourning, we face a fundamental paradox within this fiction or within all narratives: can one ever know another's tale? At stake in the final moments is the larger problem of what it means to respond to someone else's story, and what we can do to acknowledge our responsibility to it. In the double lights of postmodern theoretics and post-Holocaust paralysis, we read a work that thematizes inaction and yet demands reaction, and pause to take note of its strange power. We may well wonder just how Malamud's story does its work to make us as readers become responsive, responsible mourners.[2]

In a 1958 interview, Malamud spoke of his artist's premise that through literature we "keep civilization alive . . . we will live on" (7). Yet recent postmodern theories have focused upon the very problem of what it is in reading that can be shared. Jacques Derrida uses that same term, *sur-vivre,* to describe a dynamic in which words and texts always breed one upon the other "to go write-on-living" ("Living On" 77). Such survival empties a text of exceptional or individual meaning, since each telling—or reading—revises what has already gone before. While vital in one sense, this process can be seen as destructive, for versions are, in Harold Bloom's term, powerful "mis-readings" of the prior text (1975). Gruber, wanting to share Kessler's sorrow, joins him in sheets of mourning. But before doing so, Gruber imagines his own rendition of Kessler's life story in an ostensibly sympathetic way: "Then it struck him with a terrible force that the mourner was mourning him: it was *he* who was dead" (25). His reaction, that is, catapults him as listener into the center of his neighbor's tale, projecting his own meanings at the heart of Kessler's grief. In this painful context such a self-centered response, while humorous, is also repugnant. But can Gruber avert such solipsism? We turn the question inward to ask: can we become mourners not simply—or not only—of ourselves?

Recoiling from Gruber's easy sentimentality, we notice that this story presents unmistakable clues to a setting that demands both Gruber's and the reader's statement of the relationship between responding to texts and asserting responsibility to them, as a test here posed. In a comment at the story's outset, the narrator notes that Kessler has unaccountably walked out on his wife and children; but with this seeming irrelevancy, Malamud prepares us for the unnerving possibility that in viewing "The Mourners" as a literary instance of sorrow and reconciliation, we too could walk out. Kessler "never saw them thereafter because he never sought them"; thereby we are forewarned against following the example of Malamud's characters, in never seeing or never seeking certain unbudging conditions that this tale contains (17).

Yet the texture of Malamud's story, I will argue, complicates and nearly confounds the reader's desires to face up to that testing. On the one hand, the plot tells of Kessler's urgent need to communicate with others in a period that is specified as "ten years after the war." Here are exiles, cut off from their past and from each other, in need of a term ironically mentioned in the first line, "social security." To that end, this story's action turns upon features such as letters and games: through an emphasis upon semiotic exchange we are reminded of opportunities that ought not to be lost or thwarted. Malamud locates his exiles, moreover, in the specific setting of New York's East Side, as if to have them dwell together in a potential house of nations within a new world scene, there to participate in a postwar era and a land of promise. Appropriately enough, the story includes suggestive references to American precursor texts—literary works that also focus upon shared dwellings, communicative potential, and regenerative or redemptive overtones—as if to include this tenement building as a house of fiction in a row of others constituting a powerful tradition. Such a suggestion is doubly effective, we may feel, since it demonstrates how this author, at least, does acknowledge others' texts in an ongoing line of influence and response.

On the other hand, it is those textual or metalinguistic features, placed against the specified background of an American setting of hope and within an American literary tradition, that instead function to underline a haunting sense of defeat for any expectation of communication. They intensify the pain of these characters' unappeased longings. For deeply personal tales of grief can be washed out within the theoretical scope of intertextuality, or within an overpowering—even though hopeful—tradition. In its complex strategy of combining insistent emphasis upon letters demanding to be answered, with equally powerful elements of intertextual suggestion, Malamud enacts a problematics for his characters and readers alike.[3] It is no wonder, then, that "The Mourners"—so troubling and so unsolvable—has been largely ignored in studies of Malamud and of American fiction.[4] Its grim quality derives neither from its whiny characters nor from Malamud's inability to convince us of Gruber's sincerity at the conclusion, but rather, I would argue, from our own unremitting stress in the face of its conflicting demands. When we acknowledge that difficulty and assert the relationship between words and deeds, we discover how Malamud's story can do its work upon us.

As if to emphasize some call to action, "The Mourners" as a title, like *The Fixer, The Assistant,* and others by Malamud, suggests a task to be performed, and the story's first word presents the name of the central figure in a form that suggests some livelihood (Kessl*er*).[5] All the other characters are similarly identified by names that would seem to indicate an occupation, job, or characteristic behavior: Gruber, Hoffman, Italian, and even Ignace are names suggestive of action.[6] And yet this story is pervaded by dysfunction and paralysis. Kessler, whose occupation as an egg-candler had been intimately connected with life potential, is now unemployed, severed from vital occupations of any sort. His precarious position is given in the first line of the story. Although he lives on social security, Kessler is so insecure in the tenement he has shared with others like himself since the war that he is unable to participate in any form of social contact and is more or less unknown, even by his neighbors. Nor are any of the others gathered together in such a house of nations more able than Kessler to perform physically or socially or in any productive sense. The Hoffmans, whose name suggests courtyards, courtiers, or social figures,[7] are identified primarily as the ones who "never said hello" to Kessler (17). The Italian mother next door, in contrast to Kessler, lives with her three children; but she is wizened, and the sons are middle-aged, with limited potential. The Hoffmans add further to this picture of devitalized households; they are "sullen, childless," and no progeny at all are mentioned concerning the others, including the landlord or the janitor. These last two, Gruber and Ignace,[8] do perform active, if violent, deeds but only to direct their forces toward Kessler's abrupt eviction—a project that is negative at best.

Some hope for communicative action is signaled early in the story's development by a quirky feature Malamud presents for seemingly little purpose. The janitor and Kessler have cooperated in one pleasant pastime together: "they had several times played two-handed pinochle" (18). Card games are the very essence of semiotic exchange; yet all too soon any promise of shared terms or socialized intercourse degenerates into its extreme opposite. Ignace's losses in pinochle arouse his malicious desire to "spread the word" in the divisive form of bad-naming Kessler (18). After the card game fiasco, Malamud focuses upon the building as site of all kinds of communicative breakdowns, as Ignace's bad language leads to the further estrangement of Kessler from everyone in the house. They reject his decrepitude, shunning him as a dirty old man. When Gruber, stirred up, demands that Kessler "scram outa here," he cuts off Kessler's attempted explanations by warning him, in specifically linguistic terms: "Don't talk back talk" (20).

With the story's early emphasis upon hellos never said and upon a card game which leads only to further linguistic lapses, the appropriateness of the apartment house as a metaphor for Malamud's disunited nations becomes even more painful: premises aren't truly shared. The action hereafter devolves from failed words and signals: the plot depends upon letters delivered only to be returned, invectives shouted through doors, eviction notices, or even the ghastly eviction itself carried out with desperate shouts and pleas to neighbors for help. Yet they are unresponsive and mute: "they looked on in a silent group outside the door" (21). It is the distortions of language—the shrieks and gesticulations of the Italian woman—that finally arouse her sons (they are unable to think of what else to do) to heft this miserable tenant back upstairs where Hoffman, too, finally adds his efforts. But all this is minimal—too little, too late—and the woman's inept verbal skills, her shrieks, her gesticulations, "loose mouth working angrily," are matched by Ignace's similarly inept screeches at everybody, calling them filthy names. Such words and gestures create a bitterly parodic scene of interaction, and at its end, Kessler once again is barricaded in loneliness; his furniture remains all piled up in his bedroom. He weeps and is silent once again. The food set out by that Italian neighbor now congeals on Kessler's plate, symbolizing, perhaps, the end of all nourishing interchange.

In such a drama, the small physical prop of a letter box draws our attention. Here is a mundane medium for ordinary communication that only emphasizes the dead-letter quality of this household's sorely limited discourse. Whatever language these characters do manage to use only further betrays a thwarted outlook. Whereas in the beginning of this story there seemed some chance of human attention in the form of personal care or notice on the stairs and in the hallways of their shared tenement, now the humane and active verb *to notice,* is wrenched into the harshly abstracting noun form, *notice.* This noun becomes the menace at the very heart of Kessler's misery, when the landlord angrily *gives notice.* The devitalized existence they all lead is even more violently brought out when Gruber claims he will act, but only to "get *a dispossess*" (emphasis added; 20), further demonstrating the way that language (like the macaroni) will harden in such an environment. Kessler's reply to Gruber is thus appropriate when he responds to his missives with hard cash; but subsequent events show that even such minimal interchange is refused. Worse still, in one terrible moment of confrontation when Gruber is "at first at a loss what to say," he adds insult to injury, showing the indifference of all his yelling, papers, and demands by then declaring, "Listen, Kessler, it's not personal" (23).

Gruber, who once had sensed his building to be falling apart, now in a fit of deeper despair feels the moment of crisis at hand and has a more specific premonition that it will collapse. He recalls, significantly, that "He had read of such things" (22–23). Gruber, that is, imagines an outcome for this story that matches—even becomes—another version of what he already knows. His willful literary response is imposed upon this story, and "The

Mourners," with its insistent focus upon texts and messages, might develop, in his reading, into the narrative of such collapse. On the next day, after one more significant confrontation, a final dumbshow in Kessler's apartment presents the climax of Malamud's tale and raises the question whether, indeed, such collapse is doomed to occur. The scene begins when Gruber bursts into Kessler's rooms to find him shoeless, swaying slowly sideways. We are now given a long passage that is rendered as if in Kessler's mind's eye: a series of moments, details, and events are recollected "in all the intervening years" (25). All his thoughts and all these years smite Kessler to the heart, and as he reviews the past without end, he is moved so deeply as to tear his flesh with his fingernails. Gruber, on his side, is frightened at the extent of Kessler's suffering and tries to understand why. He tries to imagine what he ominously calls the bad news of Kessler's life story, only then to see himself falling down stairs, lying at the bottom, at the center of the mourning: "it was *he* who was dead." His emotion is intense; that we know. He is agonized and feels an enormous weight within him, until his head is nearly bursting. Yet he cannot conjure any bad news other than his own. In the minute that ensues, he endures a stroke of total silence, signaling the very end of all language or tales and their sharing.

Suddenly, however, Malamud shifts the scene to describe the setting of another version that quite miraculously assuages Gruber's bursting silent misery: "When after a while, he gazed around the room, it was clean, drenched in daylight and fragrance" (26). With the words "daylight and fragrance," Malamud appears to suggest a new and redemptive vision ("it was clean") of a room that, a short time before, had been but a stinking East Side tenement. These regenerative terms are appropriate to a new-world habit of turning toward new beginnings in nature, with rebirth always possible in some verdant transcendent version. It is such pastoral elegiac settings that belong to all great transformations of darkness into light and mourning into rebirth and celebration.[9] In this vein Gruber reads his neighbor's text and self-reliantly presumes to know it, as if in sharing. Only then does he feel remorse for "the old man"—whether for himself or Kessler, since their stories correspond—and he cries as he enwraps himself in sheets of consolation.

But the contrast between Kessler's swaying and thinking-through of past events that "smote him to the heart" in a process of recalling the "past without end" and Gruber's cry at the prospect of a comforting elegiac vision is enormous. It is in this impasse that Malamud's evocation of a post-Holocaust East Side urban elegy become most brilliant and disturbing. It asks us to recognize our conflicting impulses in reading as a means of sharing and solace or of facing our *in*ability ever to fully share the text of another's private experience, reading another's text as unbudgingly other or alien and *thus* feel its call to response and commitment. Harold Fisch, in his study of literature as covenant, points to the essential difference between what he would call poetry "with a purpose," and the "endlessly self-referential pastoral elegy" (*Poetry* 63). Texts can in their very "nagging presence" serve as a call to action, he agues, and it is this recognition that would make reader response no consolation at all, but would cause it to become an "urgent historical task."[10] Malamud's silent hallways, returned letters, failed exchanges, and literary allusions in a house of language that must not collapse, all, have built to a final scene that requires some answer. A great deal hangs in the reply, since, as Kessler's behavior has from the first forewarned us ("never saw . . . never sought") and as Gruber's glib interpretive habits ("it's not personal") have continually shown: escaping this story's conditions can also "do so much wrong" (25).

Books and pages shared in Malamud's works—noticeably within this same volume of *The Magic Barrel*—serve a particular and forceful function. They can be a medium for courtship, a tool for a successful career, or even an enticement in seduction.[11] The question posed for the reader of "The Mourners" is how this text, too, can function. While it is true that Gruber's elegiac vision offers little true consolation for Kessler's grief, we may wonder whether there is some nagging presence within this text requiring a deeper commitment to Kessler's mournful tale. "The Mourners," as I have noted, uses metalinguistic devices to focus attention upon the hunger for personal communication among the boarders in this text. Yet we can measure the extent of a second pervasive element in "The Mourners": there are provocative hints of literary reference that point beyond the borders of this text, especially to other challenging and well-known American works. There is, of course, nothing new in noting that Malamud was, in his words, "influenced by literature" (Field and Field, *A Collection* 11).[12] Many echoes have been identified throughout Malamud's writings—heroes that seem to repeat biblical, mythic, and literary archetypes or other literary precedents. If such references have been overlooked by critics of "The Mourners," it could be because the story itself has been deemed too frail to carry a weighty message. Yet, as I have suggested, it is not the brevity or frailty of this work which has deterred attention to its pages, but rather its troubling, even haunting quality, a quality in which the very element of literary reference is located at the center. It is the attraction yet danger inherent not only in the games, language, or letters described within this tale, but also in the deeper play of interrelation with other works it evokes, that poses this story's fundamental and important paradox.

Two particularly challenging resonances of American precursors recur throughout the pages of "The Mourners": Herman Melville's "Bartleby the Scrivener," and Stephen Crane's "The Blue Hotel." All three works are tales of shared houses characterized by failed communication among the inhabitants—a failure that culminates in threatened ejection of a central figure. Thematically, "Bartleby the Scrivener" (its title also suggesting some *-er* action), most clearly echoes in Malamud's later tale, as the lone scrivener, like Kessler, refuses offers of food and help. Both elicit at last a strange response when Gruber, like the lawyer, seems compassionate, as if also to sigh in true and mournful understanding, "Ah, humanity!"[13] Crane's "The Blue Hotel," like the Malamud tale, centers upon characters who are known by names that suggest action: Easterner, Swede, cowboy, gambler, and so on.[14] In "The Mourners," after Gruber announces to Kessler, "This is trespassing and you're breaking the law. Answer me," his startled tenant's reply is hauntingly like that of the cowboy in Crane's tale. When the Easterner declares that we are "all kind[s] of an adverb. Every sin is the result of a collaboration," the cowboy responds, "Well, I *didn't do* anythin', did I?" So, too, Kessler questions his implication or guilt, demanding from Gruber, "What *did I do?*" (emphasis added; 23).

"The Mourners," like its precursors, dwells upon the theme of responsibility in the face of questions posed about what "did I do" or of the onlookers' failure to "do anythin'"; all three, moreover, are linked by being consciously self-reflexive. Crane's "The Blue Hotel," like Melville's "Bartleby the Scrivener," pays insistent attention to linguistic or semiotic exchange in the form of letters, proofreading, or signs, and even another failed card game. It is as if these famous works, so appropriately evoked in Malamud's later tale themselves are not to be reread as an indication of what it is that one ought, collaboratively, adverbially, to do.[15] Yet these themes, repeatedly evoked, are only part of Malamud's strategy in this tale of an exilic household longing for meaningful terms or collaborative versions. It is the fact of echoing itself that is enacted in Malamud's problematic telling, as it interposes versions of Melville's or Crane's message in the midst of this postwar household's problems. As Gruber and Kessler weep, the jarring contradictions are not those of light and fragrance as against the stinking environment of the tenement.[16] The contradictions lie, rather, between this story's two powerful textual strategies as they are played off against each other. It is precisely because its call for personal messages and direct responsibility ("what did I do?") is made within an undercurrent of endlessly repeating, thus decentering versions—of pastoral elegies, themselves self-reflexive, or of American redefinitions of redemptive outcomes—that in the end we as tested readers can *not* join Gruber and weep.

Parting ways with Malamud's reader of self-gratifying versions, we question the very premise of consolation in literature and will not, after all, walk out on Kessler and his unpleasant tale. Whether Malamud himself fully comprehended the extent of his story's rich challenge, or whether his artist's sensitivity to his place and time—"ten years later" than the Holocaust in an American setting within a national literary tradition newly tested—helped him reach toward profound depths in this very brief work, we cannot know. We feel the weight of Gruber's response upon our shoulders especially in our time, and see how Malamud's work pushes us toward acknowledging tensions implicit between intertextuality and responsibility (tensions, I believe, that are ingrained in these same American literary precursors and in the American tradition itself—but that is another study).

As a form of acknowledging others' statements or works, intertextuality does promise reaction and renewal. Harold Bloom's explanation of reading as a process of rereading prior texts in newly assertive terms in a form of powerful response, would seem the very answer to the needs of Gruber's band of exiles.[17] More promising still for this vitiated tenement would be the concept of survival as linguistic regeneration offered by Jacques Derrida in an essay entitled, appropriately enough, "Living On: Borderlines." When all language is beyond controlled borders, it can never be limited; meanings are derived through shared texts always and already there without fail in the ongoing life of language itself. Thus, instead of the card games that in Malamud's story are threatening when not played according to delimited terms, Derrida perceives an everlasting play or *jouissance* that celebrates the variations inherent in all intercourse. If Malamud's dwellers feel uncertainty, since "None of the tenants in the house had held a written lease since the war" (18), Derrida instead calls attention to the way unsettled conditions, linguistically speaking, are normal ("Living On" 83–84). In contrast to the sterility of Malamud's bereft household, Derrida's theoretics show how narratives thrive when words breed one upon another—to *sur-vivre.*

Here then is reader-responsive action considered in its widest implication as a universal cooperative principle. But can these concepts provide a cure for the pain felt by those who have dwelt (since the war) in the house that Malamud presents? Despite theorists' suggestive language of breeding and vitality, these concepts most certainly do not assuage the postwar dwellers' pain or repair their broken world. Misreading in Bloom's sense presumes a fundamental inability (however powerful one may be) to know the text of some other person's story or version. There is, moreover, as Bloom puts it, an inherent anxiety in the very drive toward incessant misreading, that is no palliative for those who want so desperately to talk back talk and demand to be understood. "The impossibility of reading," says another deconstructionist critic, "should not be taken too lightly,"[18] and that is precisely the crux of the problem. The fertility that any theory of intertextuality promises can never help the mourners, any more than concepts of living on as linguistic regeneration in some automatic sense can bring assurance to one who wants others to know how it was, barely, brutally, with every mite of personal resource, to survive.

In a story specifically contextualized, the author has evoked a house full of tragic postwar exiles to dramatize their desire to be heard, only then to nearly entice his readers into imaginatively walking out on them through his technique of intertextuality. While Gruber and Kessler live in this decrepit tenement with all their colorful, if quirky and querulous individuality, Malamud's literary echoes place them in an American house of fiction or tradition, headed by authors such as Herman Melville and Stephen Crane. The problem is not whether the literary reference or tradition invoked be the right one—either too American or not enough Jewish.[19] The question, rather, is whether such recourse to literary reference (however elegantly evoked or appropriate the theme of Bartleby's or the cowboy's tales) in the mood of his time—and ours—be morally justified.

Malamud himself at one moment insists upon facing this issue. Although it is true that the names of the characters seem provocatively to imply action in some sense of occupation, livelihood or social intercourse, there is one more case—one that in this paper goes still unmentioned—of a similarly named "-er" person who could never be identified by some generalized trade or calling, and most certainly not broadly grouped among those who might learn to become mourners. Malamud's story contains the significant utterance of another name that could suggest a businessman—perhaps a hatter or some related trade—and his name is blurted out in the central climax, after Kessler is unceremoniously returned to his apartment. When Gruber angrily confronts Kessler with threats about breaking the law, Kessler first responds to the demand "Answer me," in broken grammar and halting query (23). Despite his brimming eyes, he slowly gathers courage to pose a terrible moral problem for his accuser: "Who hurts a man without reason?" And finally, gaining an even stronger voice, Kessler raises the question that becomes definitive for Malamud's presentation and for any considerations a reader may have, of responding to this story. Kessler continues: "Are you *a Hitler* . . . ?" (emphasis added).

"A Hitler," unlike a kessler, hoffman, gruber, or some fiery personality, is a term whose status cannot be reduced to the designation of an occupational category, despite Kessler's use of the "a" before the name. Malamud's inclusion of games, letters, and other linguistic features has emphasized the importance of shared texts and lives. Mention of a Hitler disorients the reader, abruptly causing us to question the validity of metalinguistic contexts or playful wordgames in understanding people such as Gruber, Hoffman, and the others. It casts doubt, furthermore, upon the adequacy of any means for imagining Hitler.[20] When Malamud shows Kessler facing Gruber (or *Schicklgruber,* perhaps in a hint of origins, of Hitler's mother's maiden name), we too face up to this encounter and try to reach beyond the borders of fiction in order to seek some relation between words and the world we know.[21] We feel it unjustifiable to continually imagine meanings, as this paper has done at the outset, in some playful spirit, spinning out echoes and lively variations possible for each term or text. Despite Derrida's concepts of "living on" or Bloom's powerful "misreadings," a Schicklgruber's fact and thus his name now surely deflects our attempts to theorize it into traces, or lightly to defer its certain meaning.[22] Malamud's identification of Gruber with Hitler in the crisis of his story foregrounds the unremitting friction between two textual strategies. Kessler's urgent need for some back talk in the form of personal understanding can not be satisfied with recourse to theoretics or broadly cultural terms, even those suggested by the attractive American tradition and the searching moral questions that Melville and Crane, too, evoke. And that is why, after all, the challenge that Malamud presents in the final scene of weeping disqualifies definition in terms of pastoral elegiac consolation.

If Gruber's participation fails to move Malamud's readers, that resistance is aroused not only by the sudden emotion, the elaborate dramatic gestures or the winding sheets that all seem so extravagant. It is because they are irrelevant to Kessler's and the others' private histories. Our very resistance finally emerging at the story's end—whether to Gruber or to Malamud's complicity in such mourning—attests to the challenge this perturbing story presents. Causing his readers to consider what it is to confront certain unbudging words, stories, and facts, Malamud's troubling work brings into clearer focus undeniable tensions of the postwar period that he, and we, feel compelled to acknowledge. Sensing his own and others' inability to face historic testimonies, holocaust diaries, or personal stories, Malamud managed in his time to expose a problematics of reading that more than ever confounds us.

James E. Young, for example, reminds us of the cruel fate of survivors who "lived solely to bear witness," believing their story "could bring the *realia* of their experiences forward in time through their words," only to discover in more recent deconstructionist theories that there was no text, and that their diaries' records carried only signs of meanings that would later be deferred and reread or misread by others who swerved from the experiences described (1988 24–25). Young's point is important; and we can see how Malamud's fiction in 1955 probes those painful lapses between recording and responding that would, with the sophistication afforded by the insights of postmodern literary theory, be iterated three decades later. Malamud's audience, troubled throughout by the story's conflicting demands of self-reflexivity and yet of some moral, historical imperative, finally parts ways with Gruber and his winding sheets of mourning. Malamud's readers find suspect a resort to literature as mere comfort or easy escape to another form of depersonalization. We remember, instead, just what it was that Kessler did or egregiously failed to do when he pathetically asked, "What did I did to you?"

Questioning and remembering thus, we refuse the double deferral of responsibility implicit in the echoing of Crane's story and of the Easterner's words: "I didn't do anythin' did I?" Despite brilliant poststructuralist affirmations (that are denials of such responsibility), we face up to the way books can relate to deeds. If the elegiac vision of Gruber's last scene allows him gratefully to sink into a pastoral vision as a curative sense of sympathetic response, joining as he does some symbolic band of mourners, yet Malamud's story instructs us as readers: that will not suffice. Moving beyond an implicit literary consolation, Malamud in this story has established demanding conditions within which survivors' stories are to be bared. The pain of both readers and tellers will stand exposed, not wrapped in available self-reflexive versions for cloaking grief.

Malamud has hinted at his own dilemma in writing "The Mourners" in that numbed and troubled decade after the war. With author and tale thus historicized, we, too, are called to reckon our position. We may read "The Mourners" as resisting readers—as women, for example—who use the verb to notice and worry about that lone wife and her children whom Kessler has so unaccountably left behind at the story's beginning.[23] What we bring to Malamud's story is our reaction as human beings—women, men, children, Americans, survivors, and dwellers upon this earth—who feel personally challenged to acknowledge our world and attest to its inhabitants' life stories. Our reckoning becomes an extension of our distinctive experiences; it makes our reading and our mourning, both, profound occasions for testing and testimony. When we respond to literature in this way, we refrain from formulating what Harold Fisch has described as the pastoral poet's "'as-if' statement—a lovely conceit," akin to Gruber's final sympathetic but self-satisfying cry. We acknowledge instead that other's stories can, as Fisch describes another kind of reading process, "point outwards, beyond themselves [to] remind us of duties" (*Poetry* 67).[24] Reading in this way, we respond to Malamud's disturbing short story not at all *as if* we have become part of a band of literary mourners in a theoretical, pastoral, or redemptive tradition. We respond, rather, by recognizing how this text, with its particular terms and demanding strategies, does its work upon us in disconcerting ways. Our testing is the vital good deed that Malamud's story requires. Inverting Gruber's indifferent plea, we each then duly acknowledge: "Listen, it *is* personal" and remember this story's facts to affirm our humanity. That, I suggest, is what reading Malamud's "The Mourners" can do.

NOTES

1. In his last interview, 1986, Malamud echoed a similar call for literary optimism: "I had to find a way for man to have a possible future" (Salzberg 237). Page references to the 1958 edition of "The Mourners" will be given in the text of this essay.

2. Stanley Cavell, speaking of another drama, raises the question: "How does it do its work upon us?" (qtd. in Bruns 622). Cavell's notion of receptiveness is especially appropriate to the scene we have here followed: *un*like Gruber who wraps or cloaks himself in the face of another's grief, Cavell speaks of listening as a process of *exposing* both the subject and ourselves, "giving up the will to explain and desire for absolute self-possession." Cavell studies the links between self-reliance and responsibility, between responsiveness and a sense of pain.

3. In a challenging essay that focuses on Malamud's use of narrative strategy, Lawrence M. Lasher suggests that a later story, "The German Refugee" (1963), first signals Malamud's "attempt to define the connection between private morality and public events," and claims that that story "is the only place in the canon where Malamud allows the Holocaust to emerge from the generalized background of his characters' lives into vivid and compelling imagery" (72). Dorothy Bilik devotes two lines to "The Mourners" and the "uncertainty and tension" its style conveys (69). It is appropriate to point out that Alvin Rosenfeld finds that "all novels about Jewish suffering written in the post-Holocaust period must implicate the Holocaust, whether it is expressly named as such or not." He includes Malamud specifically as one of those whose art "might

succeed in oblique or indirect representation of this most horrific of all Jewish tragedies" (*Reflections* 68).

4. One brief study of "The Mourners" is typical, in categorizing Gruber as a "stock figure in Yiddish and Malamudian fiction, a schlemiel" (Solotaroff 34–35). In the lengthiest critical look at "The Mourners," Irving Halperin devotes four pages to an overview of its plot to show the "theme of responsibility" (465). How it is that Malamud "compels us to recognize" the landlord's spiritual death and later transformation, however, is not explained.

5. Other variations include: "The Glass Blower of Venice," "The Refugee," and *The Tenants*. Many stories, moreover, open with an immediate description of some figure's occupation: "Feld, the shoemaker," "Davidov, the census-taker," "Rosen, the ex-coffee salesman," "Leo Finkle, a rabbinical student," and so on.

6. On the subject of "name as symbol" Malamud was diffident; his own mother's name was Fidelman, we know; but when asked in as interview why he used that name in "The Last Mohican," Malamud replied, "I used my mother's maiden name because I needed a name I liked" (Field and Field, *A Collection* 14–15). Nevertheless, we do have at least one figure in "The Lady of the Lake" whose name-switching—from Levin to Freeman—is indicative of personal attitude, and thus in keeping with Levin's play with names, and with reader response theories later considered in my essay, I here expand upon various possible meanings this reader might derive from the names, taken in the context of Malamud's suggestive drama. One can imagine that since a "kessler" in German might be a *kessel* maker or a teapot maker, Kessler's behavior could have been more social—in keeping with the homely utensil and the atmosphere of sociability which often (though not always, to be sure) pervades terms such as tea-time. See *The Random House Dictionary of the English Language: Unabridged Edition* (1967 Appendix: German-English: 1850). My point in such word-play is that Malamud's suggestion of action in these names not only hints at a character's habits, but also enforces the reader's tendency toward action in the form of linguistic play as well.

7. *The Random House Dictionary,* Appendix: German-English, offers the following: *Hof* means court, or courtyard, and may be related to another word, *hoflich,* meaning polite, courteous: 1849. German usage can suggest that a hoff-man is a courtier, or social, courteous person.

8. If *Grube* is a pit, or mine (*Random House:* 1848), then a grubeer very freely translated might suggest a digger as in the word *Grubenarbeiter;* in Yiddish, *Grube* as an adjective implies an uncouth quality, perhaps related to English usage in which a grubber is one who grabs for material reward. Ignace, or Ignatius, a name that appears in German and

Spanish, conveys a violent or fiery type, since the source in Latin may be *ign(is)* meaning fire (*Random House Dictionary:* 708). See *Ignace,* "akin to L[atin] *ignis,* hence lit. fiery" (*Webster's New World Dictionary* 1957:722). Ironically, the name may also be an inversion (somewhat as in the devilish meanings possible for *The Fixer*), of St. Ignatius, since Malamud's fiery maintenance worker, *un*like the famous spiritual ascetic saint, is hateful, hot-tempered, and basement-located, another clue to his nether-world undertone. See also Soltaroff, "The story several times refers to Gruber's bulk, and his name (which in Yiddish would signify 'the gross one') emphasizes both his physical and moral grossness" (34); and Halperin, "the name evokes the Yiddish term for coarse, *grubber yung*" (462).

9. Peter M. Sacks comments upon the "necessarily dialectical movement of the work of mourning" (36). Light and fragrance are associated with rebirth and flowering, characteristic concepts of pastoral elegy. (See, for example, Sacks 33.) Commenting on other works James Beyer sees Malamud's penchant for the pastoral, and notes that "Malamud is rooted in pastoral literature" (193). The American Romance tradition, with its emphasis upon what Hawthorne calls the "Imaginary . . . at one remove from the Actual" and with its firm basis in Puritan utopian and later Emersonian optimism, contains elements of the Pastoral. Conflicts within that tradition, however, raise self-doubts that cause American literature also to veer towards anxiety and skepticism as well. See the definition of the American Jeremiad by Sacvan Bercovitch; and Emily Miller Budick's emphasis upon the strains of skepticism within the American Historical Romance.

10. Fisch describes the covenental relationship between reader and text as an "urgent historical task" (58), denominating such a relationship as distinctively "anti-pastoral" (76). Fisch's insight becomes especially useful in regarding Malamud within the wider context and definition of an American literary tradition. Taking Fisch's argument for a covenental project together with the insights of the above-mentioned critics (n. 9), indeed, one could see that it is within an American "anti-pastoral" tradition that Malamud makes his place.

11. In "The First Seven Years" a courtship is conducted through books borrowed and shared; in another story, "A Summer's Reading," books read one summer may be a tool for a young man's successful career. The reverse may be the case when a Macy's book-salesman is unable to gain a bride because he fails to pass a kind of literary competency test, in "Lady of the Lake;" manuscripts serve as enticements, in "The Girl of My Dreams."

12. There would seem to be a sharp distinction between conscious literary reference and the process theorists call intertextuality, or "influence." In the case of "The Mourners," I would argue that even Mal-

amud's seemingly purposeful *use* of reference goes beyond his own borders, and thus the problematics of his referentiality remain the same—with or without (if such distinctions can be made) his control. For a discussion of Malamud's "sources" see, for example: Field and Field (1975, Introduction 5ff.). In their interview, moreover, Field and Field raise other specific questions of literary reference concerning Hawthorne, James, Turgeniev, Stephen Crane, and others. See also Bluefarb: "Malamud has borrowed from a variety of sources; yet, excellent craftsman that he is, he has both assimilated and transformed them into something peculiarly his own" (72). Richman discusses "literary traditions" (307ff.). Fisch remarks that "virtuosity is the mark of Malamud's use of myth and archetype" ("Biblical Archetypes" 163).

13. In Melville as in Malamud there are deeper references implicit in the onlookers' failure to show compassion: the eviction scenes evoke, I suggest, a Passion, including echoes of Matthew or Luke: "And as they led him away . . . there followed a great multitude of the people . . . " (Luke 23:26–28). Leo Marx argues for a redemptive mood at the end of "Bartleby." The "presence of the grass at Bartleby's death scene is the clue to Melville's affirmation" (73).

14. Throughout his works Crane's figures are often known by their characteristic habits or jobs—sheriff, drummer, oiler, correspondent, easterner, lieutenant. Malamud, too, is fascinated by the subject of a person as a "kind of adverb" (the phrase taken from "The Blue Hotel"). Perhaps both for Malamud and for Melville such *-er* names suggest a fundamental rift between our ability to act out an identity and the forces that impose themselves upon us; this sense of persons as adverbs does, however, at the same time allow for interaction as a minimal but necessary (ad)verbal and social condition.

15. Michael Fried notes the textuality of Crane's numerous allusions to pages, writing, inscription. Fried points out that "upturned faces may be understood as figures for the sheet of paper on which the work of literary writing is taking place" (117). Although Fried does not discuss "The Blue Hotel" in these terms, his point about textuality in Crane is useful in stressing Crane's focus upon readers or beholders—both within and outside the borders of the text itself. Melville criticism considering the reflexive nature of Melville's fiction was initiated decades ago by Charles Feidelson and continues in a long chain of critical history to such modern and postmodern readers as Charles Olson, Edgar Dryden, Joseph Riddel, Barbara Johnson, and Eric Sundquist, among others.

16. Two critics discuss the sense of resolution at the end: Earl Rovit perceives a "poetic resolution" in Malamud, especially in this story (7). Sidney Richman more convincingly argues that "the resolution despite numerous anticipatory clues, offers less relief than a weird shock" (307).

17. See a now-famous discussion of interpretation as play, not exile, in Derrida (1970:264).

18. Bloom states, "There is always and only bias, inclination, prejudgment, swerve; only and always the verbal agon for freedom, and the agon is carried on not by truth-telling, but by words lying against time" (1975, 9). It was Paul de Man, significantly enough in the light of recent controversy concerning his stance toward the Holocaust, who declared that interpretive irresponsibility or "impossibility" could not be lightly presumed (245).

19. For a discussion of Malamud in a Jewish-American tradition, see Sam B. Girgus, (chap. 2); see also n. 9 above.

20. In a recent critical study of Holocaust literature Rosenfeld uses a title that is appropriate: *Imagining Hitler.* Another survey of Holocaust literature by Sidra Ezrachi includes one chapter entitled, "The Literature of Survival."

21. Joining a person named Gruber with the idea of Hitler here, we speculate that Malamud may well have been playing further with names—the one often used for Hitler was "Schicklgruber." Such a denomination was probably derived from the fact that Hitler was the illegitimate son of Maria Anna Schicklgruber. See *The New Columbia Encyclopedia* (1975:1249).

22. Such consideration of the suggestiveness of that name and the further speculation upon whether Hitler ever "really was Schicklgruber" continues today. A letter to the New York Times, published May 6, 1990, uses language uncannily appropriate to this paper in discussing the "case of Hitler's presumed last name" as an effective lie based upon the way that:

> 'Schicklegruber' sounds more ridiculous than 'Hitler' even today. Therefore, the lie lives on, being more preferable than the truth [that at the time of his birth his mother had married and her name had by then become Hitler] . . . So, the mundane truth is, Hitler was always Hitler, having been born so. But [the lie's] triumph lives on, for a good lie, it seems dies hard, even in your pages—Eric Leif Davin.

23. Judith Fetterly has used this phrase in her specifically feminist and American book, *The Resisting Reader: A Feminist Approach to American Fiction.* (See especially "Introduction, On the Politics of Literature.") But her historicist point is well-taken for Jewish readers reading "Hitler," or for anyone responding to texts, as individuals within some specific and personally understood time, place, hence "political" view.

24. Instead of elegiac consolation, Harold Fisch provides a model of covenantal poetics that is more provocative. Basing his discussion upon biblical poetry, Fisch shows that writing "assumes responsibility for the future" when we respond to its challenge "not as echo or audience" but

as "witnesses to a lawsuit." (*Poetry* 67). Malamud's conflicted urban tale thus fulfills the poetic requirements set forth by Fisch, when it demands response (or mourning) as an act of historical testimony. Elsewhere, Fisch addresses the case of Malamud's *The Fixer,* to show that in that novel, too, "Malamud is trying to find a myth of continuance" in the survival of Yaakov Bok, who "survives as a witness" ("Biblical Archetypes" 71).

REFERENCES

Bercovitch, Sacvan. *The American Jeremiad.* Madison: Wisconsin University Press, 1978.

Beyer, James. "'A Repetition He Was Part Of': Bernard Malamud, *A New Life,* and *Dubin's Lives.*" *Studies in American Jewish Literature* 7 (1988):189–204.

Bilik, Dorothy Seidman. *Immigrant-Survivors: Post-Holocaust Consciousness in Recent Jewish American Fiction.* Middletown, CT: Wesleyan University Press, 1981.

Bloom, Harold. *The Anxiety of Influence: A Theory of Poetry.* New York: Oxford University Press, 1973.

_____. *A Map of Misreading.* New York: Oxford University Press, 1975.

Bluefarb, Sam. "The Syncretism of Bernard Malamud." In *Bernard Malamud: A Collection of Critical Essays.* Ed. Leslie A. Field and Joyce W. Field. Englewood Cliffs, NJ: Prentice-Hall, 1975.

Bruns, Gerald. "Stanley Cavell's Shakespeare." *Critical Inquiry* 16 (1990):612–32.

Budick, Emily Miller. *Fiction and Historical Consciousness: The American Romance Tradition.* New Haven: Yale University Press, 1989.

Crane, Stephen. "The Blue Hotel." 1898. Reprint. *Great Short Works of Stephen Crane.* New York: Harper & Row, 1968.

De Man, Paul. *Allegories of Reading.* New Haven: Yale University Press, 1979.

Derrida, Jacques. "Living On: Borderlines." In *Deconstruction and Criticism.* Ed. Harold Bloom et al. New York: Seabury, 1979.

_____. "Structure, Sign, and Play in the Discourse of the Human Sciences." In *The Structuralist Controversy: The Language of Criticism and the Sciences of Man.* Ed. Richard Macksey and Eugenio Donato. Baltimore: Johns Hopkins University Press, 1970.

Ezrachi, Sidra. *By Words Alone: The Holocaust in Literature.* Chicago: Chicago University Press, 1980.

Fetterley, Judith. *The Resisting Reader: A Feminist Approach to American Fiction.* Bloomington: Indiana University Press, 1981.

Field, Leslie A., and Joyce W. Field. *Bernard Malamud and the Critics.* New York: New York University Press, 1970.

———, eds. *Bernard Malamud: A Collection of Critical Essays.* Englewood Cliffs, NJ: Prentice-Hall, 1975. This volume includes the editors' Introduction and their "Interview with Bernard Malamud."

Fisch, Harold. *A Remembered Future: A Study in Literary Mythology.* Bloomington: Indiana University Press, 1984.

———. "Biblical Archetypes in *The Fixer.*" *Studies in American Jewish Literature* 7 (1988):162–76.

———. *Poetry with a Purpose: Biblical Poetics and Interpretation.* Bloomington: Indiana University Press, 1988.

Fried, Michael. *Realism, Writing, Disfiguration.* Chicago: Chicago University Press, 1987.

Girgus, Sam. *The New Covenant: Jewish Writers and the American Idea* Chapel Hill: University of North Carolina Press, 1984.

Halperin, Irving. "The Theme of Responsibility in Bernard Malamud's 'The Mourners'." *Judaism* 36 (1987):460–65.

Lasher, Lawrence M. "Narrative Strategy in Malamud's 'The German Refugee.'" *Studies in American Jewish Literature* 9 (1990):72–83.

Malamud, Bernard. "The Mourners." 1955. Reprint in *The Magic Barrel.* New York: Farrar, Straus & Cudahy, 1958. "The Mourners" was first published in *Discovery.*

Marx, Leo. "Melville's Parable of the Walls." In *The Pilot and the Passenger.* New York: Oxford University Press, 1988.

Melville, Herman. "Bartleby, the Scrivener." 1853. Reprint in *Great Short Works of Herman Melville.* New York: Harper & Row, 1969.

Richman, Sidney. "The Stories." In *Bernard Malamud and the Critics.* Ed. Field and Field, New York: New York University Press, 1970.

Rosenfeld, Alvin. *A Double Dying: Reflections on Holocaust Literature.* Bloomington: Indiana University Press, 1980.

———. *Imagining Hitler.* Bloomington: Indiana University Press, 1985.

Sacks, Peter M. *The English Elegy: Studies in the Genre from Spenser to Yeats.* Baltimore: Johns Hopkins University Press, 1985.

Salzburg, Joel. "Malamud's Last Interview? A Memoir." *Studies in American Jewish Literature* 7 (1988):233–39.

Soltaroff, Robert. *Bernard Malamud: A Study of the Short Fiction.* Boston: Twayne, 1989.

Young, James E. *Writing and Rewriting the Holocaust: Narrative and the Consequences of Interpretation.* Bloomington: Indiana University Press, 1988.

CHAPTER 12

"The New Covenant" and the Dilemma of Dissensus: Bercovitch, Roth, and Doctorow

Sam B. Girgus

For more than a century, Jewish authors and thinkers have written themselves into a contract with the American idea as Jeremiahs fighting to protect and promulgate the moral imperatives of American democracy, freedom, and consensus. The deep roots of this covenant go back to the coincidental date of continental discovery during the year of Jewish expulsion from Spain, to the institutionalization of civil and religious freedom under the Founding Fathers, to the emergence of America as an asylum and sanctuary for all peoples, who would attempt to form for the only successful time in history a new universal national entity and ideology composed of all the nationalities and races in the world. The list that forms this covenant includes innumerable men and women: Mary Antin's *Promised Land,* Emma Lazarus' "New Colossus," Abraham Cahan's conversion to democracy, Anzia Yezierska's compulsive drive for success and identity, the writers and thinkers who advanced civil liberties and the principles of liberalism, Philip Roth's linguistic innovation, Saul Bellow's humanism, Norman Mailer's celebration of "the mysteries of America buried in these liberties to dissent," E. L. Doctorow's jeremiads for reformation and revolution in the name of the ideology and promise of America.

This thesis of a "New Covenant" assumes the validity of Sacvan Bercovitch's theory of the rhetoric of the jeremiad and the ideology of consensus in America. Bercovitch, of course, argues that the ideology of America promises individual renewal and moral regeneration. Structured by the Puritan's rhetoric of the jeremiad, the ideology envisions America in Utopian terms so that consensus incorporates all people and discourse includes all points of view. Seeing America through the language of mission and ultimate moral value, both dominant and exploited groups, insiders and outsiders, shape their dreams according to the ideals and values of the promise of the American idea. The physical frontier formed an external sign of a social and political understanding of institutionalized marginality. All Americans belong to the group but also exist on its borders. American identity, therefore, is achieved through the route of radical individualism. Thus, for Bercovitch, "our classic literature" represents "the aesthetic flowering of an ideology adopted from the start precisely for its ability to transmute radicalism of all kinds, from religious protest to revolutionary war, into varieties of ideological consensus." Based on the "*controlling* metaphor—'America' as synonym for human possibility," the desire for building the consensus eventually "redefined radicalism itself as an affirmation of cultural values" (1986:645, 646). Accordingly, for Bercovitch dissent comprises the heart of the American idea. In this context, the term "dissensus" comes to mean for Bercovitch a kind of intensified and heightened form of cultural and social consensus based on dissent. All Americans form a permanent standing guerilla army of nay-sayers and rebels. A consensus founded on a permanent condition of dissensus promises all participants renewal within the world of national unity and identity.

Bercovitch has delineated this theory of ideology, consensus, and the jeremiad in several essays and works, most articulately and completely in *The American Jeremiad*. However, as the theory developed, dissensus assumed a life of its own. Bercovitch, in Frederick Crews' terms, moved beyond his "preradical" stage to a form of "radical politics" in several works that proved instrumental in launching a "dissensus movement" of "New Americanists." The New Americanists, according to Crews, see themselves as "unmaskers" of the ideology and false consciousness that define earlier studies of American literature and criticism. Crews says, "What gives the New Americanist critique a special emotional force, however, is its connection both to our historic national shames—slavery, 'Indian removal,' expansion, imperialism, and so forth—and to current struggles for equal opportunity. . . . In short, the New Americanist program aims at altering the literary departments' social makeup as well as their dominant style of criticism" (Crews 68, 70).[1]

The dilemma for this dissensus movement constitutes the need to reconstruct a new social and cultural philosophy and a feasible and viable praxis to supplant what has been deconstructed. Few so far have attempted to suggest such alternatives outside of offering revisions to the canon and rereadings of both literary texts and historical and social contexts. Bercovitch himself, of course, understands that ultimately radical rereadings and revisions require a broader program of social and cultural thought and action. Ironically, the so-called New Americanists now lack the kind of holistic vision that they criticized as "totalization" and ideological in such figures as F. O. Matthiessen, Lionel Trilling, Henry Nash Smith and, to a certain extent, even Bercovitch. Furthermore, in *The American Jeremiad,* Bercovitch anticipates how the destruction of consensus and the disarray of dissensus can lead to dangerous domains and unknown territory. In his discussion of the anti-jeremiad, he acknowledges the intellectual and emotional fate of those who historically have gone outside of the consensus and the jeremiad. "When they abandoned their faith in America, they had no other recourse. . . . In this country, both the jeremiad and the anti-jeremiad foreclosed alternatives: the one by absorbing the hopes of mankind into the meaning of America, the other by reading into America the futility and fraud of hope itself" (1978:191).

In contrast to this movement toward dissensus among so many critics, it is interesting how some authors continue to engage moral, social, and cultural issues in terms of the structures and ideology of "The New Covenant." For example, at the time of the publication of *The Facts: A Novelist's Autobiography,* Philip Roth emphasized that his experience of living in Great Britain brought him home, so to speak, to his identity as an American and Jew. He said that "eventually I came to understand the dimensions of my Americanness better than I ever had before." While critics over the years have excoriated Roth for allegedly fleeing from or ridiculing his Jewish origins, Roth, in fact, evidences a mordant sensitivity to the inexorable connection between his work and his personal life and between his Jewish and American roots and qualities. He argues that "for me being a Jew and being an American are indistinguishable, the one identity bound up and given shape by the other" (Brent 46). Instead of apologizing for being Jewish, Roth charitably implies an apology for the failure of the British because "what's driving the society isn't dramatized with anything like the turbulent intensity that animates America." Roth goes on to say,

> I'm speaking of intellectual and literary intensity no less than the intensity behind all the American trash, the intensity that's generated by the American historical drama of movement and massive displacement, of class overspreading class, region overtaking region, minority encroaching on minority and the media cannibalizing the works. Try to imagine England inviting, on the scale that the U.S. does, the cultural and political clashes—and, above all the linguistic and racial 'impurities'—that are the inevitable consequences of permitting millions and millions of foreigners alien to the mainstream society, language and political heritage to settle into one's developed country year in and year out. The wholesale colonization of England's major cities by third world immigrants—and only little more than half a century after those cities had been colonized by tens of millions from the impoverished classes of eastern and southern Europe—is unthinkable. (Brent 3)

As evidence of the continued vitality of the New Covenant for Jewish American writers, this comment from Roth is no less than extraordinary. It is remarkable for its direct descent from a history of more than two centuries of seeing America as a unique and special event in human history. He reminds one of Thomas Paine: "We have it in our power to begin the world over again. A situation similar to the present has not happened since the days of Noah until now. The birthday of a new world is at hand, and a race of men, perhaps as numerous as all Europe contains, are to receive their portion of freedom from the event of a few months" (Paine 120). The passion and intensity of Roth's images and ideals appeal to the idea of America as a home for all immigrants where they can begin a new life and form a new culture. As such, they echo the young Melville in *Redburn:* "Let us waive that agitated national topic, as to whether such multitudes of foreign poor should be landed on our American shores; let us waive it, with the one only thought, that if they can get here, they have God's right to come; though they bring all Ireland and her miseries with them. For the whole world is the patrimony of the whole world, there is no telling who does not own a stone in the Great Wall of China" (Melville 281–82).

Like Paine, Melville and so many others we could cite, Roth uses the structure of the jeremiad to make a moral statement in terms of the meaning of America to the world. American experience, history, and language establish an ideal dimension from which to criticize the failure to meet the moral standards and expectations of American democracy. Conceivably, Roth's association with authors and works from Eastern Europe, such as Milan Kundera, partially explains his vigorous defense of freedom. His work with these writers suggests that in helping so many of them to publish their fiction and to achieve international recognition, he has found another avenue to express his own identity and inner strengths. Of course, such associations of ideas and beliefs do not provide a final or total answer to Roth the man and writer. They do not explain his interest in the self-referential nature of fiction and language and his fascination with the intimacy of fact and fiction. They do, however, suggest an important context for his consideration of these matters and his creative expression of them.

Moreover, anyone familiar with Roth's unforgiving political and social humor knows better than to accuse him of being an apologist for popular American conventions and beliefs. Over the years, his sardonic attacks on dominant political figures, such as Presidents Nixon and Bush, his parody of contemporary political debate and discussion, and his satiric commentary on wide-ranging political subjects appear frequently in publications such as *The New York Review of Books* and *The New York Times*. For example, during the 1988 presidential election, he could not resist ridiculing both Michael Dukakis as a poor excuse for Zorba and the Republicans as "Poppa Bush" and "Sonny Boy Quayle." For Roth, politics and culture commingle so that political slogans manifest deep cultural notions and patterns of "Ethnic Pop" and "Native Corn" ("Ethnic" 23). A student of American literature who did graduate work at the University of Chicago, Roth may have been thinking of Mark Twain's wonderful exposure of the economic basis of politics in "Corn-Pone Opinions" when he wrote this article. Nevertheless, his recent parody of George Bush's language and thought during a fictional press conference on the abortion issue, headlined in *The New York Review of Books* as "Pro-Life

Pro," is worthy of a classic Mark Twain monologue. In this piece of about one thousand words, Roth captures the horrible hokum of modern political debate—the mindlessness of what passes for discussion in the media, the manipulation of mass opinion, the banality and vulgarization of appeals to morality and religious belief. In this piece Roth takes a pattern of twisted syntax and perverse double-talk and obfuscation that has become something of a standard for many of our recent presidents and uses it against Bush, in a sense strangling him with his own words and "pone." Enveloped securely in brilliant political parody, the piece is charged with a powerful moral subtext of the abuse of power and the corruption of the American mind and body politic. First, on the new program concerning illiteracy:

> These are gonna be kids born to teen-age mothers and impoverished mothers and homeless mothers, and if we're lucky, they're *all* gonna be illiterate because of, you know, the lack a some a the wonderful things we're all so prouda like education and family values, and that's gonna give a real big boost to this literacy program. Cause the more illiterates we got, the more opportunity for Americans to volunteer to wipe it out. I have a kinda dream about this. I see a country where we have illiteracy on such a scale, that every American even half able to read will be out there pitchin in, voluntarily, and helpin somebody who can't. ("Pro" 5)

Roth follows this political satire with the President's program to ban both menstruation and masturbation in the name of advancing the principle of the right to life.

> Menstruation is the murder of a human egg. And down the road a human egg is a potential human life. Right now that life is being allowed to flow out of all those millions of American uteruses—well, I don't like to think about this anymore than anybody else; I don't like to think about anything more than anybody else, but when ya have stuff like this goin on with the frequency that this thing is—heck, it's just wrong. When I look at my grandkids out sailin and playin ball, and they're great kids, and I think that they were once little defenseless eggs of the kind that women are. And every twenty-eight days. This is documented. Every single woman in America between puberty and menopause, every twenty-eight days, well, it's just plain wrong. Menstruation is murder and masturbation, of course, is worse. Masturbation is killin not just one egg. It is murderin sperms by

> the millions, and every one of them a potential life. Beyond that, we are talkin about somethin that isn't happenin only once a month. If ya look at the figures—I've seen them, I've studied the reports on this, and when I saw those figures, I was staggered, I was horrified, I said, 'You know, hey, look at all this.' I look at those wonderful grandkids of mine and I think about masturbation and I want this matter remedied. *All* the wonderful grandkids around America—it doesn't bear thinkin about. Nothing does. ("Pro" 5)

The remarkable accuracy of Roth's language prove a point of great importance to E. L. Doctorow, namely the power of myth and fiction to render facts and history. Roth's imagination puts presidential prose into a moral and political dimension that objective reporting would find difficult to convey. In addition, like Twain, Roth heightens the political drama by internalizing it within the speaker. Listening to the speech, one can only guess about the degree of the speaker's self-deception and hypocrisy. Leaving this question open intensifies the felt sense of danger to the nation brought about by ignorant and corrupt leadership. It also personalizes the moral issue of the betrayal of the principles of democracy.

Such political and cultural discourse from Roth fits contextually, what many today would call intertextually, into his understanding of the American idea. The ability of his humor to deflate pretention, pomp, cant, and to expose blatant deceit achieves extraordinary power partly because it functions within a broader moral vision of reconstruction. Roth's humor does not work in isolation. Often it succeeds to the degree that it contrasts reality with the ideal. He simply makes humor part of his linguistic armory. Thus, when Roth rambunctiously celebrates the way ethnic, racial, and social differences in America regularly revitalize the American way of thinking by revolutionizing our use of language, he certainly includes humor as one of the most important of linguistic tactics. Humor, as a means for literary and linguistic invention and cultural inclusion, participates in his program for individual and cultural renewal. Accordingly, his exuberant expression of beliefs about cultural and literary democracy in the 1988 interview reiterates his ideas about American authors and culture in *Reading Myself and Others* (1975). The pluralism and radical individualism of American democracy as structured by the moral rhetoric of the jeremiad continue to be his platform for condemning any diminuition of diversity and dissent. Thus, Roth's radicalism as it has been articulated for at least two decades remains rooted in the inherent radicalism of American consensus.

In a similar vein, E. L. Doctorow's radical philosophy of the intertextual relationship of narrative, history, and fiction, perceives the energy for regeneration to exist in the past. Thus, in a 1986 interview with George Plimpton, Doctorow said, "History is a battlefield. It's constantly being fought over because the past controls the present. History is the present. That's why every generation writes it anew" ("Fiction" 33). For Doctorow, this conception of history and contemporary reality as conveyed through narrative and myth becomes especially relevant to the American experience because of his understanding of the renewable and reusable nature of American history and democratic ideology.[2]

Doctorow's insight into the relationship of history to the present and to American culture causes him to reconsider the very notion of the "revolutionary." Whereas for many the word conveys certain preconceptions about political views and cultural life-styles and values, Doctorow regards revolutionary as a kind of permanent condition and consciousness that links the past, present, and future to the power of individual and cultural invention. In a 1980 interview, he responded to a question about the revolutionary nature of his work by saying, "If the work helps create another kind of national composition or national self-consciousness then something is changing and in that sense you're contributing to some sort of revolution. Whether that's good or bad, I don't know. The Constitution is just about a perfect document, and if we truly lived up to it we would have social perfection. That's as radical or revolutionary as anybody can ever get" ("Creators" 48).

Of course, seeing the Constitution, one of our most "conservative"—in the sense of preservative—founding documents as a seminal source and veritable hotbed of radical initiative and potential, certainly seems to situate Doctorow at the very heart of the rhetorical tradition of the jeremiad and American consensus. This view of Doctorow finds confirmation in his response in the same interview when it was "*pointed out that your novels have a leftist political point of view.*" "I think every writer who writes is doing something political. Every novel has a political meaning or content. It may be that to the extent that a writer's politics in a book are not the prevailing politics, they become more visible in a work. I'm not even sure what my politics are. I always thought of myself as a reformed Democrat, but I may be a Social Democrat with some kind of vague inclination or wish that wealth should be redistributed without affecting or cutting into the democratic institutions we have in this country" ("Creators" 48).

Certainly, such "covenantal" ideas about the universal nature of "politics" and the importance of traditional "democratic institutions" might be seen to alienate Doctorow from the presumed "prevailing politics" of the dissensus movement as described above. Thus, it is not surprising that in a brilliant piece, Geoffrey Galt Harpham recently implied serious objection to Doctorow for beginning "to conceive of his art in nearly capitalistic terms" (Harpham 93). In fact, it seems to me that Harpham misconstrues the meaning of Doctorow's presumably reactionary comment about subscribing to "the American entrepreneurial sense of novel writing" ("Creators" 48). In this remark, which was made during his 1980 interview, Doctorow was comparing American attitudes toward writers and the novel as a form to those of the British. He said:

> American novelists in particular don't take the form of the novel lightly. I think in this country there's some sort of presumption on our part that it's a major act of the culture. Therefore, every time you start a novel you go for the moon. You don't hold back. You take the biggest chances and the greatest risks and the most dangerous gambles you can possibly imagine in order to somehow bring it off in a great way. It may be our weakness. The English literary community doesn't understand the American entrepreneurial sense of novel writing, and it may be a flaw of ours. But I subscribe to it. Each time out, you go for broke. ("Creators" 48)

Branding such an attitude capitalistic, imputes an obsession for remuneration and economic gain to Doctorow, whereas Harpham himself recognizes that the idea grows out of Doctorow's increasing sensitivity "to the possibilities for self-invention" (Harpham 93).

What needs further emphasis, however, is the ideological context for this view of literature and history. As a source and a weapon for "self-invention," fiction in America for Doctorow serves to make American history into a theater of invention and regeneration. Doctorow's most recent novels are designed to perpetuate such invention. In *World's Fair* and *Billy Bathgate,* Doctorow clearly continues the role he adopted with his earlier novels of speaking for the moral and democratic demands of a culture of renewal. Significantly, Doctorow sees no conflict between his role as author and inventor of fiction and his guise as Whitmanesque social prophet, a harmony of voices that was central to his previous novels, especially *The Book of Daniel* and *Ragtime.* Thus, he told Plimpton and the audience at the Young Men's Hebrew Association (YMHA) in New York, "Modernism made us think of writing as an act of ultimate individualism. But, in fact, every writer speaks for a community" ("Fiction" 42).

In reading Doctorow, therefore, it is important to remember the importance he places in going beyond the facts of history and biography to the invention of a self within a social and cultural text. Forgetting this has caused some reviewers and interviewers to place undue emphasis upon the similarities between Doctorow's fictitious voices and his own life, especially in *World's Fair* and *Billy Bathgate.* Regarding the former novel, one reviewer noted that it was about "a boy named Edgar—born on the same day as Edgar Laurence Doctorow—whose parents bear the same first names as Doctorow's own" (Clemons 69). However, Doctorow responded to a question about a similar identification of "the fictional Billy Bathgate to the young E. L. Doctorow, who also once lived in the Bronx" by noting, "Only in the sense that every book encodes your life am I in this one, too. . . . My criminal career as a boy was nonexistent. If I claimed any firsthand knowledge about crime as a way of life, it just wouldn't be true" (Mitgang 17). Accordingly, in his last two novels, he continues to speak not only for himself, but for at least two communities as well, Jewish and American, with the idea of seeing them meld together as they do in Roth's work and consciousness. It is no accident that Jewish life and Jews are crucial to these two novels. In these works, he still writes as a modern American Jeremiah in the tradition of the New Covenant.

Significantly, the elements of what I have called the "new hero of thought" apply with equal vigor and relevance to Doctorow's most recent novels (*New Covenant* 17–23). In both *World's Fair* and *Billy Bathgate,* a Jewish hero of thought with gifted intelligence and sensitivity becomes the central consciousness for a modernized and urbanized myth and narrative of America in which an urban wilderness of danger and violence replaces the geographic frontier of regeneration. Instead of geographic mobility across frontiers and beautiful natural landscape, we get a story of upward mobility in terms of both success and ultimate moral understanding and awareness. Also, the love goddess or *shikse* theme, in a somewhat different form, continues to help structure and dramatize the hero's representative encounter with the dominant culture, which is femininized in the figure of a Christian girl or woman who embodies the dangers and rewards of freedom and success in America.

Moreover, the consciousness of consensus as structured in the apocalyptic terms of the jeremiad pervades the novels. Accordingly, toward the end of *World's Fair,* the father of the narrator delivers a jeremiad that provides the central political statement of the novel. In the course of their visit to the 1939 World's Fair in New York, the father explodes over the injustice of the contents of the Time Capsule buried at the Westinghouse building. The father's outrage repeats the ideology of expansion and inclusion that reverberates through Paine, Melville and Roth.

> He asked my brother and me why we thought there was nothing in the capsule about the great immigrations that had brought Jewish and Italian and Irish people to America or nothing to represent the point of view of the workingman. "There is no hint from the stuff they included that America has a serious intellectual life, or Indians on reservations or Negroes who suffer from race prejudice. Why is that?" he said as finally we edged him away from the Immortal Well and into the Hall of Science. (1985:284)

Obviously, the father's anger and bitterness over the failure of the ideology of democracy are encapsulated and structured by the ideology itself. Indeed, the sensibility and values of the ideology of consensus fuel the anger. The speech exemplifies the idea of consensus as a process of continual expansion and tension that perpetuates itself. Interestingly, David, the father, remains within the consensus of American values and ideals while advocating a politics to the left of and critical of Franklin Delano Roosevelt. In contrast, for Edgar, who functions as the novel's most important narrative voice from his fifth to ninth year of age, Roosevelt exists as a sort demi-God. In spite of this difference, for father and son consensus both encourages and contains dissent, once again revealing the startling combination and conflict of radical and conservative elements in the ideology of America.

In the novel, the circumstances of the family's visit to the Fair, which provide the stage for the father's speech, also articulate the ambivalent tension and uncertainty at the center of the American idea of consensus and regeneration. They are there because of the young narrator's triumph as one of six honorable mentions in a contest sponsored by the Fair on the subject of the "Typical American Boy." Other events surround the actual composition of the essay that compound the irony of exclusion dramatized by both the Time Capsule and Edgar's secondary honorable mention status. First, the boy is assaulted by young Christian thugs immediately after deciding to enter into the essay contest. He cannot forget the terror of the assault nor can he forgive himself for his cowardice in denying being Jewish. The memory of his humiliation over his inability to prove his Christianity by crossing himself or repeating what one says at confession chafes at him. "'Let's see you cross yourself.' I did not know what this meant. 'You're a Jewboy,' he said. He pushed the knife point into me. I could feel it. One shove and it would go right through me" (1985:237). This experience helps determine his view of the world outside his family and immediate Jewish background.

> For weeks afterward, whenever, I went out, I looked for those two boys, and the fact that I never saw them did not remove them as a threat from my mind. I could go about my business only by the accident of their not being there, a matter entirely of their choice, and so even when absent they had me. But at the same time I knew it wasn't even these two in particular, because Christian boys were like this all over, and you were free only at their collective whim, only if they happened not to walk down your street or lope through your backyard or otherwise see you. I struggled to understand Christianity as something that would shove a knife into my belly. (1985:238)

The incident certainly dramatizes his existence on the perimeter of the American experience. More important, however, such "marginalization," so to speak, constitutes the essence of the idea of being American and frames his response to both past and future experience. The facts of his victimization and his position as an outsider become less important than his response to his situation.

He acts with what Edgar terms elsewhere in the novel, "the fervent pride of the assimilationist," an epithet suggesting the overcompensation of the insecure alien (1985:200). The incident tests his faith and his idea of himself. Rather than proving the fallacy of the ideology of consensus, the attack actually demonstrates the importance of consensus and inclusion. In essence, Edgar turns alienation around by centering the situation on himself and exposing his persecutors as the outsiders. He becomes the insider's outsider. Structuring alienation and marginality within the ideology of American consensus becomes the means for finding one's own identity as an American, a Jew and an individual. "But my resolve to enter the World Fair's contest for boys was unshaken. In fact, writing an essay on the Typical American Boy had now the additional appeal of an act of defiance. I, not those miserable louts, would propose the essence of American Boyhood. They were no models for anything. I doubted they could even read" (1985:139). Accordingly, Edgar's essay brilliantly conveys this complex body of experience through the thought processes and language of a nine year old boy:

> The typical American Boy is not fearful of Dangers. He should be able to go out into the country and drink raw milk. Likewise, he should traverse the hills and valleys of the city. If he is Jewish he should say so. If he is anything he should say what it is when challenged. He roots for his home team in football and baseball but also plays sports himself. He reads all the time. It's all right for him to like comic books so long as he knows they are junk. Also, radio programs and movies may be enjoyed but not at the expense of important things. For example he should always hate Hitler. In music he appreciates both swing and symphony. In women he appreciates them all. He does not waste time daydreaming when he is doing his homework. He is kind. He cooperates with his parents. He knows the value of a dollar. He looks death in the face. (1985:244)

The precocious and endearing reference in the essay to appreciating all women deserves comment. In the novel, as in so many other examples of work in this tradition, the ideology of consensus and the urbanized form of the myth that dramatizes it also serve as a convenient means for focusing the anxieties and fears of the rite of passage into young manhood. Thus, it is during this period of his life that Edgar develops an important relationship with a girl of his own age, Meg, and her mother, Norma. The two clearly represent a world of alienation and otherness. Rose, Edgar's mother, gossips about Norma and obviously questions the circumstances surrounding Meg's birth. "'Everyone knows. It's common knowledge in the neighborhood,'" she argues with her husband, further questioning how Norma lives: "'How has she gotten by all these years?' my mother said. 'Do people change that much?'" (1985:247)

Almost immediately Edgar senses the infectious nature of the freedom that characterizes the girl and mother: "Yet it gradually came to me that I now had a private life. Nobody in my family saw Meg and Norma, only I did. I liked that. Living in a new neighborhood had made me independent. I ranged now. I did not run right home after school. I could see Meg without even telling anyone. This was an unusual household, this mother and daughter. It had no father. It brought out in me a certain feistiness. My loins stirred with protective feelings. This was my secret life of adventure" (1985:232). Living independently in the midst of poverty, working as the titillating object of the lecherous arms of a fake octopus in a sexy underwater sideshow at the World's Fair, Norma presents a congeries of challenges as powerful in their own way as the aggression of the Christian hooligans. "When I went upstairs to Meg's I always hoped Norma would be there. I had to acknowledge that to myself now, and with a weird feeling in the chest, some breathable excitement, as if I had done something terribly wrong although I didn't know what it was" (1985:167). Toward the end of the novel the importance of Norma's influence upon Edgar to break boundaries and to open himself to new experiences grows especially apparent. "I knew no one like her. She acted free. I did not think of her as a bad woman but as someone who probably took a different view of things. . . . Norma's freedom made life more thrilling and more dangerous. I felt the danger now. Meg had been born to the thrilling freedom that I only now suspected was possible. The burden of it made her quiet and beautiful. I loved her" (1985:270).

Clearly, the young narrator is intended to function as a spokesman for a "thrilling freedom" that extends beyond breaking sexual and ethnic barriers to cultural inclusion, innovation, and experimentation. He embodies that freedom, as his father hints, by personifying the individuality and uniqueness that ironically undermine the theme of his essay. "My father said, 'Don't be disappointed that you didn't get first prize, Edgar. You are not a typical American boy and that's all there is to it'" (1985:279). There is, of course, more to it. Failing to win first prize emphasizes the importance of the process of consensus itself. Also, as the father himself implies, the unconventional should be the convention, the untypical the standard. In other words, the narrator exemplifies the notion of a nation of nay-sayers, a culture of dissenters, a form of dissensus structured by a frame of consensus. To paraphrase the young narrator's essay, the really Typical American Boy breaks the mold and is true to himself. It is this conception of freedom that helps account for Doctorow's continuing effort to reinvent Huckleberry Finn in his fiction. Thus, responding to a letter from me, Doctorow says, "In view of your idea of Daniel [*The Book of Daniel*] as a kind of Huck Finn, you may find it [*World's Fair*] interesting" (1985). Interesting indeed. The Edgar of *World's Fair* must learn to become Huck, a difficult process of linguistic, cultural, and literary revolution. On a river of language that defies final linguistic definition and cultural and individual conformity, Edgar escapes protection and security to search for a freedom that proves as enticing and as elusive in New York as it was on the Mississippi.

Billy Bathgate extends the search for a modern Huck, a deceptively passive character whose inner life and consciousness become a central stage for the active engagement of conflicting and contradictory cultural forces. Billy mirrors a world of urban Jewish violence in which classic cultural symbols of Huck, Billy the Kid, and Gatsby coalesce. His apprenticeship to the gangster Dutch Schultz and his education on the streets of New York leave little room for nurturing false idealism and illusions. A Jew who is a non-Jew according to the orthodox, a boy who is abandoned by a Jewish father and lives like an orphan with a nearly insane Irish mother, Billy personifies a society of the dispossessed. He is an underdog's underdog, a charity case among those who have less than nothing. Like Huck, Billy initially is even on the periphery of a gang of outsiders.

Nevertheless, Billy is no mere victim of circumstances beyond his control. No philosophy of fatalistic acquiescence applies to either the author or his character. Billy chooses a mentor for himself, Dutch Schultz, and begins a series of adventures from the sexual to the criminal that leave him in awe forever of his own experience under the gangster's tutelage. Obviously, a character of the pure violence and rampant individualism of Dutch Schultz is incompatible with democratic institutions and culture. The perverted extreme of a society of outsiders, Dutch cannot survive. However, in the process of self-extinction, Dutch transforms Billy's consciousness. Dutch is to Billy what Ahab and Gatsby are to Ishmael and Carraway. The gangster serves as the source of violent energy for physical action, for cultural transformation and for the expansion of experience. Epitomizing the anarchy of unstructured democracy, Dutch kills at will and crosses barriers to his whims by obliterating them, whether in illegal businesses or in a hypocritical conversion from Judaism to Catholicism, a move which is designed to endear him to Italian mobsters. Neither a revolutionary nor reformer, Shultz represents a process of continuing change and cultural fluidity. Doctorow does not romanticize or apologize for Dutch. Instead, in him Doctorow finds the violent origins of American culture and character. At the core of the American ideology and experience Doctorow discovers death, destruction, and evil. Like Fitzgerald, however, he also sees courage, renewal, and the opportunity for transcendence. Billy's story and language, like Huck's and Gatsby's, become part of a bigger story. For Doctorow, Billy's narrative of Schultz' violent career incorporates the mythic and ideological constructions through which the past and present merge to define and make history. Dream and nightmare, transcendence and corruption, regeneration and decadence, freedom and violence, opportunity and anarchy exist together. The novel suggests a replication by Billy of a cultural process of balancing these forces as part of a continuing fulfillment of the democratic impulse. The novel further suggests that within a consciousness and social structure of democratic values and institutions, these contending and contradictory forces promise individual renewal and cultural regeneration.

Significantly, when Doctorow received an honorary degree at Brandeis University on May 21, 1989, he chose the form of the jeremiad as the structure for the commencement address he delivered on that occasion. The address sustains and advances the moral fire of Thoreau and Whitman. Like Thoreau in "Civil Disobedience" and "Life Without Principle" or Whitman in *Democratic Vistas* and *The Eighteenth Presidency*, he speaks with the moral authority of American idealism and values and argues in the tones of a prophet of political and cultural destiny. He rails, condemns, and castigates; but ultimately he also offers the hope of renewed idealism and effort to achieve political salvation. Arguing that "something poisonous has been set loose in the last several years," Doctorow says:

> The philosophical conservative is someone willing to pay the price of other people's suffering for his principles. And so we now have hundreds of thousands, perhaps, millions, of our citizens lying around in the streets of our cities, sleeping in doorways, begging with styrofoam cups. We didn't have a class of permanent beggars in this country—in the United States of America—fifteen or twenty years ago. We didn't have kids selling crack in their grade schools, or businessmen magnifying their fortunes into megafortunes by stock manipulation and thievery—I don't remember such epidemics of major corporate fraud. A decade ago you did not have college students scrawling racial epithets or anti-Semitic graffiti on the room doors of their fellow students. You did not have cops strangling teen-age boys to death or shooting elderly deranged women in their own homes. You did not have scientists falsifying the results of experiments, or preachers committing the sins against which they so thunderously preached. A generation or so back, you didn't have every class of society, and every occupation, widely, ruggedly practicing its own characteristic form of crime. (Nation 352)

Thinking of Abbie Hoffman as a modern example, Doctorow significantly evokes the names of Hebrew prophets to suggest how the nation should respond to such injustice. "Wasn't it Isaiah who walked abroad naked to prophesy the deportation of the Jews? And wasn't it Jeremiah who wore a yoke around his neck to prophesy their slavery?" (Nation 354) Equally significant, Doctorow describes this moral collapse in terms of the failure to meet the demands of the American idea. He sees "a national regression to the robber baronial thinking of the nineteenth century," as "nothing less than a deconstruction of America." He says, "So that, finally, our country itself, the idea, the virtue, the truth of America, is in danger of becoming a grotesque" (Nation 354). Accordingly, in this address, Doctorow suggests that the moral reconstruction of America will be achieved by reinventing "the truth of America." Thus, the myth and ideology of America continue to define the boundary and the structure of political discourse and the moral imagination.

A controversy regarding the publication of Doctorow's address followed quickly after its presentation. When the address failed to appear in the *Brandeis Review* as Doctorow expected, he assumed that the university had censored him because of the hostile reaction of some in the audience to his talk. *The Nation* then published it, followed by a public apology and explanation from the university and the ultimate appearance of the talk in the university's alumni review. Summarizing the situation for *The New York Times,* Doctorow said, "An American ideal has been upheld. If a university can't be a place for open discussion, where can one be held?" (Scardino 24)

The continuing interest of writers such as Roth and Doctorow in the democratic culture and ideology of consensus is intriguing, not only because it occurs in the face of the trend in academic criticism toward the dissensus movement, but also because it happens at a time of extraordinary events in world history. The horror of Tiananmen Square, the tentative emergence of democracy in Eastern Europe in the midst of the deepening dissolution of communist hegemony, the continuing challenge to democratic values, and the increasing fragmentation of Israeli society in the confrontation with Palestinian aspirations for liberation—all of these developments suggest by comparison a vitality and permanence to the ideology of consensus in America that may surprise many of its current critics. Moreover, the ideology of consensus, with "The New Covenant" that nourishes it, proffers an important context from which to engage and correct inequalities and injustices that inspire the dissensus movement. The history of totalitarianism and the proliferation of the politics of terror and violence testify that the ideology of consensus and "The New Covenant" are necessary for the protection and advancement of the kind of vital dissensus that is indispensable to a relevant and real democracy.

NOTES

1. Crews adds, "It ought to be clear, then, that we have here something more definite and consequential than the latest permutation of 'theory' as we know it in the Sixties and Seventies. To be sure, the New Americanists are broadly poststructuralist in sympathy; they refuse to draw categorical distinctions between literature and history, foreground and background, art and advocacy, and they distrust all 'foundational'

claims, whether they be for fixed aesthetic quality, authorial autonomy, a specifically literary kind of discourse, or scholarly detachment. But they scorn the daisy chain of indeterminacies with which the once dandyish but now crestfallen Yale deconstructionists used to caper. For a New Americanist, social struggle must always be kept in view, and any concepts obscuring it—concepts, for example, of the'American character,' of the representative masterpiece, of the impish freeplay of signifiers—are to be not just rejected but exposed as ideology" (70).

2. As I wrote in *The New Covenant,* "As a Jewish writer and thinker, Doctorow contributes to the development of the American idea by being at once both the most conservative and the most radical of Americans. He is the most conservative because of his concern for preserving those institutions and values of democracy that constitute the American idea. At the same time, he is the most radical because he extends and modernizes the ideology and meaning of America to make it relevant to contemporary American life, thought, and needs" (182).

REFERENCES

Alter, Robert. *The Pleasures of Reading in an Ideological Age.* New York: Simon and Schuster, 1989.

Bercovitch, Sacvan. *The American Jeremiad.* Madison: University of Wisconsin Press, 1978.

———. "The Problem of Ideology in American Literary History." *Critical Inquiry* 12 (Summer 1986):631–53.

Clemons, Walter. "In the Shadow of the War." Rev. of *World's Fair. Newsweek* 4 November 1985, 69.

Crews, Frederick. "Whose American Renaissance?" *New York Review of Books* 27 Oct. 1988, 68–81.

Doctorow, E. L. *Billy Bathgate.* New York: Random House, 1989.

———. *The Book of Daniel.* New York: Random House, 1971.

———. "The Art of Fiction: E. L. Doctorow." Interview with George Plimpton. *Paris Review* 101 (Winter 1986):23–47.

———. "Creators on Creating: E. L. Doctorow." Interview with Hilary Mills. *Saturday Review* Oct. 1980, 44–48.

———. "A Gangsterdom of the Spirit." *Nation* 2 October 1989, 348–54.

———. "The Rise of Ronald Reagan." *Nation* 19–26 July 1980, 1, 82–84.

———. *World's Fair.* New York: Random House, 1985.

Girgus, Sam B. *The New Covenant: Jewish Writers and the American Idea.* Chapel Hill: University of North Carolina Press, 1984.

Harpham, Geoffrey Galt. "E. L. Doctorow and the Technology of Narrative." *PMLA* 100 (Jan. 1985):81–95.

Melville, Herman. *Redburn*. Garden City: Doubleday Anchor, 1957.

Mitgang, Herbert. "Doctorow's Characters: Old Souls, New Bodies." Interview *The New York Times* 9 March 1989, 17.

Paine, Thomas. *Common Sense*. Ed. Isaac Kramnick. Harmondsworth: Middlesex: Penguin, 1980.

Roth, Philip. "Ethnic Pop and Native Corn." *The New York Times* 19 Sept. 1988, 23.

_____. "Pro-Life Pro." *New York Review of Books* 17 August 1989, 5.

_____. "What Facts? A Talk With Roth." Interview with Jonathan Brent. *The New York Times Book Review* 25 Sept. 1988, 3, 46–47.

Scardino, Albert. "Doctorow vs. Brandeis: 2 Winners." *The New York Times* 8 October 1989, 24.

Twain, Mark. "Corn-pone Opinions." *Great Short Works of Mark Twain*. Ed. Justin Kaplan. New York: Harper and Row, 1967.

CONTRIBUTORS

Sharon Deykin Baris teaches in the Department of English at Bar-Ilan University where she is the Director of the Kaplan Fund for American Literature. She has published on Nathaniel Hawthorne, Henry James, and Wallace Stevens.

Daniel Boyarin holds the Taubman Chair of Talmudic Culture in the Department of Near Eastern Studies at the University of California, Berkeley. He is the author of *Intertextuality and the Reading of Midrash* and *Carnal Israel: Reading Sex in Talmudic Culture.*

Emily Miller Budick teaches in the American Studies Department at the Hebrew University of Jerusalem. She is the author *Fiction and Historical Consciousness: The American Romance Tradition,* and the forthcoming *Engendering Romance: Women and Men and the Hawthorne Tradition.*

Gerda Elata-Alster teaches comparative literature at Ben-Gurion University of the Negev. She has published articles on medieval and classical literature and on psychoanalysis and literature. She is currently working on a book about midrash and literary theory with Rachel Salmon.

Menachem Fisch teaches the history and philosophy of science at Tel-Aviv University. He has published on confirmation theory, rationality, and ninteenth-century English mathematics and physics. His study of William Whewell was published in 1991 and a book on the rationality of Jewish learning is forthcoming.

Elizabeth Freund teaches in the English Department at the Hebrew University of Jerusalem. She has published on Shakespeare and literary theory, including *The Return of the Reader: Reader Response Criticism.* She is working on a book on the concept of wit in the English Renaissance.

Sam B. Girgus teaches American literature at Vanderbilt University. He is the author of *The New Covenant: Jewish Writers and the American Idea,* and *Desire and the Political Unconscious in American Literature.* His most recent book is *The Films of Woody Allen.*

Betsy Halpern-Amaru teaches in the Department of Religion at Vassar College. She has just completed a study of land theology in post-biblical Jewish literature, and is currently working on the characterization of the matriarchs in the same period.

Susan Handelman teaches in the English Department and the Jewish Studies Program at the University of Maryland at College Park. She is the author of *The Slayers of Moses: The Emergence of Rabbinic Interpretation in Modern Literary Theory* and *Fragments of Redemption: Jewish Thought and Literary Theory in Benjamin, Scholem, and Levinas.*

Betty Rojtman teaches French at the Hebrew University of Jerusalem, and writes about the conjunction of contemporary literary theory, Jewish tradition, and hermeneutics. She is the author of *Feu noir sur feu blanc: Essai sur l'herméneutique juive,* and *Une grave distraction.*

Rachel Salmon teaches English at Bar-Ilan University. She has published on Henry James and on varieties of religious poetry. She is currently working with Gerda Elata-Alster on a book on the hermeneutics of midrash.

Ellen Spolsky teaches English literature and literary theory at Bar-Ilan University in Israel, where she is also the director of the Lechter Institute for Literary Research. Her most recent book is *Gaps in Nature: Literary Theory and the Modular Mind* (SUNY Press, 1993). She is working on a study of skepticism in Renaissance paintings and texts.

Daniel Statman teaches in the Philosophy Department at Bar-Ilan University. His interests include moral and legal philosophy, moral psychology and the philosophy of religion. He is the author of *Moral Dilemmas,* and co-author of *Religion and Morality.*